D0887730

Public
Testimony
on Public
Schools

NATIONAL COMMITTEE
FOR CITIZENS IN EDUCATION

COMMISSION
ON EDUCATIONAL GOVERNANCE

McCutchan Publishing Corporation
2526 Grove Street
Berkeley, California 94704

ISBN 0-8211-1306-2
Library of Congress Catalog Card Number 75-20296

PREFACE

    The National Committee for Citizens in Education is a nonparti-san, nonprofit organization dedicated to increasing citizen involvement in the affairs of the nation's public schools. It was previously known as the National Committee for Support of the Public Schools, which was founded in 1962 by the late Agnes E. Meyer with the assistance of former President Harry S Truman, General Omar Bradley, James D. Conant, and other distinguished citizens. During the 1960s the Committee concentrated on advocating increased federal assistance to public education and was highly successful in this effort. With the death of Mrs. Meyer the Committee reduced its activities until mid-1973, when it was reorganized and was given a new name and a new set of goals. Initial grants from the Ford Foundation gave the Committee its new start. The financial goal of the NCCE is to become self-sustaining for general operating funds through membership dues, the sales of publications, and individual gifts.

    The nation's public schools have a longer record of public involvement than any other American institution, and the NCCE believes that active citizen participation is vital to the healthy functioning of democratic institutions. It seeks to restimulate active citizen involvement in public education through a mass-membership advocacy organization, a Common Cause for public education. The strategy is to mobilize citizen action around issues that have great impact.

To further its purposes, the NCCE established a Commission on Educational Governance in November 1973. The Commission was to develop a report and a set of recommendations on the citizens' role in the establishment of policy and in decision making in the operation of the public schools. Its task was to conduct public hearings around the country to examine issues related to the question "Who controls the public schools?"

The Commission, consisting of citizens from various parts of the country selected for their interest in education and of members of the governing board of the NCCE, are: Karen Blank, Lawrence, Kansas; Susan Blaustein, Claremont, California; R. Stephen Browning, Washington, D.C.; Daniel A. Collins, San Francisco, California; Mrs. Merrimon Cuninggim, St. Louis, Missouri; Frederick T. Haley, Tacoma, Washington; Calvin J. Hurd, Elizabeth, New Jersey; Mary Conway Kohler, New York, New York; Ethel M. Lichtman, Palo Alto, California; Susanne Martinez, San Francisco, California; Donald Rappaport, Philadelphia, Pennsylvania; Charlotte Ryan, Manchester, Massachusetts; Phyllis Wiener, Portland, Oregon; Paul Ylvisaker, Cambridge, Massachusetts.

The Commission held hearings in Minneapolis, Minnesota, St. Louis, Missouri, Portland, Oregon, Atlanta, Georgia, and Los Angeles, California. In addition, testimony was taken from citizen activists from Alabama, Mississippi, Florida, and South Carolina.

Testimony was taken from 190 witnesses, including eight state or local school board members, seventeen official community advisory council members, thirty-five legislative or executive commission or committee members, six ad hoc legislative or executive committee representatives, six Title I committee members, ten official representatives of teachers' organizations or students' organizations, four PTA representatives, six League of Women Voters representatives, four quasi-official advisory committee members, two American Friends Service Committee representatives, one quasi-official representative of a teachers' organization, three quasi-official members of a citizens' organization, thirty-six representatives of unofficial organizations, and fifty-two people who did not represent an organization or who testified as private citizens.

The public hearings were designed to assure the fullest opportunity to question and gather information from teachers, students, educators, administrators, legislators, and citizens about their experiences and knowledge concerning citizen participation in the decision-making process of the public schools. Following a brief opening statement by each witness, there was extensive dialogue between the witness and the Commissioners.

Field interviews were conducted prior to each hearing to develop background information on the public schools, the communities, and citizen organizations. Approximately 2,350 organizations or individuals were contacted and contributed directly or indirectly to the information gathered.

Ten days to two weeks prior to each hearing all the Commissioners were mailed packets of information, consisting of facts gathered in the field, interviews, administrative profiles, regulations, socio-economic data, site information, and relevant current and past issues.

Each Commissioner was asked to attend one or more of the hearings. The staff of the Commission conducted a briefing for the impaneled Commissioners. Data and information presented at the briefings included an overview on the school community, profiles of witnesses, demographic and geographical information, and prefiled testimony. In addition, local resource people were available at each briefing to answer questions. All information presented at these briefings was distributed both to the Commissioners present and those who were not.

As the field interviewing and research proceeded in the early stages of the project, several central questions began to surface as overriding themes. How did the growth of the teachers' organizations directly affect the role of the citizen in the decision-making process? Was there a historical role for the citizen within the institution, and had it changed? Was the expanding alternative movement an answer to the issue of school governance? How did the present governing arrangements come into being, and what would constitute desirable change? The testimony at the public hearings clearly needed understanding and analysis grounded in the history of the growth of the public schools.

The Commission established, therefore, a panel of consultants to review and develop papers on the major governance issues and to assure the continuity of focus on the central themes that emerged from the testimony. The consultants were asked to serve in both a

research and advisory capacity. Each member of the consultants' advisory panel agreed to tackle separate parts of the complex issues and to review the development of the Commission's report: Dr. Mario Fantini prepared the section on alternatives; Dr. James W. Guthrie wrote the history of governing policies in American schools; Dr. Lawrence Pierce researched and wrote the section on the growth of teachers' organizations; Donald Reed researched the chapter on some significant history of citizen participation.

All consultants had access to and reviewed the materials for pre-hearing information, hearing summaries, and testimony. The researchers met and conferred as a panel to review the development of the Commission's report and each others' work.

The papers appear as separate chapters; the opinions stated in each are those of the author and do not necessarily represent those of the NCCE Commission on Educational Governance.

Below are listed the Commissioners followed by the cities in which they attended hearings:

Blank, Minneapolis, Portland, St. Louis, Atlanta, Los Angeles;
Blaustein, Los Angeles;
Charles Bowen (resigned), St. Louis;
Browning, Minneapolis, St. Louis, Portland;
Ms. Sarah Collins Carey (resigned), Minneapolis, St. Louis;
Collins, Minneapolis, St. Louis, Portland;
Cuninggim, Portland, Atlanta;
Haley, St. Louis, Portland, Los Angeles;
Hurd, Minneapolis, Los Angeles;
Kohler;
Lichtman, Portland, Los Angeles;
Martinez, Minneapolis, Atlanta, Los Angeles;
Rappaport, Los Angeles;
Ryan, Atlanta;
Wiener, Minneapolis, Los Angeles;
Ylvisaker, Atlanta.

Observers representing various organizations were also present at the hearings. Following are the organizations, their representatives, and the cities at which they were present:

Education Commission of the States, Christopher Pipho, Minneapolis, Portland, Atlanta, Los Angeles;
Citizens Conference on State Legislatures, Willie Campbell, Minneapolis, Los Angeles, and Elton McQuerry, St. Louis;

National Conference of State Legislatures, Richard Merritt, Minneapolis, St. Louis;

National Urban Coalition, Robert Bothwell, St. Louis, Los Angeles.

The National School Boards Association was unable to send an observer to any of the hearings, but attended two Commission meetings.

Commission members and observers attended four meetings of the Commission on Educational Governance between April 1974 and March 1975, at which time interim reports and analyses of the hearings were discussed and approved.

The staff of the NCCE is indebted to many people for their assistance in the development of the project on educational governance and offers its thanks to all who extended kindness and help throughout the country.

It was a privilege to work with the Commissioners, whose diligence and good humor are exemplary. Their outstanding tact and sensitivity overcame the crises we encountered in working with hundreds of witnesses. In every city the Commissioners devoted themselves completely to the task. They never complained; nor did their physical stamina diminish in the face of the incredible hearing schedules. We extend our deepest thanks for their patience and support at each of the public hearings and Commission meetings.

The senior staff of the NCCE, Carl Marburger, J. William Rioux, Stanley Salett, and associate, Stuart Sandow contributed their years of experience and expertise throughout all stages of the project. Their support and encouragement contributed greatly to whatever success the project may have.

At each of the public hearings and Commission meetings five national organizations attended as observers and commentators. The individuals representing these organizations took great interest in the project and became a part of all that we did. They never refused a task, and they contributed in large measure to the information we collected through their questions and comments. In particular, Chris Pipho of the Education Commission of the States and Dick Merritt of the National Legislative Conference shared vast amounts of their time and knowledge with us. We are grateful to all the observers for their faith in the project and to our "unofficial" observer, Donald U. Honicky, for his consistent and dependable support.

We appreciate the time, advice, and help of the consultants who contributed to the project: Mario Fantini, James W. Guthrie, Laurence Iannaconne, Michael Kirst, Lawrence Pierce, Donald Reed, and Jay Scribner.

Our special thanks is extended to Michael Bowler, education writer for the *Baltimore Sun,* who wrote the summaries of each hearing. Despite transcripts that arrived very late and deadlines that came very early, he never failed us. His facility with the English language has been of inestimable value in this report.

We extend our appreciation to the field research assistants who interviewed potential witnesses. Adrienne Smith warrants special thanks for her dedication, the thorough completion of her tasks, and her very "special touch" in helping the community to understand the nature of our project and obtain its cooperation.

Because of the limited time, funds, and staff, one of our more difficult tasks was identifying resource people, key actors, issues, and the individual character of the cities in which we held hearings. Citizens, educators, community leaders, and students furnished us with their knowledge and experience. We are very grateful to the many hundreds of people who assisted us with both small and large tasks.

In each city, however, there are those who must be mentioned separately since they made the whole project possible. Because of their assistance the public hearings were a success.

First in this group are the many school superintendents and their staffs who cooperated with us. They are: John B. Davis, Superintendent, and August Rivera, Assistant Superintendent for Information Services, Minneapolis Public Schools; Howard Casmey, Commissioner of Education, Minnesota; Clyde Miller, Superintendent, St. Louis Public Schools; Robert Blanchard, Superintendent, and Donald McElroy, Assistant Superintendent, Charles Clemans, Intergovernmental Relations, and John Nellor, Public Information Officer, Portland Public Schools; Dr. Milton Baum, Assistant State Superintendent, Oregon; Alonzo Crim, Superintendent, and Barbara Wittaker, Assistant Superintendent, Atlanta Public Schools; William Johnston, Superintendent, James Taylor and William Rivera, Assistant Superintendents, Los Angeles Unified School District; and Jessie Heinzman, Special Assistant to the State Superintendent, California.

In the five cities we had the opportunity to meet and work with outstanding citizens and business leaders. Without the time and efforts of the following individuals the public hearings and the many and varied tasks would not have been accomplished. These people were, in part, responsible for our success in gathering broad and diverse information from the communities.

In Minneapolis they were Anthony Morley, Director S.E. Alternatives; Maxine Nathanson, Minneapolis Citizens for Better Public Schools; and Betty Svetnson, Director St. Paul Volunteer Services. In St. Louis they were Alice Muckler and Jane Paine of the White House Conference on Education; Robert Elsea, Cooperating School District; Daniel Schlafly, Chairman of the school board; and Andrew Doyle and Katherine Nelson, members of the school board. In Portland they were Mollie Weinstein, City Hall; Mary Rieke, state legislator; Donald Barney, assistant to the mayor; Charles Clemans, Department of Education; and John Nellor, Public Information Officer, Department of Education. In Atlanta they were K. C. Chavitz and Dorothy Routh, Leadership Development Program; Winifred Greene, American Friends Service Committee; Roger Mills, Southern Regional Council; Junie Brown, *Atlanta Journal*; Lonnie King, NAACP; Esther LeFevre, "The Patch"; and Jules Sugarman, assistant to the mayor. In Los Angeles they were Roy Azarnoff, mayor's office; Rosalind Cooperman, Women For; Clive Hoffman, public relations; Walter Jones and Robert Singleton, Education Finance Reform Project; Jack McCurdy, *Los Angeles Times*; Lois Nevius, Community Relations Council of Southern California; Connie Schiff, League of Women Voters; Robert Scott and Beth Milwid, San Francisco Service Center; and Robert Loveland, Los Angeles Unified School District Goals Committee.

Lending their secretarial skills, administrative support, and encouragement to the staff were Beverly Norbeck, Katy Bagierek, Sharon Cuthbert, Janis Harris, Jenny Dee Glassberg, and Rita Goff.

It is not unusual to leave for last those individuals who were most responsible for ensuring the success of a project. Leslie Glassberg contributed her administrative excellence to implement the many hundreds of details in so large an undertaking and, in general, served as the vital source of energy to keep everything moving. As the administrative assistant, she deserves all of our appreciation and thanks for the completion of the project.

Douglas Mitchell, research associate, served a unique function: to express the intentions of the staff and to analyze the testimony of the witnesses. With unfailing patience and great endurance, he applied himself to this enormous task.

There are two people whose continuing constructive criticism and unfailing faith in my work will always enforce the drive for excellence—James Kelly of the Ford Foundation and Arthur E. Wise of the National Institute of Education.

Shelly Weinstein, Project Director

CONTENTS

1

SCHOOL GOVERNANCE IN TROUBLE

In November 1973 the National Committee for Citizens in Education convened the Commission on Educational Governance. The Commissioners were enjoined to develop a report and a set of recommendations on the role of citizens in the establishment of policy and in decision making in the operation of the public schools. The task laid before the Commission was to conduct public hearings around the country to gather information on the experience of citizens with decision making in public schools. The NCCE Board said: "We propose to focus attention on the issue of educational governance as a way of helping the American people inform themselves that their public schools are undergoing significant changes which do affect their rights, responsibilities and ability to control what is happening in their schools."[1] The NCCE Charge to the Commission on Educational Governance stated in part: "Much has been written about the problems confronting American education today. In spite of a decade of creative energy, vast sums of money and widespread research, however, these problems have not diminished . . . . Now more than ever, there exist no mechanisms for public concerns to be expressed in any systematic, meaningful and productive way on the issue of educational changes."[2]

1

Was the concern for citizen participation in public education a new issue? Since 1965 interest in the role of citizens in public education and their right to access to and response from the schools were the themes of several national conferences held by the predecessor of the NCCE, the National Committee for Support of the Public Schools. Along with issues of school finance, decentralization, accountability, and performance contracting, the problems of community control and citizen participation had been studied by the NCSPS. In 1968 a special report to the NCSPS stated: "Highly centralized and bureaucratic, insulated from the public, growing in lower class and non-white population, and unable to adjust their programs and institutions to changing needs, many of our big city school districts could hardly have worse relations with the communities they serve . . . ."[3]

Six years later the NCCE still found itself confronted with such questions as: What determines where a school is built? Who decides how much money should be requested in a school budget? Who decides what programs schools will have? How does a parent obtain his child's school records? How does a teacher get hired? Who controls the public schools? Who *should* control the public schools? What are or should be the roles of citizens in public education?

It is universally accepted and firmly rooted in most state constitutions that the future of society rests solidly on the foundation of education. "If," said Thomas Jefferson, "a nation expects to be ignorant and free, in a state of civilization, it expects what never was and never will be."[4] Our forefathers expected and planned for both freedom and civilization, and as federalism emerged it was only natural that it was the states' fundamental responsibility to provide adequate, free and efficient, thorough and uniform education.[5]

Educational governance encompasses the constitutional, legislative, regulatory, and administrative bodies that are charged with running our schools. The constitutional responsibility rests with the state; the authority for policy making, raising revenues, and operating the schools has been assigned to the state and local school boards. At present there are pressing demands for new kinds of services and responses from educational institutions at each of these levels.

Over the last several years, at the federal level, the executive branch espoused the notion that the public was interested only in peace and prosperity—bread-and-butter issues. Federal allocations dipped below 6 percent of the total national education budget of

$52,000,000,000 in 1972, placing education as a low-priority item following ten years of major attention. In this same year 45,700,000 children between the ages of five and seventeen were enrolled in public schools, and 92.9 percent of the fourteen- to seventeen-year-olds were enrolled in school. It is estimated that elementary and secondary expenditures will exceed $70,000,000,000 in 1982-1983. In thirty-five years expenditures per pupil have grown from $100 to over $1,000. The nation's counties spend more on education than they do on highways, hospitals, or police protection. By 1972 life-time earnings almost doubled for a person with four years of high school as compared to a person with eight years or less of schooling.[6]

Despite the statistical dominance of education, in recent years citizens have become frustrated over their inability to influence decisions concerning it. The frustration has many sources. It is tied to domestic and foreign turmoil, the national economy, the "participatory ethos" of the late 1960s, and the desire of the poor, blacks, Mexican-Americans, and others to gain a voice in education. There is also a strong movement espousing the return to "basics" in the public schools, and citizen groups have organized to protest such school policies as the selection of textbooks; they feel they have been eliminated from decisions that are vital to them. When one adds all of this to the continuing protest over bussing to achieve school desegregation, he finds that America is entering its bicentennial with its public schools in a state of malaise, if not depression.

Voters are responding negatively to spiraling educational costs, as the financing of public education is tied to local property taxes. Traditional supporters of public education have become disaffected by overdependence on the local property tax as the major source of revenue. Bond issues have been defeated in middle-class suburban districts during the last ten years, and some big-city school systems have closed briefly for lack of funds. Although most of those who use the system are still favorably disposed to the schools, an outspoken portion of the public is seeking basic changes in public education.

As was mentioned above, such feelings are reflected in school bond and tax elections. Results of public school bond elections during the ten-year period from 1961-1962 to 1971-1972 show a dramatic decline in public willingness to support bonds for new school construction. While the public approved over 72 percent of all school bonds in 1961-1962, less than half of such bonds were approved during the school year 1971-1972. It is difficult, of course, to generalize from such statistics regarding public attitudes toward schools. While it would be plausible to conclude that these voting patterns reflect lack of public confidence in schools, other explanations are equally possible. Perhaps they simply reflect the frustration of voters over increasing taxes and demands for expanded public expenditures at all levels of government. But, for whatever reason, citizens have become gradually aware of their potential for exercising financial control.

Background

Formal education was historically left to the smallest unit—the family. In the early colonial period schooling was a private matter, and families provided training in reading and writing either in the home or in private schools. In 1642 an organized effort began in Massachusetts to provide a system of education, and by the late 1600s the number of schools began to increase. Local communities were, without exception, responsible for the functioning of these schools. School affairs were routinely considered part of the regular business of town government. Joining together in town meetings, parents, as well as other citizens, selected teachers and provided their board in local homes. They also evaluated their performance. The local community constructed school buildings, often with volunteer labor and materials.

As communities grew in size and complexity, decisions concerning schools were delegated to separate committees of the town councils. Gradually these separate committees of selectmen became special boards that were elected to set policy and run schools. By the turn of the nineteenth century these special boards for each school became city-wide boards responsible for several schools.

One factor remained constant, however, throughout this transitional period. Local communities continued to control school policy directly. Thus, prior to 1900, American schools were properly characterized as being highly decentralized. Decisions about day-to-day operations of schools were left to local communities, and so reflected local values, regional differences, and community vocational needs.

In 1900 school governance was still embedded in the local community. Even though the national population had grown to 72,000,000, there were approximately 110,000 local school districts with an average of five members per school board. Community residents were able to have close contact with local school board members, and disagreements over schools could be settled on a personal basis.

Since 1900 the population has continued to expand, and there has been a continuing effort by state legislatures to consolidate school districts. This has meant that the ratio of representatives to those represented has decreased dramatically. Today there are 16,000 operating school districts, while the national population has increased to more than 210,000,000.

Another factor in the decline of local influence on education was the desire in the early 1900s to depoliticize the schools, which resulted from a call for professionalization of both teachers and administrators. It was a movement parallel to the expansion and professionalization of government that reached every level of the executive branch by 1935. As matters became more and more complex, schools grew in numbers and school populations expanded, the school committees or boards became more and more dependent on the professionals for day-to-day decisions. Educational policy making was turned over largely to these educators, either formally through delegation or informally through reliance on professional judgment. The skills of teaching and of school administration were considered as sciences to be taught by institutions that trained teachers. The less measurable skills deriving from an educator's upbringing and character became increasingly less important; education was considered a science more than an art.

The technical principle of competence was highly valued, and legislators at every level turned to educators for the specifications of school laws and policies. School governance was severed from such regular political processes as partisan elections on the assumption that professional expertise would more effectively serve the common good if "we could get politics out of the schools and get the schools out of politics." Efficiency thus became the criterion for policy making in schools, as in industry.

Professional influence on day-to-day policy decisions was not confined to intradistrict governance; it was also influential at the state level. Organizations of teachers and administrators lobbied to secure standards for certification, curriculum, and personnel policies. Professionals, for the most part administrators who had served at the local level, comprised the staffs of state education departments and promulgated regulations in the process of administering the state codes. The twentieth century, then, gave rise to centralized educational governance, to the increase of the power of the state to ensure minimal standards and to oversee programs and the strengthening of the authority of central city boards and superintendents at the expense of ward-based, politically controlled boards.

Beginning well beyond the middle of the century, there were several attempts at countervailing reform, as seen in the experiments in community control and decentralization. The movement for community control and later efforts to achieve "accountability" in education stemmed from complex factors: the failure of city school systems to educate poor, black, and non-English-speaking children; lags in reading scores; high dropout rates; and the failure of integration in big cities.

In the years since the Supreme Court ruled that racially separate schools are not equal it has become clear that desegregation has not proceeded "with all deliberate speed." Whether because of an absence of will, fervent opposition to bussing, or the fact that school populations in many large cities have become overwhelmingly black, making desegregation almost impossible within city boundaries, community control was seen by many as a possible answer. Some people asserted that if schools are to be desegregated, and neighborhood schools are to continue as the mainstay of the system, then neighborhood schools should be controlled by neighborhood parents and residents. They maintained that only people living in the neighborhood can know the kind of education most relevant for their children.

During the last few years several major cities enacted decentralization plans, notably New York and Detroit, both of which gave a measure of control over school personnel to citizens. The typical decentralization scheme involved the division of a school district into several smaller units, each serving a cluster of elementary schools and one or two high schools. Each unit was headed by a regional or district superintendent who answered to the central superintendent. Citizens were encouraged to take their concerns and complaints to the regional office, where the central office functions of planning, pupil personnel services, curriculum development, and teachers' in-service work were duplicated on the regional scale.

Most of the decentralization plans were accompanied by citizen and/or parent councils whose function was to advise the regional superintendent and his staff. The advisory bodies usually were given no policy-making roles, and they had little or no control over the budget at the area or regional level. Their role in the hiring and evaluation of teachers and administrators was, with a few exceptions, advisory. Even when decentralization was in this formative stage, teachers' organizations and administrators' organizations usually opposed it, fearing any loss of authority.

And teachers have gained considerable authority, particularly in the past two decades; their professionalization and organization added yet another layer of complexity to the problem of governance. Over the past twenty-five years the number of teachers has tripled from slightly over 1,000,000 in 1940 to nearly 3,000,000 in 1971. It has been estimated that by 1980 membership in the two national organizations of teachers (National Education Association and American Federation of Teachers) could reach 3,500,000, and their ability to generate funds, through dues and other assessments, could attain the annual level of $500,000,000.[7] Over the past fifteen years these two organizations have grown substantially closer ideologically and more active politically; the movement to merge them, which began in the 1960s, has continued to gain momentum. In 1972 the New York State Teachers Association (an NEA affiliate) voted to merge with the United Teachers of New York (an AFT affiliate). This merger made the New York organization of teachers the largest state organization of public employees in the nation. Similar mergers took place later in Florida and several major cities.

Teachers used these professional organizations to consolidate their power to influence local decision making. Even though statutes in many states prohibit strikes by public employees, teachers' organizations successfully withheld or threatened to withhold their labor in order to improve their working conditions and to gain financial benefits. This power to strike—or to threaten to strike—in many instances had a positive influence by upgrading depressed salaries and improving teachers' working conditions. As strikes by teachers increased from thirty-five in 1965-1966 to over 114 in 1967-1968, however, public confusion grew over who was running schools. Though the public may initially have been sympathetic to teachers' demands for salary increases, since the 1960s these increases outstripped other indicators of economic growth.

Other matters that have been negotiated by teachers include class size, transfers of teachers within districts, assignment to nonclassroom duties, working hours, and pupil-teacher ratios. In some cases, teachers are seeking to expand the scope of bargaining to include curriculum development, selection of textbooks, and selection of subject matter by department heads.

One consequence of the growth of teachers' organizations has been that school boards have been forced to share decision-making power with the teachers. In the past this power was largely in the hands of laymen and top-level school administrators.

The courts also played a major role in such policy matters as discipline and suspension, testing, school finance, teachers contracts, desegregation, districting, curriculum, and special education. Courts represent the rights of citizens, and many of these decisions have provoked badly needed and long-awaited action that school boards and other legislative bodies have not been willing to take on their own initiative. Legal action has often been the only effective means for citizens to gain access to school policy making. Recent U.S. Supreme Court decisions have significantly expanded the rights of due process for students. But court decisions in recent years, particularly those mandating school desegregation, have estranged a growing number of citizens. Many have withdrawn their children from the public schools. These citizens have viewed the courts as uncompromising and unreasonable. It is ironic that while the desegregation orders were designed to secure the rights of one group of children, they were regarded as diminishing the rights of another group.

Whatever direction the demands and expectations for our schools may take, and however great the efforts to reexamine our institutions to guarantee their viability in achieving these demands, the purposes of the public schools remain deeply rooted in our constitutional concept that "diffusion of knowledge and intelligence is essential to the preservation of the rights and liberties of the people."[8]

A public school serves a public purpose rather than a private one. It is not maintained for the personal advantage or private gain of the teacher, the proprietor or the board of managers; nor does it exist simply for the enjoyments, happiness or advancement of the individual student or his parents. It may, indeed it should, enhance the vocational competence or upward social mobility or personal development of individuals, but if that were all a school attempted, the job could be done as well by a private school catering to particular jobs, or careers, or leisure time enjoyment. Rather, the prime purpose of the public school is to serve the general welfare of a democratic society . . . .[9]

Typically from many views the schools may not appear to be fulfilling their public purpose. As things now stand, educational policy appears shaped by time and circumstances, with the result that few reforms have been fully achieved, and almost none seems manageable.

More than ever before, technology, mobility, differences in and expansions of population are contributing, however subtly, to an ever greater degree to the confusion of how the system works and who influences it. The problem is further complicated by the addition of the issues of unionism, parents' and students' rights, local control, citizen participation, ethnic and minority cultural interests, and special education to the more traditional issues of structure, financing, and community goals.

Two hundred years ago most of our citizens lived on farms and in villages. One hundred years ago education was only for an elite few. Today two-thirds of the American people live in metropolitan centers and depend on industry and commerce instead of agriculture for their income. Universal education has become an integral component in the quality of American life: it is no longer a luxury for the few. The growth in mass education and the search for knowledge will continue in our demand for excellence and quality in a civilized and technical world.

This effort to educate all our citizens entails certain consequences. It means mass education. It means crowded schools and huge universities . . . . It means devising educational programs for youngsters who will grow up to be plumbers and farmers as well as for those who will grow up to be philosophers and art critics. In short, it is a very different system from one designed to educate young aristocrats for the role of cultivated gentlemen. And having set ourselves these objectives, we cannot weep because our educational system no longer resembles the cozy, tidy world we deliberately put behind us.[10]

The Findings

Who controls the schools? No one person or group does, but in a ranking of the degree of control exerted by individuals and groups, students are least influential, and professional educators are most powerful.

Besides these two groups—the one the clients of education and the other among its purveyors—there are vast numbers of people and organizations. These include parents and others with interest in what happens in the schools, special-interest groups, teachers, principals, state-level educators, school board members, members of advisory councils and committees, and groups such as the League of Women Voters with only partial interest in education. It is a vast, overlapping system, and it is not a system at all. It is a public service but also a mammoth business enterprise. It is highly political, but strives at the same time to rid itself of the taint of politics. It is the springboard to success in our society and the conveyer of culture. It is at once the great leveler, treating students of all races and incomes equally, and a promoter of values that tend to be white and middle class.

Within this system, professional educators, particularly superintendents and their staffs at the level of the school district, enjoy considerable power and respect for their expertise in what generally is considered a highly technical enterprise. Teachers have become extremely powerful in very recent years through collective bargaining agreements at the same level and extremely effective lobbying in state legislatures. Statewide collective bargaining legislation and national collective bargaining for public employees are no longer remote possibilities, but are close to reality.

At the NCCE hearings school board members were optimistic about the influence of "citizens" on school governance, but they were outnumbered by those citizens who accused the school board members of being influenced almost exclusively by central administrators.

The hearings produced much talk of the new "advisory councils" that were formed in most urban districts as they were decentralized in the past decade. Though there were some exceptions, most of the talk was discouraging. The advisory role of these councils and committees renders them vulnerable to being used for the purposes of administrators. A direct relationship exists between the effectiveness of the advisory group and the willingness of the local school principal to listen to it. If advisory committees do not work in schools where principals are strong willed and uncompromising, the Commission was asked, why have them at all?

Much of this could have been expected. In any enterprise, particularly one as large as American education, there are many on the outside who want to get in and very few on the inside who want to get out. But education is not a profit-making business; it is an enterprise rooted in democratic ideals. On its success may depend the future of the nation.

Overall, the inquiry into educational governance resulted in conclusions covering seven broad areas.

Education is highly valued. Education continues to be a service that is highly valued by all sectors of society. Recent critics of education who have proposed the elimination of schooling carry little weight in America's cities. Despite the considerable problems of public support and conflict over policy management, the overwhelming view is that education is and will remain a vital public service that is an important part of growing up for every child. Even the school's harshest critics remain deeply convinced that there is little opportunity for success in contemporary society for people who have not acquired an extensive and high-quality education.

There are, of course, many suggestions, proposals, and demands for changes that would improve the effectiveness of the public school system. Citizens present this drive to change the schools, however, in a mood of disappointed expectation, loving criticism, or sometimes outraged betrayal, but virtually never do they dismiss what they consider their inherent right to education. Even those few individuals who would do away with formal schooling never suggest there is no need for high-quality, carefully organized educational experiences open to everyone in the society.

There are problems in the responsiveness and control of school policy. There is a serious striving to participate in the making of school policy in America's cities. In an open democratic institution this effort should be welcome, but there are serious problems in the present structure. Not only are there some inequities in the provision of educational services to our children but also the response of school policy makers to those seeking change is uneven. As a result the schools are widely seen as unresponsive to basic needs and desires, and they appear to be undemocratic in their decision-making processes.

One can detect this striving for control of school policy in the following:

1. The emergence of new organizations among both citizens and professional educators. Prominently included among these new

groups are teachers' organizations, proponents of alternative schools, citizen advisory councils, and issue-oriented groups supporting and opposing desegregation, bussing, selection of textbooks, and many other issues.

2. The changing purposes of existing and traditional groups, most notably the PTA and professional associations of teachers that are seeking more influence.

3. An increased interest in "accountability" and similar issues on the part of state and federal lawmakers.

4. The widespread intervention of the courts in educational policy making, particularly in matters of constitutional rights, especially desegregation and school finance.

5. The number of strikes, boycotts, mass meetings, picket lines, and other forms of direct political action focused on school policy decisions.

6. The concern of teachers that they do not contribute significantly to school policy.

7. The greater determination by legislators to frame laws that will alter school programs and practices.

Poor people and blacks are underrepresented on school boards, while wealthier middle-class whites are overrepresented. There is poor communication among key decision makers in the schools, a lack of effective judicial review for students and families with grievances and a tendency of schools to disregard students' opinions and rights.

There are problems in the organization of schools and in the access to school governance. Students and parents find it difficult, if not impossible, to influence school governance or to participate in the structures established to operate the schools.

Though there is some agreement on the universal goals of school operations, there is extensive disagreement on how to balance priorities in the schools. Should they emphasize quality academic programs over equality of opportunity, give greater importance to the communities they serve than to individual needs and desires, emphasize socially and economically relevant skills over character building and cultural values? These disagreements over priorities mean that proposals for educational programs often meet intense resistance; most often the reaction is to leave existing programs untouched.

School organizations also are failing to provide effective procedures of accountability. The result is a fragile autonomy for educators, one that alternates between isolation of the classroom from all external influence and conflicts that disrupt it almost completely.

The inaccessibility of the school organization is evidenced by:

1. The widespread demands that school systems be broken up into much smaller units with board members drawn from neighborhoods close to the students and their families.

2. The number of citizens who are filing court suits seeking to force the schools to respond to their desires.

3. The extent to which professional educators preempt policy making and limit the participation of nonprofessionals.

4. The number of new state laws that have sought to define and force professional "accountability."

There are problems in the flow of the information that is vital to policy making in the schools. Information is the essence of intelligent policy making. When one party or group controls information, the result can be uninformed and uncritical policy making.

Among important barriers to the flow of information are:

1. Collective bargaining between teachers and school boards that is conducted most frequently behind closed doors and without public knowledge until after decisions are made. This is an alarming trend because negotiations are moving increasingly from bread-and-butter matters to matters of intense interest to school patrons such as discipline policies.

2. The increased difficulty for citizens to obtain information about school policies and practices, even when this information is theoretically in the public domain and covered by statutes concerning public disclosure.

3. The remoteness of school board members from the average citizen, especially in urban school districts. Even when information is available to them, some school board members are not particularly skilled in collecting and using it.

4. The control of information at state and regional levels by lobbyists for groups of professional educators despite growing sophistication on the part of citizens' groups.

5. Local school boards' overreliance on state school boards and departments of education for information on state educational policies. In addition, citizens appear to be ill informed about the relation of state-level actions to their educational programs and needs.

These difficulties lead, of course, to school policy that is inflexible and oriented to the status quo, to the appearance that school policy is made on the basis of little hard information, and, perhaps worst of all, to the hostility of citizens toward policy makers.

There is a connection between demands for educational alternatives and increasing dissatisfaction with existing public education. There are widespread and significant demands that schools adopt alternative goals, procedures, and programs. Although there are a growing number of fairly small-scale experimental alternatives in most major school systems, generally the response to these demands has been inadequate. The demands come from parents, students, and community leaders who point out the inadequacies of traditional school programs. Federal and state policy makers recognize that the stimulation of alternative programs is timely and desirable, and parents and many educators respond enthusiastically to well-planned and effectively implemented alternative programs.

But dropout rates remain alarmingly high. Some students are pushed out of school because of discriminatory discipline practices, and many leave because they are alienated. A number of other factors have led to the failure of school systems to provide alternatives, among them the abandonment of urban schools by many middle- and upper-class families and the high cost of providing alternatives. And school systems have been reluctant to start programs without federal or state funds.

Decisions in education are too often made at points far away from where those decisions will affect people and programs. One result is inequality in educational services. There are three basic levels in education: the local school level, the school district level, and the state level. All too frequently, the formal authority for making school policy is not vested in the mechanisms of governance closest to the appropriate level. Decisions concerning school finance, for example, are generally made at the state level, but the responsibility for raising the revenues to finance the schools is too heavily borne by school districts with limited resources and diverse local populations. The overdependence on local wealth for school funds leads to unequal services and inequality of opportunity. Desegregation is another example. Responsibility for action is usually given to the local school district. But in urban districts that are becoming racially more homogeneous, it is increasingly difficult to provide an integrated education for all students.

In judging the job teachers and principals are doing, those connected with the local school should be most involved, but the evaluation function usually rests with the school district. The evaluation and planning of school programs is also tightly controlled by district-level bureaucrats, and yet these are clearly the everyday concern of parents and students. The results of misplaced responsibility are negative. Social and political pressures tend to build up in school systems because there is no effective method for citizens to participate in evaluation and planning, and school boards come under direct attack for nonresponsiveness to concerns over which they often have little control or authority.

Students are surprisingly alienated from school affairs. They express a deep disappointment with the quality of their educational experiences, but they seem to have given up hope for meaningful improvement. Had the hearings been held in the late 1960s, angry, dissenting students would have flocked to testify, as some of their parents, in fact, did in 1974. But the students who appeared before the Commission did so with an air of resignation. With few exceptions schools have done little to encourage meaningful student participation in matters of curriculum and governance. As the Commission was told abundantly, the students' role in the school continues to be that of junior prom planner, pep rally promoter, senior class fund raiser. The testimony of students was sometimes cynical, sometimes naive, sometimes hostile, but consistently left the impression that the clients of the schools are emotionally withdrawing from participation in what they view as a burdensome and boring situation.

These are but the major findings from the Commission's inquiry into educational governance; other conclusions about the central issues can be found in the evidence. The ones here, however, form an overall pattern that should help the reader to understand the context of this report and to provide a basis for constructive reform of public school governance in America. The time for such discussion, on the eve of the nation's bicentennial, is appropriate. The Commission's hearings indeed pointed to deep problems in the governance of education, but they also showed that over the two hundred years of the nation's history it has developed a system of education with variety, depth, and considerable vitality. It is hoped that these findings and the Commission's recommendations will help shape educational reform for a third century.

Notes

1. Agenda Item D, NCCE Board Meeting, November 1973.

2. Charge to the Commission, April 12, 1974.

3. "The Roots of Discontent," in "1969 Report of National Committee for Support of the Public Schools."

4. As quoted in R. Freeman Butts, "Assaults on a Great Idea," *The Nation* (April 30, 1973), 553.

5. Harold J. Ruvoldt, Jr., "The Horizon Just Moved," paper presented to the National Tax Association-Tax Institute of America, September 12, 1973.

6. All of the statistics in the preceding paragraph can be found in W. Vance Grant and C. George Lind, *Digest of Educational Statistics* (Washington, D.C.: National Center for Educational Statistics, Office of Education, 1973).

7. Myron Lieberman, "The Union Merger Movement: Will 3,500,000 Teachers Put It All Together?" *Saturday Review/World* (June 24, 1972), 53.

8. *Serrano* v. *Priest,* 483 P.2d 1241, 1244 (Cal. 1971).

9. Butts, "Assaults on a Great Idea."

10. John W. Gardner, *No Easy Victories* (New York: Harper and Row, 1968), 68.

2

THE PUBLIC HEARINGS: PRESSURE SYSTEMS

Between the call to order at 9 a.m., April 22, 1974, in Minneapolis, and the closing gavel at 5 p.m., October 18, in the Los Angeles Board of Public Works hearing room, the Commission on Educational Governance of the National Committee for Citizens in Education heard nearly sixty hours of testimony on the key issues in public school policy making. Witnesses included executives, legislators, teachers, and clients of the school as well as a broad spectrum of organized and unorganized interest groups. They expressed views on every important aspect of school policy making in five metropolitan centers: Minneapolis, St. Louis, Portland, Atlanta, and Los Angeles.

Transcripts from the five hearings fill more than two thousand typewritten pages and are recorded on video tape. The initial impression given by the testimony is one of tremendous variety. The witnesses displayed moods ranging from ebullient pride in recent accomplishments to biting anger and deep frustration at the failure of the schools to respond to the most basic needs. Testimony covered a bewildering array of topical concerns, ranging from the selection of school boards to sex education programs, from the energy crisis to the nature of democracy and the "good life." Speakers addressed immediate and practical issues of life such as teachers' salaries and reading scores. They ranged over every imaginable level of educational activity from the family, the classroom, and the local schools to the administrative subdivision, the local school district, and the metropolitan area. They touched on the activities of state-level executives and legislators and matters of regional and national policy making.

The process of public hearings provided a unique contribution to the currently widespread inquiry into the role of citizens and others in the organization and governance of the public schools. Although several important studies of the problems of school governance have been undertaken in recent years, none has used the vehicle of public hearings on a national scale. Even when such hearings have been held, generally they have been sponsored by government agencies. Thus these hearings represented a special source of information and a special contribution to this ongoing inquiry.

There are several reasons for believing that public hearings are vital to the development of sound policy for the governing of schools. First, as the transcripts show, the witnesses felt they were speaking "for the record," and so they frequently spoke in somewhat muted tones and guarded language (though there were occasional exceptions). In fact, forty-nine of the witnesses (about 25 percent of the total), despite their extensive personal involvements with organized groups and agencies, insisted they were testifying merely as "private citizens" and not as designated spokespersons for any organization. They wanted to be careful not to put their organizations on the record in ways that had not been approved formally by these groups.

This quality of being on the record had both strengths and weaknesses. Though the Commission was not able to hear many of the witnesses' opinions, it was able to look carefully at how the various speakers were prepared to act in public in relation to each other and in relation to the basic issues. This aspect of the testimony is almost certainly a critical element in understanding how school policy is made. When people are ready to assert themselves in public, they are no doubt also ready to commit their personal and political resources to seeing their positions realized. These insights into the public posture of the various witnesses became all the more significant in the context of the interviews and communications by the staff of the Commission with nearly two thousand other persons who did not give formal public testimony.

The public hearing not only gives witnesses a chance to express opinions on the issues but to display their skills in the politically significant processes of public articulation, presentation, and debate. Through dialogue with the witnesses, the Commission was able to understand to a greater extent the full significance of the testimony. In talking on a give-and-take basis with each witness, cultural and social barriers that frequently prevent communication in education could be surmounted. Since five or more Commissioners were listening to each witness, and since the Commission itself was made up of members from wide social and ethnic backgrounds, it was able, as the hearings progressed, to gain singular insights into the feelings of Americans about their schools.

The Witnesses

When one is interpreting the testimony, it is helpful to look at school policy making from the standpoint of the kinds of pressure exerted and the various individuals and groups exerting it.

Thinking of school policy in this way is complicated by the fact that there are a number of different reasons for pressure groups to form. Many have formed around explosive national issues, such as desegregation and textbook controversies. Other factors also important in shaping controversies in education are religious identities; the tension between urban, rural and suburban interests; and the growing conflict within school systems between teachers and administrators.

Three key characteristics of the pressure groups represented at the hearings are ethnicity, social and economic class, and the role each person occupies in relation to the schools. Of the three, the last is by far the most important. The easiest way to guess what a person was going to say about school governance was to determine if he was a student, parent, teacher, or person holding some other functional role in the schools. The 190 witnesses fell into eight different groupings of this kind.

Students

The students were variously referred to as the products, the clients, the consumers, citizens, workers, learners, and "the kids." Assessment of their importance to school policy making ranged from Atlanta Mayor Maynard Jackson's opinion that "There is evidence of growing political sophistication among young people in the high schools, especially eleventh and twelfth graders, and also among college young people (A., III, p. 46*)" to a Los Angeles teacher's conviction that "there isn't really any student power that I can see at all (L.A., Fri., p. 204)," with nearly every shade between these extremes.

There was, on the whole, little evidence that students are an effective force in school policy making. Unlike teachers' and parents' groups, students did not rush forward to present their views on school governance in the public hearings. They tended instead to be either a bit cynical, believing that no one would take their involvement in governance seriously, or "turned off" and withdrawn entirely. There were few signs of the student activism and aggressive efforts at reform that were sweeping the country a short time ago. One student in St. Louis seemed to summarize why students generally are changing in their response to school: "The student began to realize it really wasn't his education, it was someone else's education; they were just doing the hard part of it . . . [there] was really no enjoyment in learning (S.L., p. 9)."

The director of an alternative school in Minneapolis reported that students attending his school were very uncomfortable in the public school because of "the sterile atmosphere of the school. Going to public school is a job for these kids. I don't feel that my students [in the alternative school] feel this way . . . . They want to come to school . . . they thoroughly enjoy it. My dropout rate is zero (M., p. 72)."

The students, then, seem to be more potential than real contributors to school policy. But their potential is quite important. Once they began to address problems of school governance they frequently were able to pinpoint issues with a freshness and clarity lacking among witnesses with other perspectives. Note, for example, the effective analysis of the complexities of student and citizen participation in decision making displayed by a black high school senior in Portland:

---

*The information enclosed in the parentheses within the quotations refers to the transcripts of the hearings. The place of the hearings is abbreviated as follows: A.=Atlanta; L.A.=Los Angeles; M.=Minneapolis; P.=Portland; S.L.=St. Louis.

There is participation in Portland public schools but very little decision-making participation by students or citizens. There are several levels of citizen and student participation. These may be defined as the local school, the area and the district level. There are different kinds of participation; there is partial participation, open participation, and closed participation. Textbook adoption is an area of partial participation. Citizens and students do not participate in the development of criteria, but are allowed to review proposed criteria. Students and citizens are not members of textbook selection committees but are permitted to review and request rejections and additions . . . . Open participation . . . [is] concentrated in auxilliary functions. The participation is in the implementation of policy but not in its evaluation or development . . . . The public is excluded from decisions regarding personnel, contract, and negotiations. Student government at present is ineffective to change policy, since its focus is on school-centered extracurricular activities . . . . As citizens, students should have the right to participate in policy-making decisions (P., pp. 57-59).

Students are by no means of one mind about how much they should have to say about school affairs. One high school student in Minneapolis expressed the view that although students have "limited" power in curriculum planning and development, nevertheless, "At our high school I think the student council has enough responsibility and power (M., p. 16)." A Los Angeles student insisted, on the other hand: "Student leaders should have a full opportunity to question, inquire, and exchange their ideas as far as their school is concerned. Student leaders should be permitted to act in administrative, advisory, and curriculum matters which pertain to student concerns. Examples should be budget consideration at the school, student body finance, security on campus, course selection, and counseling . . . (L.A., Thurs., p. 92)."

Some witnesses indicated that patterns of student participation in school governance may be changing. The Minnesota commissioner of education reported, for example, that his "state board right now is researching legally how we can put a student on the state board of education (M., p. 196)." In Atlanta it was reported that it was possible, in suburban DeKalb County, "to get two students to attend the school board meetings as nonvoting representatives (A., II, p. 97)." The dominant theme, however, was that "Students do not play any role in negotiations in the State of Washington (staff member, Washington State Department of Education, P., p. 10)" and "The whole system is built around the student, but for *educational* purposes. I'm making a distinction between the student as learner and the student with rights and responsibilities (member, Missouri State Board, S.L., p. 192)." Or, as the students put it, "The student council really tries hard, but they're not doing anything . . . nobody offers us an opportunity (A., II, p. 76)."

Parents, Citizens, and Community Interest Groups

Ninety-four of the speakers were parents or citizens whose interest in school governance springs from their reactions to the results of schooling either on the community that supports the schools or on the children who attend them. Some of these witnesses belong to relatively permanent organizations like the PTA, the League of Women Voters, and the new parent advisory committees. Others belong to groups devoted to specific purposes and may or may not be permanent. Examples are the Goals Committee of the Los Angeles Unified School District, the court-appointed biracial committee in Jackson, Mississippi, and Mothers for Children, Portland, Oregon.

A second division within the group of ninety-four parent-citizen witnesses is that between those who belong to school-related groups, like parent advisory councils, PTAs, parent congresses, and goals committees and those representing groups with roots in, and support from, the wider community. Examples of the latter are the NAACP, Citizens for Integrated Education in Minneapolis, the League of Women Voters, and Portland's Schools for the City. Witnesses who had no known group affiliation were thought to be representing their family group, and thus to be reflecting community-based perspectives. There were, therefore, fifty-four witnesses with community-based affiliations and forty speakers representing school-related groups. Table 2-1 breaks down the two divisions within the parent-citizen witnesses.

Table 2-1
The ninety-four parent-citizen witnesses

	School-based groups	Community-based groups	Total
Groups with specific purpose	9	20	29
Groups with wider purposes	31	34	65
Total	40	54	94

It should be noted that the Commission staff, in scheduling the hearings in each city, made no effort to provide an exact breakdown of types of witnesses or affiliations. To do so would have been unwise and restrictive. The single goal was to hear as wide a variety of views as possible. There was evidence of jockeying for position on the hearing agenda, both before and during the actual sessions. Some speakers wanted to testify just before or after the local superintendent (or his designate), while others wanted to be on the agenda at a time when it was believed the educational establishment would not be present.

One thing that was documented throughout the hearings was the increasing determination, resourcefulness, and sophistication of the parent-citizen groups. The motivations for the expansion and organization of parental pressures on school policy are diverse, but their common theme is the poor job the schools are doing in meeting parental expectations. A black grandmother in the South explained: "I had been a victim. My children were victims at that time. Now I have grandchildren who are being victimized. And I look to the generations to come that's still going to be victims of this vicious cycle (A., I, p. 51)." A Chicano mother in Los Angeles insisted: "Most of the teachers I feel have the idea that they are just babysitting our children (L.A., Thurs., p. 108)."

White parents, too, are sensitive to the apparent failure of the schools to prepare children for meaningful adulthood. A parent in Minneapolis suggested that "The critical issue is what are the goals of education, what are the goals for an educational institution (M., p. 202)?" As if in answer to her question, a mother in San Francisco pointed out: "Educators traditionally trained to dispense facts are not doing that very well, and are now being asked to dispense culture (L.A., Fri., p. 157)." And in Los Angeles a mother who was a member of the PTA underscored the point by suggesting that "The schools do not necessarily meet society's needs, the students' needs, or the parents' aspirations for an education that will prepare students to fully participate in the mainstream of society (L.A., Fri., p. 208)."

Teachers

Traditionally the term "educator" has embraced classroom teachers, school administrative personnel, and the members of university faculties who train teachers and conduct research into educational practices and problems. It is difficult to say whether it was appropriate in the past to categorize these people as belonging to a single pressure group exercising unified influence on school policy, but that is clearly not the case today. James Ballard, the president of the AFT in San Francisco, put it this way: "Too often I think there is some confusion. We talk about professional educators, and there is no pure distinction between that person called a teacher and that person called an administrator . . . . It has been just recently that we have grown to accept that there is something called management of a school system (L.A., Fri., p. 115)."

There is a deep and widening gap between the teaching and administrative staffs of the public schools. The testimony indicates that public school teachers are the most effective emerging pressure group. Teachers in St. Louis and Los Angeles have recently conducted successful strikes, and in Portland the teachers' association has recently raised dues by 17 percent in order to increase staff and improve the training capability so as to sharpen influence on policy. In the testimony of the teachers, there is ambivalence about the adversary relationship developing with other groups interested in school policy, but teachers in all five cities wanted a "piece of the action." As a Portland teacher said,

Teachers are citizens, and maybe teachers have, as a group, more expertise in what goes on in the schools than anyone else. Not necessarily about what should go on, but we certainly do know an awful lot about what does go on . . . . What [the teachers] are talking about is staff input to the administration, the management, so that they can make the decisions . . . . The effect [of not having input] on staff is to create apathy because they never get a chance to help make the decisions. They are never members of a democratic society in the school district (P., pp. 25-27).

Demosthenes Dubose, an organizer of teachers in St. Louis, echoed these sentiments: "What we're really trying to do is to work out some arrangement where the working professional, the teacher, has as much to say about what happens in the classroom as does the school board member (S.L., p. 202)."

In contrast to this strong, singular stance taken by most organizers of teachers, the Commission heard from a number of teachers who were concerned with the preservation of an intimate quality in the student-teacher-parent relationship. A teacher in Portland was mindful that education needs to be "shared by parents, students, and school personnel (P., p. 151)." Another teacher in Portland expressed fear that the adversary process is destructive and insisted that "Interactive educational governance is necessary . . . this would require an active interest and participation by parents, by students, by teachers, by administrators, by city residents . . . everybody else. This is difficult . . . it requires many skills (P., p. 155)."

The clearest articulation of why teachers have been sacrificing this "interactive" for the collective bargaining style of policy making was found in the testimony of Ballard:

> Up until a few years ago, teachers were told that "they could have their input" even before the word input became so popular. Teachers could have their input by simply informing their principal about what they thought should occur and the principal would inform the divisional superintendent, and this is how the teacher would have his or her "input" on what should or should not occur in that particular school. Well, a few years ago this broke down, if it ever really worked, and the teachers, in searching around for some kind of model to develop a voice that would have an effect upon decision making that affected education in their classroom . . . after trying several things, they came up with the model that has been used in other places, and that is known as collective bargaining (L.A., Fri., pp. 116-117).

Administrators

The hearings confirmed once again that superintendents of local school districts and their immediate staffs exercise extensive influence in school policy making. Evidence for this was presented by witnesses of many backgrounds and perspectives. Oregon State Representative Howard Cherry affirmed that "the most important single person in each community that a legislator goes to is his local superintendent. They know them, they know them personally, they respect them, and they know that they are well aware of the problems (P., pp. 149-150)."

The director of the Southern Regional Council, a widely respected civil rights monitor, said: "With the help of the school attorney and the help or acquiescence of the school board chairman, it is the superintendent who basically decides where your children will go to school, what budget the system will have, and what kind of education is going to be provided (A., III, p. 148)."

Most, though not all, witnesses put the school principal in the same general category as the school superintendent. It does appear, however, that there is a widening gap between upper and middle management in the school system. The more districts have become large and complex bureaucracies, the more it seems to be natural and necessary for parents, students, and teachers to relate directly to the school principal as the key policy maker.

Local School Boards

"The local school boards, they run the schools (S.L., p. 24)." With these words Representative Wayne Goode of Missouri expressed the characteristic view that school boards are central in the policy-making process. From the citizens' perspective this matter is not so clear. There is fairly widespread agreement that there is "a pass-the-buck situation that has developed in our district, from Tinker to Evers to Chance, which becomes, for a local school person with this problem, from teacher to principal to area superintendent to down-town staff to the board. And then he is told, 'Have you dealt with it at your local school level?' (L.A., Thurs., p. 207)."

Even among school board members themselves there is a fair amount of uncertainty about just how much they "run" the schools. A school board member in Atlanta said: "One of the biggest prob-lems with education is you can't fire anybody. They almost have to hang a child at mid-noon in the middle of the street before you can get enough on them (A., II, p. 39)."

Robert Hoover, a school board member from a medium-sized school district just outside San Francisco, painted a vivid picture of how difficult it is for board members to exercise their legal powers effectively.

Let me give you an example of what I am talking about. About three years ago we decided that before we were going to grant any more tenures in the district that we were going to take a look at all of the personnel records of the teachers who were being recommended for tenure. So we asked the superintendent to bring all those records in, and the board sat down and went through them and looked at the evaluations of those teachers. And what they showed was essen-tially information that was of no use to the board in determining whether or not a teacher was a good teacher. It had nonsense information as far as I was con-cerned. The things like: "She comes to work on time, dresses neat, gets along well with the rest of the staff," but didn't tell me a thing whether or not she could teach, didn't say the students in her classes were learning anything. And as we went through the evaluation we also could not find any indication that one single teacher had any weaknesses in any area. I said, "It is impossible for me to believe that all thirty of these people have absolutely no weaknesses in teaching. If that is the case, then all of our children ought to be reading at grade level, ought to be well educated. There is something wrong."

And as we began to grope through this problem we suddenly began to realize that there was no way . . . we told them to take these evaluations back, that they had to be redone, and told them what kind of information we wanted. And, of course, they came back with, again, the things I said, all the teachers were good. There is no way the central board or administration, because of the lack of personnel, can go out to the individual schools and observe these teachers, find out whether or not they really are good teachers, where their strengths and weaknesses are (L.A., Thurs., pp. 172-173).

This board found that even though it moved every principal in the district—and some of them two or three times—it was still not possible to get an effective evaluation of the teachers.

State Legislators

The Commission heard testimony from eight state legislators and from the representatives of three others. Senator Jerome Hughes of Minnesota asserted that, as in other states, "The constitution of the State of Minnesota determines that it is the *duty* of the legislature to establish a general and uniform system of public schools in the state [italics added] (M., p. 46)."

In addition to this constitutional mandate, state legislators have important political reasons for playing a significant role in school policy making. It was one of the designated spokesmen, representing a California state senator who had been appointed lieutenant governor just a few days before the Los Angeles hearing, who summed up the reasons for legislative interest in educational matters: "Legislators are deeply concerned and interested in education for at least two opposing reasons. One is that it is one of the most important services . . . whether they are intellectual, social, or political because of concern of their constituents they have to pay attention. And the other is that it takes such a large chunk of money (L.A., Thurs., pp. 22-23)."

Despite a universal recognition of their responsibilities for educational policy, legislators are by no means of one mind about how those responsibilities should be discharged. Some legislators, like the chairman of California's Joint Legislative Committee on Educational Goals, pointed with satisfaction to the "marked movement away from centralization of power in the legislature and the governor . . . such that it is much more decentralized. We have seen, for example, the abolition of the uniform statewide textbook system. And we have seen this year passage of a bill to make our educational code permissive rather than restrictive (L.A., Thurs., p. 184)."

The chairman of Minnesota's Senate Education Committee, on the other hand, focused on the role of legislative activity in directly affecting education in his state. He pointed with pride to the fact that over 47 percent of all of that state's revenues is expended on education and indicated that the legislature "pushed for an equal education opportunity program, and we now fund at the state level 70 percent of education. We feel that we are constantly aware of what's happening within our school districts by our testimony and our approach, at a legislative level (M., p. 28)." He went on to argue that "the legislature really is the body that ought to be making legislative policy with respect to education . . . . We ought to know what the concerns are, and we ought to make the policy (M., p. 38)."

The legislators demonstrated, on the whole, a keen awareness that they have a large and probably growing role to play in resolving major conflicts concerning school policy. California's Assemblyman John Vasconcellos put it this way: "At this point in time it is particularly important that we take a good, strong look at governance structures and control on power. There is a convergence of a lot of forces that could well signal the end of public schools in terms of credibility and/or physical support and/or morale unless there is something really creative . . . undertaken and accomplished (L.A., Thurs., p. 187)."

Doing something creative does not appear very easy, however. First a legislator from Missouri suggested: "Most legislators are not very much innovative. We're pretty much copy cats (S.L., p. 122)." And a legislator from Oregon with more than twenty-five years in public service added: "the priorities of education in peoples' minds and in the legislature's mind is not as high as it was previously. I think that school boards, at least in the communities that I see, and teachers and the public have lost a good deal of mutual respect that was present just a few years ago (P., p. 148)."

There is ferment at the legislative level. In every state represented in the hearings significant legislation has been passed affecting school finance, teacher organization and contracting, and new educational programs such as early childhood education. State legislators, like parents and teachers, seem to be emerging as a force to be reckoned with in public school policy making in the next few years.

State-Level Executives and State School Boards

The state legislature uses the state school board and state department of education as its conduit to implement, regulate, and administer legislative policy. These agencies have considerable latitude in establishing regulations and administrative bylaws. How they work or should work in school policy making is poorly understood at many levels. As a state legislator from the St. Louis area remarked, "The state board is so remote that citizens and persons who have a concern think lastly of the state board. They think first of their local board; they think second of the legislature . . . . Teachers are more cognizant of the state board than lay citizen people . . . very seldom do lay citizen people even appeal to the state board for any help in their problems (S.L., p. 167)."

There appear to be two reasons for this low-profile image of state school boards and their executive staffs. First, there is a decided tendency to view the state-level operation as providing support services rather than leadership or control over education. A state school board member in Missouri summed up the situation: "The State Department of Education has the technical staff who can bring to the local districts such expertise as may be needed . . . . I view the state department of education as something of a staff function. We can assist the local school district in providing and bringing a certain amount of expertise in the field of education (S.L., pp. 181-182)."

A second reason for the remoteness of the state-level staff from day-to-day school operations is the widespread belief that education is best managed at the level of the school district. An official of the Washington State Department of Education, for example, told the Portland hearing: "I believe in local control of education. If you move negotiations and all of those decisions around negotiations from the local level to the state level, I think you will have weakened the base of support of citizens for education (P., p. 9)." And the state board member from Missouri declared: "I happen to be a real advocate of local control and autonomy as much as possible and as much as practical . . . . If there is a real problem in the citizens being heard on a local basis . . . I'm not too sure there's a whole lot that can be done on a statewide basis (S.L., p. 177)."

The spokeswoman from the California State Department of Education was more aggressive in her views of state-level responsibilities, declaring: "Delegation of authority does not relieve the state of the responsibility for quality and equality of the educational programs in the local schools (L.A., Fri., p. 92)." This responsibility of the state does not, however, lead the department into direct intervention in the operation of schools. Using the Early Childhood Education Program as an illustration, she noted: "We discharge our state responsibility for quality and equality by providing proper guidelines. We do not fund programs where plans and implementation are not a joint responsibility of parents and teachers (L.A., Fri., p. 93)."

The commissioner of education of Minnesota raised the most basic question about the role of state boards of education: "We might have a full-time legislature in the State of Minnesota. If that happens I'm not sure that we will need a state board of education—that they will become the board of education . . . why have an agency or board promulgating rules and regulations when you have a legislature in session who can make the laws (M., p. 198)?"

Other Significant Pressures

Three other sources of pressure affecting school governance were frequently mentioned in the hearings. The first is the courts. In each of the five cities major school policy questions are being or have recently been litigated. The most important question for litigation has been the matter of desegregation. Rights of parents and students, school finance, due process procedures, teachers' contracts, and collective bargaining are, however, also significant topics for court action. Certainly the involvement of the U.S. Fifth Circuit Court of Appeals in the desegregation of the Atlanta schools and the California Supreme Court decision in *Serrano* v. *Priest* represent far-reaching intervention of the courts in day-to-day school operations. In Atlanta the court has mandated the attendance of students, the redistribution of teaching and administrative staff within the school district, a detailed specification of job titles, distribution of departmental and school personnel along with the regular reports for court review. In addition, the court has ordered transportation for parents wishing to attend after-school activities and meetings.

In summarizing the significance of the court, a longtime civil rights advocate in Atlanta asserted flatly, "The only hope that the parent has, has been through the court (A., I, p. 20)."

A second source of pressure identified frequently by witnesses was the executive agencies of the federal government. Federal money and federal policy were often cited as having brought about changes in education. The director of an alternative school in Minneapolis said this was a deliberate policy: "What the federal government was interested in in 1970 and 1971 was the concept of comprehensive change. ... What Washington was interested in doing was ... to test the notion of comprehensive change (M., p. 112)."

At the same hearing, the director of Indian affairs of the Minnesota Department of Education was questioned about what his office was doing to try to relieve the hostility of parents in the public schools. He replied: "Well I guess we're looking to [a] federal project ... to do a lot of this for us (M., p. 169)."

Several witnesses seriously questioned the effectiveness of federal intervention. For example, a staff member of the American Friends Service Committee in Atlanta charged: "HEW's efforts to combat racial discrimination have been weak and frequently useless (A., III, p. 133)."

The Commission received only limited testimony from elected state and local officials and from federal level policy makers. Both groups influence school policy making significantly, if indirectly.

Ethnicity and Social Class Groupings

Not only were witnesses speaking from the perspective of their role in the educational system; they were also speaking as members of a particular social, ethnic, and economic class. Black teachers spoke differently from white teachers, and residents of the ghetto and the barrio had a different perspective on schools from that of middle-class and suburban families. An Asian-American mother in Los Angeles insisted that, "Parents, whether in high socioeconomic level or in the ghetto are concerned about their child's education (L.A., Fri., p. 136)." But a Chicano mother from East Los Angeles said, "the problem we have in America is a social class problem. Racism keeps the juices going of the class problem . . . . We are going to have to realize that if you belong to the lower classes . . . you are not going to get an education (L.A., Fri., p. 67)."

This same view was offered by the regional field director for the

American Friends Service Committee in Atlanta who has spent more than ten years working for desegregation in the South. She said: "issues are now more complex and tend, in many instances, to deal with class as much as they do with race (A., III, p. 137)."

Many witnesses from minority groups felt that racism and cultural insensitivity are the major sources of the failures of urban schools. In Los Angeles the Commission was told that the decentralization of that school district "added another layer to the previous bureaucratic structure which had minimal flexibility, sensitivity, and . . . [was] sporadic in its attempts to meet the needs of the diverse ethnic and socioeconomic communities it served (L.A., Thurs., p. 5)" and that "We need people who are sensitive to the black community, who will note things that happen in the black community. Very little things, not only learning, but just things that make you feel like a human being (L.A., Fri., p. 29)."

The prevailing message of the hearings is that ethnicity, race, and economic class are real forces in determining what people think and feel about school governance and school programs.

3

THE PUBLIC HEARINGS: THE CENTRAL ISSUES

The hearings demonstrated that five major policy issues concerning school governance account for most of the conflict between and among the witnesses.

The Control of Policy: Access and Responsiveness

Surely the most pervasive issue presented by the witnesses is heard in the questions: Who controls school policy? How do they control it? Who should have more—or less—control than they do now, and why?

The control of school policy is crucial. First, public school programs and policies are widely felt to be both inadequate to contemporary society and inflexible in meeting all the needs of individuals and ethnic groups. Second, school policy is felt to be unresponsive to the various groups seeking change. Finally, the process itself seems to be closed off from public view and democratic participation, particularly from minorities and the poor, but also from large numbers of other citizens. Witnesses representing minority groups presented the most compelling description of the inadequacies of schools. Some sketched the problem in stark statistical terms. For example, the director of the Hispanic Urban Center in Los Angeles presented a

graph showing the relationship between the reading scores for Los
Angeles schools and the percentage of minority students in each.
That graph alone is compelling evidence that there is something fun-
damentally wrong with school programs. He summarized the problem:

In East Los Angeles [a predominantly Mexican-American area of the district],
60 percent of the youth between the ages of sixteen and nineteen are neither in
school nor gainfully employed . . . 60 percent of our young people have been
blanked out from any participation in society, because by the time they are in
the sixth grade, they are reading at the third-grade level, by the time they are in
the twelfth grade, they are reading at the fourth- or fifth-grade level, and they
are blanked out from our society (L.A., Fri., p. 18).

A parent from one of the predominantly Mexican-American schools
put the same point in blunt personal terms: "The reason I decided to
come here is that the children [in my school] are illiterate. You
know, I don't mean semiliterate; I mean they are illiterate (L.A., Fri.,
p. 42)."

The problem of failure to teach is not confined to Mexican-Americans or to Los Angeles. At the hearing in Atlanta there was testimony that "in Georgia the rate of dropouts before they graduate
from high school is 50 percent . . . I don't think General Motors
would stand for that kind of rejection rate . . . (A., II, p. 146)." In
Portland a black witness related: "Our children come to where I
work, and they do not know what they want to do. They can't read;
they do not know how to make out an application (P., p. 159)."

In St. Louis a black attorney with the state Advisory Commission
on Civil Rights cited as evidence for the failure of the schools his
discovery that "none of the board members at the present time have
children in the public school system (S.L., p. 152)." He continued:

I also have children who are school age . . . they are attending private schools
because the public schools don't offer the educational opportunities that I think
my children should have. And I think the same thing is evident in the fact that a
great majority of your principals and your school superintendents and your
teachers have moved out of the city primarily for the purpose of providing better educational opportunities for their children (S.L., p. 152).

A black woman from the same agency argued that "there would be a
greater return to the public schools if the public schools were effective . . . when our children finish high school they are not able to

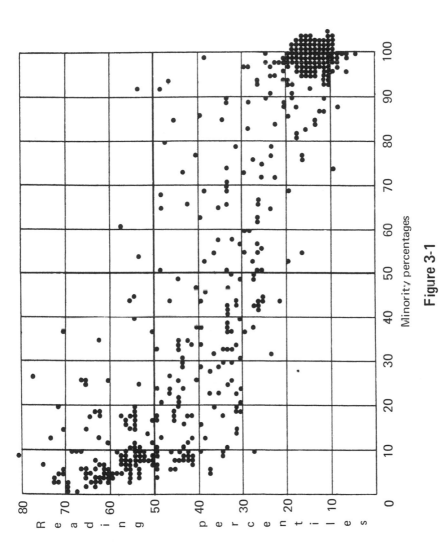

Figure 3-1

Los Angeles city schools, sixth grade, fall 1971, reading scores
(from a chart by Vahoc Mardirosian prepared from L.A. Unified School District Summary Report #321)

Minority percentages

pass a SAT and PSAT examination which is necessary for them to go to college. And, I also believe that . . . public schools . . . have the great responsibility of providing education which is relevant to today's society (S.L., p. 149)."

Though the problem is not limited to minority students, the poor and minorities are stuck with the school's inadequacies, while wealthier and more mobile white families are able to flee the worst of the schools and attend private schools or move out of the cities altogether.

The widespread, if sometimes inarticulate, feeling shared by parents and citizens that something is deeply wrong with the conduct of public schools in America's major metropolitan centers has touched off an intense effort for control of school policy.

One white mother from a suburban district near Portland put the issue of control in dramatic terms. With barely constrained outrage, she said of her family, "We have reluctantly reached the decision that wherever else our boys might go, they will not attend the public schools until parental control of curriculum is acknowledged and respected . . . the objections of literally thousands of irate parents and taxpayers about what is happening in the public schools have had absolutely no effect on the arrogant educators (P., p. 142)." She also complained of "behavior modification techniques" and the abandonment of "all theocentric beliefs."

A more general complaint was that schools are failing to provide democratic experiences or basic skills. Among minority witnesses the outrage was frequently suppressed and took the form of a kind of cynical challenge to the Commission. Witness a black leader in Los Angeles: "I am going to make this short because I have testified before groups before, and really, I have gotten to kind of wondering what is going to happen. I hope you guys do something. Obviously I keep hoping something is going to happen, and nothing ever has (L.A., Fri., p. 20)."

No matter how intense the loss of confidence, merely demanding a shift in control of school policy is not sufficient to produce intelligent or effective reform. School administrators and school boards are not responding to these demands for change in a way that is likely to ease the tensions or restore confidence in their leadership. A city councilwoman in Atlanta reported: "The response from the system has been too often a defensive posture that says 'all is well,' and reiterates what is the goal of many educators . . . . What is amazing to me is the denial that [the problems] exist. I mean that's where we lose credibility (A., III, pp. 110, 111)."

Perhaps the most important result of this loss of credibility is the deepening of a chasm between professional educators and lay citizens. As one witness put it, "I think there are some who are beginning to question whether it should be left to the professionals (A., III, p. 191)." Another witness, representing the Southern Regional Council, insisted, "In leaving education to professionals . . . we have seen the children tossed and thrown about . . . . Standard curriculums and standard methods produce boredom and apathy and often bear no relations to the reality of the world . . . the job of educating our children is too big to leave to the professionals alone (A., III, p. 150)."

While most witnesses believed that the gap between professionals and nonprofessionals was the natural result of different ways of looking at education, there were many who accused school board members and school administrators of bad faith. The education director of the Community Relations Council of Southern California, for example, insisted that "the school administration effectively maintains control of the schools by several influences which are most clearly visible . . . such as powerful administrative structures and strict control of information (L.A., Thurs., p. 15)."

In Los Angeles the Commission heard from several black and Chicano witnesses that they were intimidated by the use of policemen in the schools and by a school board that prevents anyone from entering the campus without permission. As one black woman put it, "This gets the parents off the school grounds. And in fact, it has done nothing to help the other things that the parents were complaining about, and that is, that two of the teachers had been raped. He [the principal] didn't get the rapists off, but he got [the parents] off . . . this is to get rid of the parents . . . . The board rule . . . is definitely not . . . binding anyone from coming on the school ground but peaceful parents (L.A., Fri., pp. 37-38)."

School District Organization: Planning and Accountability

The second major issue emerging from the hearings was whether present structures of school governance lead to effective policy making. A spokesman for the California state senator who sponsored a bill to break up the Los Angeles School District into a number of smaller units described the school organizational problem this way:

It became quite clear that insofar as the very large school districts of California were concerned, and one in particular [Los Angeles], the organizational form that had its origin more than a hundred years ago unfortunately was not particularly relevant to the latter part of the twentieth century because of its worn-out organizational heritage. The district fell short in providing quality education, and its policy making failed to afford adequate and healthy presentations to the public it served. Superintendents, principals, and teachers were not held accountable for performance. The protections of self-interests by all employee groups within the district relegated consideration of improvements for better education to a secondary significance (L.A., Thurs., pp. 6-7).

The president of San Francisco's Urban School Administrators' organization painted a similar picture of school organizational structures unable to cope with pressing needs. She summarized: "The governance of schools in San Francisco, from our viewpoint, is in the hands of an inbred few who hold top-level positions in the management system, and who use the techniques, along with a few board members, of ignoring or nondecision making to maintain the status quo, and to effectively prevent any meaningful impact by community or anyone else on changes (L.A., Fri., p. 162)." A witness in Minneapolis insisted: "The system as it is presently constituted cannot respond . . . . It can't respond because it is organized as a hierarchical pyramid with power starting at the top (M., p. 257)."

The Commission repeatedly heard the insistent claims that the school system is organized as an "inaccessible" and "very self-protective type organization (A., II, p. 31)." These structural problems are preventing the schools from performing their tasks adequately; what is worse, they make it virtually impossible for those seeking change to influence or control school policy and practice.

Witnesses who addressed the problems of school organization took two different approaches to the problem. Some identified the activities made ineffective and/or inaccessible by the structure. Two major activities—planning and program implementation—were singled out by these critics. Others focused on the breaking up of schools into various levels of operation and indicated that there are major barriers preventing the effective passing of policy from one level to another. The levels of operation that received at least some attention were the classroom, the school site, the decentralized administrative area, the school district, the state, and the federal government.

The inability of the school organization to plan effectively was most obvious to witnesses who have statewide experience with the schools. Said the chairman of Missouri's House Education Committee: "the problem, as I see it, in this system centers around the long-range planning and implementation of these plans. The system of governance that we have in Missouri does not provide anything in this area (S.L., p. 23)." A legislator in Oregon expressed the same sentiments: "I do see a great need for school districts to widen their scope of planning to do a greater amount of planning with other services which affect them: land use, subdivision development, health, mental health, transportation divisions, and so on (P., p. 45)." A similar remark was made by an official in the Washington State Department of Education: "We observed that there was inadequate mechanism for planning in education, and so we developed a thing called Imaging which is a long-range planning device . . . a mechanism involving the public and others in . . . helping to reach the goals of what education ought to look like in the future (P., p. 4)."

A second major problem area concerns the implementation of school programs. The term "accountability" has become both the description of the problem and the battle cry for its solution. Accountability legislation has been proposed or passed in most states and has been the topic of study by legislative committees and community groups alike.

The central feature of the concern for accountability was well stated by a black activist teacher in Los Angeles: "Today our problem arises in that parents are demanding decentralization to increase the learning capacity of their children. Their theory is that the inadequacies are caused by local school staffs not being accountable to the local parental control. But the contrary view of the school district is that inadequacies of academic achievement result from the local administrators' lacking resources and the power to . . . use efficiently whatever resources are available (L.A., Fri., p. 198)." A witness in Minneapolis who focused his complaint on the power pyramid also found a conflict between the explanations of school officials and citizens for the failures of various programs. He said that "The argument of [the superintendent] has been, in conversations . . . that what Minneapolis needs is more money in the system. I do not believe that. Lack of money is not why schools fail; lack of money is not why students drop out; lack of money is not why kids quit learning (M., p. 257)."

The movement for accountability has grown steadily in the past decade. It seems to be built on the widespread conviction that schools are not using their resources in the most effective way. Many people feel that the universal response of school officials when a program fails is that there were inadequate funds to make the changes or improvements. This has led to a strong desire to penetrate the school organizations and directly shape the performance of the teachers and administrators who are making the classroom program what it is. These efforts to reach into the classroom are being made at every level from federal agencies and state legislatures to parents existing at the poverty level. A legislator in Missouri framed well the state-level perspective: "We spend eleven hundred dollars on average per child in the city of St. Louis or about thirty-five thousand per classroom on an average of thirty-two. And we have a situation where up to two years ago one out of three was getting a certificate of attendance [rather than a graduation diploma] when they all finished high school. Well, there was a lot of objection raised to that . . . people will demand and are demanding educational accountability (S.L., p. 127)." The legislator in Florida who was responsible for that state's recent Assessment Accountability Act indicated in testimony that the act "also emphasized a much expanded program of accountability with the focus . . . being on the individual school (A., III, p. 92)."

In Los Angeles a Mexican-American mother told the Commission in vivid detail how the culturally different child suffers painfully in the typical school. She added hopefully: "All these things have to be taken care of, I believe, by real, honest breaking down of this tremendous school system which we have, and we have to have areas that are really accountable to the people that live there, and they must serve these areas in order that they will function (L.A., Thurs., p. 109)."

Despite the widespread support for some kind of accountability, however, there are serious problems in using it to improve school performance. California's Assemblyman John Vasconcellos reported that "[Accountability] threatens to inundate the schools with paper, charts, checklists, over-the-shoulder watching, and so little energy and time for that kind of personal involvement that students have a right to, if they are going to feel good about themselves, and learn more adequately what they need to learn (L.A., Thurs., pp. 188-189)."

An organizer of teachers in St. Louis said accountability as a measurement of classroom performance is meeting powerful resistance from teachers: "The teachers' main problem with accountability is who is supposed to be accountable to whom, and for what. This usually ends up with the teacher being accountable and no one else . . . evaluations themselves are usually built on the principle of retribution, not on the principle of helping a person to perform a job in the classroom . . . as long as we have this principle of retribution involved in accountability and involved in evaluation, then teachers must fight this kind of accountability (S.L., p. 204)."

The director of the Minneapolis Accountability Project declared that accountability of teachers may not be very easy to handle for a quite different reason: "Assuming that there was 1 percent of the teaching force . . . incompetent . . . you were talking about establishing some criteria which would eliminate them. You'll spend all your time working on that 1 percent and not upgrading the skills of the other 99 percent (M., pp. 228-229)." He warned that those seeking access to school performance through accountability may be frustrated if they seek to root out failures rather than promote successes, and there is no doubt that eliminating failures is the dominant motive behind efforts to make teachers accountable.

James Ballard, mentioned before as an organizer of teachers in San Francisco, sees a conflict between accountability and the thrust toward decentralizing the schools. He said that, "Once you start spreading responsibility too thin, then you can't hold anyone accountable (L.A., Fri., p. 127)."

Several witnesses said effective accountability is much more complex than living within the letter of a law dealing with accountability. For example, the regional field director for the American Friends Service Committee, who has more than ten years of experience in the South, said: "People are beginning to realize that legal programs don't mean that the programs are well organized, efficient, or meeting children's needs. It takes more than legislation to obtain sound educational programs (A., III, p. 133)." She added: "Local parent involvement is a good means of monitoring the effectiveness of the programs . . . . Local and state department officials should be providing parent advisory councils with the support and technical assistance needed for real involvement (A., III, p. 133)."

It appears, then, that success with regard to accountability is much more complex than merely toughening up legislative mandates. There is little evidence that the recent spate of accountability legislation has, in fact, significantly altered school programs.

Witnesses perceived the problem of access to the school organization—whether to planning activities or to implementation of programs—in two quite distinct ways. On the one hand, many witnesses equated access with formal control through voting on policies, personnel, or budgets. On the other hand, some witnesses believed that access is, or ought to be, much more subtle and informal. They spoke of creating an "atmosphere" that would shape planning and program activities or of "influencing" the votes or the decisions.

A school board member in Portland made this distinction: "There are two aspects of power. One aspect is the ability to be consulted and to have your views listened to very carefully and taken into account in making a decision. There is a second aspect of power: that is being given the right to make the decision (P., p. 77)." He added that school advisory councils have influential or informal power: "I disagree when you say they [the advisory councils] don't have any power because they don't have the final right to decide. I think they have a great deal of power. They certainly have influenced my vote on issue after issue during the last two years (P., p. 78)."

In Los Angeles a school board member said that even the school board does not exercise direct control in decision making. His was the typical view of the relationship between actions of the school board and organizational activities of the school: "It has been my experience, both as a citizen volunteer and a member of the board of education, the best thing the elected public officials can do to improve the quality of education, in this case in our community, is to provide an *atmosphere* that gives the school principal and teacher in each individual classroom the notion that they are the key to the success of that educational program [italics added] (L.A., Thurs., p. 57)."

The chairman of the Los Angeles Goals Commission explained the reason for preferring this informal, atmosphere-creating access: "I am convinced that education takes place in the interface between the teacher and students, and everything else basically has to be supportive of that role (L.A., Fri., p. 84)." A student in Los Angeles made the same observation: "Teachers should have additional authority, additional to what they have now, because they are the front liners; they realize what kinds of problems occur on a day-to-day basis in a classroom; they realize what sort of problems occur in the curriculum, in teaching and disciplinary methods (L.A., Thurs., pp. 72-73)."

This need to bring decision making as close as possible to the front lines detracts from the capacity of the school organization to specify exactly what teachers should do, and it destroys accountability of the type found in industry where the nature of the work often makes possible a precise specification of the workers' responsibilities.

Many witnesses opposed this view. They maintained that the autonomy of teachers and administrators tends to close off the organization from responsible access by those who have legitimate interests in its performance. These witnesses found deep and unmanageable difficulties in trying to influence the behavior of teachers through informal processes, and they insisted on substantially increased formal power.

One of the most important results of a system that leaves much decision-making control in the hands of teachers and administrators is that the professionals tend to worry more about their careers than about the needs of effective programming. This problem was seen at all levels in the system. A black citizen in St. Louis found it in the principal's behavior: "The principal is in a unique position because he's the school board's man, and naturally he has to cater to the board (S.L., p. 83)."

In Los Angeles a black citizen saw the problem as running all the way up the administrative ladder: "There are many things wrong with the school system here. One is the buddy system we have of bringing up administrators. What happens in this buddy system is that principals always help other principals [whom] they know . . . . So by the time you get to the top you don't have any creative people: you have people who have expertise in bootlicking (L.A., Fri., pp. 22-23)."

Perhaps most distressing in the testimony was the consistency with which those who have a significant amount of formal control over decision making felt that others should be content with informal processes. School board members, state legislators, and school administrators were startlingly consistent in the view that parents should not feel such a strong need for more direct control over planning or implementation of school programs.

Many witnesses identified the school principal as the key to access to the school organization. Those who found principals cooperative and accessible generally reported good success. Those who found the principal closed to their concerns were generally frustrated in their attempts to get any satisfaction from other levels in the school organization.

Teachers' Organizations and Collective Bargaining

The third conflict encountered in the hearings concerned teachers' organizations and collective bargaining. In one sense this is an extension of the problems of access and accountability just discussed. The emergence of teachers' organizations has become so important to questions of school policy making and control, however, that it must be treated as a separate issue.

The militancy of teachers' organizations was vividly expressed in each of the public hearings. An official with the Washington State Department of Education summed up the situation with the declaration that, "The most pervasive and newest element in the decision-making structure was the emergence of a thing called negotiations or collective bargaining (P., p. 3)." There was significant evidence in the testimony that the teachers' organizations are already beyond the point of "standing in the wings, waiting to come upon the stage with the power to act in the arena [of school policy making] (L.A., Fri., p. 199)," as a black teacher in Los Angeles described them.

The official in Washington pointed to a "rapidly rising number of strikes" among teachers in that state. And an official of the Oregon School Boards Association indicated that "It may appear that we are in a state of panic over collective bargaining in Oregon (P., p. 13)." He quickly explained, however, "I want to assure you that this is far from true (P., p. 13)," and even asserted, "I don't think any process, including collective bargaining, is going to do that much damage to our traditional system of governance in education (P., p. 13)."

The most obvious fact about the relationship between teachers and others concerned with school policy is that the situation is changing very rapidly. Whether they are legal or not, teachers' strikes have increased in frequency, and the settlement of these strikes has had a very substantial impact on school budgets. There has been, furthermore, a flood of enabling legislation aimed at restructuring the process by which the contracts for a teacher's professional services are negotiated. It is hard to put the question of teachers' organization and collective contract negotiations in proper perspective since the issue is so immediate and so easily lends itself more to rhetoric than to careful thought.

Legislation concerned with collective bargaining does, however, have at least four common features: First, in every state that has passed or tried to pass legislation, the right of teachers to organize and negotiate their professional service contracts collectively has been strengthened, not weakened. Second, in each hearing, teachers and their advocates assumed that the teachers should adopt the basic model for labor relations developed in private industry. Dubose, the organizer of teachers in St. Louis, put this idea as succinctly as anyone: "I see the relationship between the school board and the teacher as being the same relationship which exists between any employer and his employee (S.L., p. 203)." It is important to recognize, however, that this commitment to the model of private industry for employer-employee relations is distinguished, in teachers' minds, from a notion that they are production-line employees. They consider collective bargaining to be "professional negotiations." As Dubose said, "We don't view ourselves in the same way as an employee or union who would be involved with General Motors. We realize very well that we are not manufacturing cars (S.L., p. 207)."

The third feature is that there is widespread resistance to the application of the model of private industry in schools. This is usually based on the model's adversary character, which is felt to be damaging to effective educational planning and programming. The hearings produced, however, no clear alternative procedure and no evidence that the unique characteristics of contract negotiations by public employees are understood very well. There seem only to be a generalized resistance to the teachers' application of the model of private industry and a determined but losing battle to weaken its implementation.

The fourth feature is that in each case only the local school board and the teachers' organizations are recognized as the legal parties to the contract, with administrators generally carrying on the negotiations for the board. Some efforts have been made to involve the public, and there are suggestions that either the school site or the state level might be logical alternatives for the vesting of contract authority, but these proposals have not yet received serious attention in legislation. Organized teachers everywhere share the view of a leader in a teachers' union in Portland: "We have been so busy trying to get ourselves as teachers into the decision-making role that we really haven't thought a lot about how to get the students and parents into it. We're fighting tooth and nail to get into it ourselves (P., p. 32)."

In each of the five hearings advocates for teachers declared forthrightly that they were determined to expand greatly the scope and content of decisions arrived at in negotiations. A leader of the Minneapolis Federation of Teachers declared: "I think that we need to be able to negotiate anything and everything that affects the job that a teacher can do (M., p. 304)." In St. Louis the spokesman for the teachers' union said negotiations "would cover everything from teacher salary to the way promotions are made, school calendar, textbook selections, the curriculum content, you name it, it covers just about the whole spectrum (S.L., p. 198)." The Atlanta spokesman insisted: "I think anything that affects public school education, teachers should have a voice in. They're not only teachers, they're taxpayers; they are parents; they are homeowners; they're voters (A., II, p. 107)."

Spokesmen for the teachers' organizations seemed to understand, however, the resistance to the breadth of their contract demands. In St. Louis, for instance, it was agreed that "Teachers do not negotiate policy decisions. So, obviously, the public should not be involved in that facet of things that strictly involve the teachers themselves and their conditions of employment (S.L., p. 199)." It turns out, however, that under close questioning it was not possible for this witness to identify where "policy" leaves off and "conditions of employment" begin. Hence he was not too helpful in limiting the scope of bilateral decision making.

The AFT spokesman from San Francisco made a similar distinction: "It is the AFT position that we don't want to run the schools. As a matter of fact, we don't want to make policy. We believe that is the job of school management. That is the reason we advocate strong, competent, intelligent, sensitive school superintendents, with competent boards, the whole process . . . (L.A., Fri., p. 126)." This position differed from that expressed in St. Louis in its confidence in the effective interaction between strong teachers and strong school boards to produce effective policy even without any advance commitment as to exactly which decisions are "policy" and which are limited to working conditions. Furthermore, this same spokesman strongly supported parents' forming unions and bargaining collectively with school managers.

In addition to the consideration over who should negotiate with whom and over what, there were a number of expressions of concern for the balance of power among the various parties in negotiations so that each party would have enough power to protect its own interests but not enough to damage those of others. In Portland it was asserted that "you see in education something different than in any other field . . . . It's only in education that we see the employees' organization really trying to get control or at least bilateral decisions over the mission of the organization and the way in which that mission is going to be carried out (P., p. 21)." And a school board member in Portland discussed this problem both in terms of the destruction of the rights of management and of the impact on the interests of citizens, which he saw as being substantially "eviscerated" by the bargaining process. He focused on the problems of change: "There is more of a barrier to . . . change than perhaps any of us realize, and that barrier . . . is the direction that we are headed in collective negotiations for public school teachers and administrators across the country (P., p. 69)."

This concern for the impact of collective bargaining on program innovation was shared by the spokesman for the Oregon School Boards Association who asserted bluntly that "more of the contracts or contract demands that I have looked at this year contain clauses to limit innovations and change and experimentation than they do to expand [them] (P., p. 19)." A spokesman for the Minneapolis Urban League was anxious about the impact of teachers' collective bargaining on efforts to integrate the teaching staff in that city. Teachers, he said, are seeking absolute freedom to move where they choose, but such freedom has a "deterrent aspect for quality education (M., p. 147)" in that it will not ensure a balanced staff in race or experience in the inner-city schools. The superintendent in Minneapolis expressed concern that the focus of organized teachers on "just the continuance of employment," through "seniority without limitation (M., p. 103)," will sharply restrain the "deployment of personnel (M., p. 104)."

Teachers, of course, do not see their contract demands as leading to an unfair dominance of the decision-making process, and they do not believe that their impact on policy will be inhibiting or negative. Instead, they make two basic points. First, they are acutely aware of the abuses that have been heaped upon teachers in the past, and thus they follow the line of San Francisco's AFT president: "We represent teachers to see that their *procedural* rights are protected. We believe that any society, like any . . . school system, is ultimately judged on how it treats the bad people, rather than the good people (L.A., Fri., p. 127)." The second point teachers make is that their views of educational problems differ from those of administrators and others, and that it is "necessary to involve the teachers, who, because of their background and training, have a special knowledge and competence which enables them to make a valuable contribution [to the solution of problems facing educators] (A., II, p. 128)." Furthermore, this contribution can be made through collective negotiations, since "For more than thirty-five years, collective bargaining has been the cornerstone of American labor relations in the private sector (A., II, p. 128)."

One keenly felt problem in collective bargaining is that the adversary character of the negotiation process seems inevitably to weaken the needed bond of trust between teachers and the parents and students who are their clients. Beyond that, the process as it is presently known seems to be an inherently private or secretive one. We are, however, at a historical moment when, as an Oregon legislator put it, "public business conducted in public is one of the most important national issues, and it has a lot to do with credibility (P., p. 48)."

Alternative Educational Experiences

At each of the five hearings substantial interest was expressed in both "typical" and "alternative" educational experiences. Many witnesses demonstrated a fairly intense commitment to the idea that the educational experiences typically available through the public schools are either inadequate in quality or insufficient in diversity. The corresponding interest in the development of alternative educational experiences constitutes a fourth major conflict. The directors of alternative schools in Minneapolis, St. Louis, and Atlanta all identified the importance of alternative educational experiences with students' different "learning styles." James Kent of Minneapolis said: "I think it fair to say that alternative schools should be viewed as one central way to demonstrate what many know so well—that children learn in myriad ways, that effective instructional strategies vary, and that parents, students, and faculty and staff have a right to be involved in school decisions (M., p. 110)." Al Chappelle of Sophia, Incorporated, in St. Louis, made the same point: "Basically what a kid has to learn in school, we think is pretty simple . . . . We find that it is important, especially with a high school student, if we can point out his learning style—his method of learning . . . (S.L., p. 262)."

A second rationale for alternatives in education came from Superintendent Robert Blanchard of the Portland school system: "There is insufficient diversity in alternatives to meet the kinds of goals that . . . the young men and women . . . may desire (P., p. 90)." From this perspective, educational alternatives are not so much a matter of matching teaching and learning styles as they are a matter of pursuing divergent learning goals.

There was a fair amount of support for this notion of divergent goals, but more often it blended into a third reason for stressing alternatives. This came from a state legislator in Oregon who lauded efforts to produce alternatives because "many of us look forward to this opportunity to improve quality [in the schools] . . . because we were working on the head count for so long and just trying to meet the demands of a growing traditional school-age population (P., p. 49)." In this statement the focus is on the refinement of educational quality through the development of experimental alternatives that could be tested. Atlanta's Councilwoman Bradley concurred in this view: "What is needed . . . is a series of schools which offer a host of different educational experiences . . . what we need are conscious models, team teaching . . . the open-classroom method, and school programs that are traditionally emphasized (A., III, p. 109)."

A number of witnesses cited additional techniques or programs that would form the basis for alternative educational programs, and Atlanta Superintendent Alonzo Crim proposed that schools should "incorporate what I call the consumer-producer concept in helping students not only to be the consumers of those things [alternative experiences] but get them interested in producing educational experiences (A., II, pp. 11, 12)."

This matter of experimental alternatives is more than a little controversial, however. Citizen witnesses denounced a number of these alternatives, including team teaching, new math, sex education, behavior modification, and sensitivity training. Another reason given for alternative education shifts emphasis from the impact on the student to the impact on the community. A number of witnesses advocated alternative experiences to enable students to become better prepared to compete in the economic and political world. In this category were requests to change the undemocratic quality of the classroom and to bring the students into direct contact with business and political institutions. Said a black personnel manager in Portland: "Our children are not given a meaningful curriculum to prepare themselves for full citizenship and competition in this city and state . . . our children are told about democracy but not how to get involved in it . . . . There is no meaningful interaction with private industry to prepare the minority students for the real world (P., p. 158)." And a student in Los Angeles echoed these sentiments with the affirmation that, "Truly to me most school subjects are irrelevant. You take them . . . but you cannot use them in the street . . . in working jobs (L.A., Thurs., p. 80)."

Another rationale for alternatives—their potential for control by the community—was suggested by a black teacher in Los Angeles: "The only thing that Los Angeles has that does seem to be a model would be a few alternative schools where parents have sat down, written the proposals for the school, actually sat down and hired the principal, dealt with the staff, and have a tremendous amount of input into the school system. There you find two or three hundred parents attending a meeting once a week (L.A., Fri., p. 206)." In Minneapolis the same feeling of shifting control through alternatives was linked to an unsuccessful effort to start a program of educational vouchers. One of the leaders in the movement said: "Vouchers are essentially an opportunity to turn the system on its head, to give parents access to the system, to make teachers accountable to teachers and parents, to make administrators accountable to both of the above (M., p. 253)."

The witnesses described four broad types or categories of alternatives.

First are organizational alternatives, such as the Atlanta Street Academy, the Minneapolis Southeast Alternatives Program, or the Los Angeles Alternative Schools. Also in this group are programs that change the operation of the school systems, for example, the voucher system proposed in Minneapolis to introduce control of the market-place by providing parents and students with "purchasing power" and the freedom to exercise that power in whatever way they choose. Other proposals for organizational change included reorganization of textbook adoption and performance contracting of educational services with nonschool agencies.

The second group of alternatives includes all those of a technical nature. That is, there were a number of demands for the use of alternative techniques for instruction, such as work experience, team teaching, use of occupational specialists who are not certified teachers, development of more open classrooms, computer-assisted instruction, sharply reduced class sizes, and individualized instruction.

A third group is concerned with the cultural role of the school. Many witnesses expressed an intense need for the schools to adopt programs that would "dispense culture." This possibility was explored by a San Francisco parent and zone council chairwoman:

The great battle for the schools is not integration but a new philosophical issue which is going to take San Francisco schools through what my husband calls a major educational earthquake. The three Rs versus life adjustment argument and open or shut classrooms seems to pale, and is mostly behind us .... The whole thrust of the community is to demand that the energy, resources, and expertise of the district respond to demands of parents not to teach their children English, but "to preserve the students' culture, heritage, language, life-style, etc."—what is now known as bilingual, bicultural education. Many black and white parents in San Francisco see this as a direct threat to their children's education. The school district and its personnel are totally unprepared, either philosophically or organizationally, to deal with these concerns. I think that educators traditionally trained to dispense facts are not doing that very well, and are now being asked to dispense culture (L.A., Fri., p. 157).

Of course, many of those who are working on the development of integrated education also regard alternatives in terms of the cultural norms of the school. More than twenty years after the Supreme Court ruled school segregation unconstitutional, however, there has been little progress in the creation of a genuinely integrated culture in the public schools.

The fourth category of alternatives relates to education that provides the student with a humane environment. One of the organizers of the Atlanta Street Academy set the mood: "Schools in general have not been designed with students in mind; nor have they been

designed with teachers in mind. The schools are designed for the jani-
tors (A., III, p. 64)." He went on to discuss the straight hallways and
orderly rows of desks as anathema to humane education. One of his
colleagues described the principle of decision making as it concerns
the provision of humane school environments: "The students do
have some input into running of the program; what they feel is relevant to them and their life-style and their needs. And we're finding
that students stand up very well to that responsibility and have much
longing for it (A., II, p. 116)." Thus, this fourth group of alternatives
is not so much a matter of organizational processes, technical learning principles, or cultural norms as it is of following the choice of the
child and his family—wherever that may lead—to an educational
experience that is exciting and interesting to the student.

With so much interest in alternatives, why are so few available;
why are they not being developed more quickly; and what can be
done to stimulate them?

A number of witnesses concerned themselves with how alternative
educational experiences can or should be stimulated. In this regard,
state and federal policies were widely credited (and occasionally
blamed) for the rate of change. In Minneapolis the development of a
fairly extensive program of experimental alternative schools was seen
as a direct result of the National Institute of Education's interest in
planned change. In St. Louis parents' veto power over the ability of
the district to acquire federal funds under Title I of the Elementary
and Secondary Education Act of 1965 was credited with an important role in the alternative experiences generated under that program.
In California the fact that the early childhood education program
provided new state money to school districts was said to be crucial to
the alternative experiences provided through that legislation. On the
other hand, vacillation and inconsistency in federal policy on desegregation were cited in Atlanta as major hindrances to progress toward
integration.

In accounting for the slow development and adoption of effective
alternatives, the professional educator tends to attribute the problem
to a lack of money. Citizens, on the other hand, are generally convinced that the problem is not money but bureaucratic inflexibility
and unresponsiveness. This conflict is increasingly important, since
those who charge educators with failure to respond tend to share the
views of a black civil rights advocate in St. Louis who actively opposed a recent revenue referendum in that city. He said:

It's a matter of how much credibility that you can give to the source that is saying that additional money will increase the public school system—I mean increase the quality . . . . There is no evidence in the past of the revenue, of the monies that they have now, that the quality of education was on the increase, or there is no evidence that we have ever had any quality education in St. Louis. So what constitutes the thinking that by adding money to a sickness that is already in existence is going to make the situation well or is going to cure the situation (S.L., p. 105)?

Another inhibitor to change is the tension between the right of parents and students to educational choice on the one hand and the public and economic purposes of schooling on the other. In other words, should the alternatives serve the needs of the student or of society? A spokesman for the Citizens' League of Minneapolis identified the tension between these two philosophies: "Public schools, in fact, serve two clients, society and the individual students (M., p. 277)." The alternatives that increase service to society may not be best for students, and those that focus on the development of students may not be directly responsive to social needs. The creation of effective alternatives will, undoubtedly, have to balance the interests of the student and society.

On the whole, citizens, students, state officials, and educators outside the regular public school system displayed a much higher commitment to alternatives than did school board members, administrators, or teachers. This certainly accounts for the intense pressure and debate related to the matter of educational alternatives. Those who are making the day-to-day decisions about educational programs are being pushed hard to expand the scope of their thinking and action.

Community Participation: Structures and Effects

The fifth issue presented in the hearings concerns the nature of citizen participation in school policy making and implementation. No issue was more widely discussed by the witnesses, and none drew a wider array of opinions and commitments. Evaluation of current efforts at citizen participation ranged from the enthusiastic to the moderate to the pessimistic. Minnesota State Senator Jerome Hughes evinced enthusiasm: "We've got plenty of citizen participation for you. I want you to know that (M., p. 34)." The superintendent of schools in Portland was more moderate: "I admit to considerable unevenness either as to the desire on the part of the individual administrator to involve, or to the desire on the part of citizens to be involved . . . (P., p. 92)." The Reverend Bryant Peterson of Minneapolis, an activist clergyman with long experience in civil rights, presented the pessimistic view: "Citizen participation is something which everyone believes in, but the style of citizen participation that is favored and acted upon in this city is the style of co-optation . . . stealing good people and buying them—maybe that's a mark of a good politician and a good administrator (M., p. 231)."

In addition to these conflicting views on the degree of citizen participation, there were also significant differences concerning the substantive meaning of "participation." The word was used in a variety of contexts, to cover a wide range of relationships between citizens and schools. One can discern in the testimony three levels or degrees of citizen participation: citizen involvement, citizen participation, and citizen control (or power or authority).

Citizen involvement is the farthest from policy making and implies that the citizens know what the schools are doing, identify themselves with the value of schooling, and feel a concern for the schools, but have little direct influence. A number of witnesses perceived too little citizen involvement and too much apathy about schools. The superintendent of the Minneapolis school system said: "An area of concern to me . . . is the absence of the articulate spokesmen in places of high calling who say that public education is worthy of support (M., p. 104)." A longtime member of the Oregon legislature reported, in a tone of disappointment: "The priorities of education in the people's minds, and in the legislators' minds, are not as high as they were previously. I think that school boards, at least in the communities that I see, and teachers and the public have lost a good deal of mutual respect that was present just a few years ago (P., p. 148)." And a representative of the Parents' Congress in St. Louis said that the task of his group is "to talk up the pride and get involved . . . . If we don't believe in it, and we don't have this pride and don't want to get involved, then education will always be the same (S.L., p. 240)."

The second level of relationship between the citizen and the schools—citizen participation—is used to indicate a closer, more active connection with decision making. Those who discussed citizen participation had in mind some mechanism through which the needs, opinions, and wishes of citizens would be reflected in decisions regarding school governance. Citizens themselves talked much more about participation than did either school board members or administrators, who generally spoke of citizen "involvement" (which they wanted more of) or "control" (which they opposed).

The most intense level of citizen participation in school policy—citizen control, citizen power, or citizen authority—was used by witnesses to mean that citizens participate directly in the formal procedures through which policy is made. The most frequent, though by no means the only, specific decisions citizens wanted to make were those concerning personnel and budgets.

There was a major conflict in the hearings between those who discussed citizen involvement and those who sought citizen control, power, or authority. In the testimony of the president of the Los Angeles school board this conflict surfaced clearly: "If you are a community control advocate, then in no way are you going to be satisfied with the school district the way it is now because the board never intended to give up control of the school district when decentralizing the administrative districts (L.A., Thurs., p. 63)." He continued:

I personally feel that [a previous witness] comes a little closer to the community control advocate that I was speaking of, not all the way, but I believe that we battled a little bit on a friendly basis when his committee . . . was attempting to get a little stronger guidelines because I am—I believe in community participation, involvement in decision making, but not control. Now we have some people in this district, citizens, who believe they should have the right as citizens to hire and fire teachers and principals. Well, I don't go that direction (L.A., Thurs., p. 65).

The hearings were filled with illustrations of mechanisms or procedures of governance that enhance or inhibit citizen participation. In addition to local school boards, which a board member in Portland called "the great experiment in American education . . . to get citizen involvement (P., p. 77)," there were two other features common to all districts: administrative decentralization and some form of community advisory councils. (There were, of course, a large number of other mechanisms of governance in one or more districts, but not in all of the districts represented by the witnesses.)

Witnesses made two basic points about local school boards in major metropolitan centers. First, the school boards are not very effective mechanisms for democratic representation. Everyone

recognizes that poor and minority citizens are substantially underrepresented among those who actually become school board members. These members are clearly identified as being part of the establishment, even though several board members agreed with Donald
Newman, the board president of Los Angeles, who said, "We are
elected to serve all of the citizens from the school district rather than
parochial interests . . . (L.A., Thurs., p. 54)." He continued: "We
have elected lay citizens to represent the citizens of Los Angeles and
to follow their mandate in an attempt to create a committee committed to quality education (L.A., Thurs., p. 55)."

Furthermore, many witnesses accused the school boards of being
out of touch with the broad community interests they claim to
represent. Several witnesses agreed with the St. Louis woman who
said, "We need the board of education to get out of that web down
at 911 Locust Street and come into the community, see the people,
let the people see them, meet with us, let us ask them questions
(S.L., p. 82)." Similar sentiments came from a Missouri legislator:
"Many people can live and die in the city of St. Louis without seeing
a school board member . . . they never have to test their ideology.
They never have to test their positions prior to arriving on the school
board. And subsequently, I don't think they have developed the
sensitivity to respond to communities (S.L., pp. 116-117)." This
legislator believed that one major reason for the ineffectiveness of
boards is that "it takes more votes to get elected to the board of
education in the city of St. Louis than it does to get elected to be a
United States congressman (S.L., p. 116)." This is true, of course,
not only in St. Louis but also in the other four cities. Because school
boards are typically elected on an at-large basis, winners in large
metropolitan districts require a great number of votes.

A number of witnesses pointed out that the cost of a campaign
and the small or nonexistent pay for serving on most school boards
make it impossible for the poor or even those with moderate incomes
to seek election. The fact that political parties do not become involved in the election of school board members makes this situation
even worse for candidates of moderate means because they have to
take personal financial responsibility for their entire campaign.

Witnesses proposed several possible mechanisms to bring school
boards closer to their constituencies. By far the most frequent proposal was that board members be elected by districts rather than at-

large. This suggestion was made repeatedly in Los Angeles and was put into sharp focus by a Mexican-American mother who said: "We want our own board of education, performed by parents, and we want to take education into our own districts and educate the children ourselves, if there is not a solution to this problem of the unresponsiveness of the schools (L.A., Thurs., p. 118)."

Some witnesses, however, vigorously resisted the idea of making school board members representative of smaller and more culturally distinct districts. Board members were the strongest opponents of subdistrict rather than at-large elections. They tended to concur with the board president in Minneapolis, who said: "If we were elected by districts, then I think we would become more political because we would have a smaller nucleus of people that would elect us, that we would have to be responsible to (M., p. 248)." But the board president in Los Angeles did indicate that "The San Diego plan has some interest to me, where we would be nominated by areas but then voted in at-large. That sounds like a logical plan to me. It would in some way ensure the possibility that at least in the primary election that minority members or people without the amount of funds that is necessary could have some representation (L.A., Thurs., p. 68)." And a spokeswoman for the League of Women Voters in California indicated that the position of her organization is that some board members "should be by election and some by appointment . . . it seems to me too often to be the case, depending upon the community, that you want some appointed representatives to round things out (L.A., Thurs., p. 131)."

Witnesses generally agreed that there are problems of board representation, but differed on the way to remedy them. Compromise is needed because any method used to select board members will benefit some groups at the expense of others. The present system of selection is most beneficial to those who have the knowledge and money to get what they want from schools, while those who are most disadvantaged in the marketplace are also underrepresented on the boards.

Even when board members attempt to represent the interests of all citizens, they do not succeed very well, according to the testimony at the hearings. There are several reasons for this. One is that the boards get nearly all of their information from the superintendent of schools and, therefore, receive a one-sided picture of school performance.

Also, board members, even in very large districts, are part-time lay citizens who do not have the energy or time to gather information necessary to represent their constituents effectively. Rules on the operation of school districts, like other laws, are not, moreover, self-enforcing, and the boards must depend on the goodwill of teachers and the diligent attention of administrators to see that policy is turned into practice. There is, in addition the increasingly comprehensive nature of teachers' contracts, which removes most of the teachers' day-to-day activities from any direct influence by the board. Finally, there are the extensive and complicated state education codes that specify school priorities in a very narrow way. Even when boards do try to make changes, they must secure the services of a highly skilled lawyer to keep from running afoul of state law.

Witnesses from each of the districts represented in the hearings reported recent moves toward administrative decentralization. Within each district, administrative areas (as they are normally called) usually number from three to a dozen and contain approximately seven to more than fifty schools. The purpose of administrative decentralization of school districts was summarized by W. Harry Davis, the board president of Minneapolis, who reported: "In the efforts to provide for parent-student involvement in our school district we have decentralized into six districts, each having a director (M., p. 236)." The superintendent in Portland indicated that city's motivation for decentralizing: "Unlike Detroit and New York, in which decentralization was legislatively mandated, . . . here these steps were undertaken voluntarily, essentially in response to . . . an attitude on the part of citizens that more and more decisions are . . . being controlled by forces over which they have little influence (P., p. 89)."

In Los Angeles, on the other hand, it was reported that decentralization was extremely difficult to effect. A promoter of the legislation that had been intended to divide the school district into smaller units reported that the bill passed by the legislature but vetoed by the governor was essential because in education "changes are hard to come by mainly because of a very powerful, well-entrenched educational establishment, one that is very comfortable with the status quo (L.A., Thurs., p. 11)." He and other witnesses were convinced that the near victory of that bill had been the essential motivation behind the decentralization of the sprawling Los Angeles Unified School District into twelve administrative areas.

In general, administrators were rather pleased with the results of decentralization. But other groups were not. Superintendent Davis of Minneapolis expressed the typical view of those favoring decentralization, describing it as "a vehicle for making the school system more responsive to those who were a part of it, the students, and the faculty, and also to the clients who are the citizens with particular reference to the parents (M., p. 108)."

In the same city, however, the Reverend Peterson bluntly asserted: "Decentralization in Minneapolis . . . failed . . . failed because the citizens' groups were given no power whatsoever, and they were simply advisory councils (M., pp. 251-252)." He returned to this point again later: "Now, that's the basic issue in the Minneapolis schools that is never talked about, the issue of power, and until we address that problem decentralization is only going to be another bureaucratic way of solving bureaucratic problems (M., p. 258)."

A black teacher in Los Angeles made essentially the same point:

Decentralization was tried in Los Angeles in the early sixties to increase the efficiency of the school system. By 1966 decentralization became associated with the demand of minority communities and groups of parents for a greater amount of input into the public schools . . . . The parents are . . . concerned with the *political* approach; the central board is concerned with the *organizational* approach. So you have two different things when you mention the word decentralization. The organizational approach is dominant at this time, and the usual rule is that the administration is decentralized, but policy making is not decentralized (L.A., Fri., p. 198).

Here we see clearly the prevailing view of citizens: whatever else its merits may be, decentralization does not in itself provide them access to participation in school policy making.

In addition to decentralization, each of the districts represented at the hearings had citizen or parent advisory groups intended to provide participation in local school policy making. As with decentralization, advisory groups are highly controversial. School administrators, school board members, and state-level officials generally are pleased with the current status of the advisory groups. Assistant Superintendent James Taylor of Los Angeles said: "We in Los Angeles made the conscious decision to concentrate our citizen participation effort at the local school level, rather than in subdivision governing boards of education or district-wide citizens' bodies. We chose to do so by the formation of school-community advisory councils at

each of the regular elementary, junior high, and senior high schools
of the district (L.A., Fri., p. 103)." In evaluating the performance of
these more than six hundred community advisory groups, he commented: "I wish I could tell you that all our councils are highly
effective and working to the full limits of their capacity. This, however, would be sheer nonsense. We have outstanding councils; we
have effective councils; we have councils which are apathetic; we
have councils which function in name only (L.A., Fri., p. 103)." He
added: "Overall, we have learned that the school community advisory groups can be a helpful means of improving the educational
program of a school . . . we have also learned that if advisory councils
are approached in the wrong way, they can be a detriment or liability
as far as the educational program is concerned (L.A., Fri., p. 104)."

Parents, other citizens, and students expressed views on advisory
committees that contrasted sharply with official optimism. The prevailing view, especially among minority witnesses, was voiced by a
member of the Los Angeles Black Education Commission: "Advisory
committees have become merely rubber stamps for the school district . . . most of them have been stacked with school board employees . . . they're only there to ratify the decisions of the school
board (L.A., Thurs., pp. 7, 8)."

In Portland the effectiveness of the Parent Advisory Committees
(PACs) was equated with that of the PTA. One member of an advisory committee said that the PAC "is involved at a more basic level
than PTA but the gist of what I want to put across here today is that
it is no more effective at [my school] in changing or raising the quality of what goes on . . . . No more effective than a PTA has ever been
(P., p. 104)." A clue to the perceived failure of this advisory group
was offered in the same parent's assertion that "The principal was
basically authoritarian and believed in direct discipline (P., p. 105)."
When faced with this principal, the advisory group "discovered . . .
more or less that it is a matter of power (P., p. 106)," and "There is
no power in an advisory status . . . . There is no power really for students or parents because administrators, principals . . . have a hegemony of functions . . . (P., p. 106)."

While the largest number of citizen witnesses shared the view that
advisory groups have no power over school policy, there were some
notable exceptions. One was a member of a Portland advisory group
who said, "I just wanted to make a few comments on parent partici-

pation possibly of a positive nature . . . what makes me feel a little bit positive is what is happening in our neighborhood school . . . we were able to get a new principal . . . who liked to mix with the community (P., p. 165)."

Lay people usually see themselves as unable to direct the educational enterprise and are therefore reluctant to exert pressure on professional educators. Only when they are dissatisfied do they insist that professionals change their ways. Actually, these so-called advisory groups operate as sounding boards and rubber stamps for the school policy generated by professional educators. Traditional PTAs are criticized for performing these very functions. The central task confronting the school advisory council is to become a partner in education with the educator. The role of the lay citizen is that of a monitor of policy and a decision maker. This is what was intended when school boards were created one hundred years ago.

The overall significance of the testimony can be put quite simply: there are three kinds of groups that can expect to change school policy. First, if it is an ongoing school group, like a citizens' advisory council, it will be influential only to the extent that school administrators permit or encourage its actions. Second, if the group is designed to solve problems, with a narrow and reasonably clear definition of the problem it seeks to solve, it will be successful so long as it can work on that problem directly. The group dissolves if the problem is solved or if it is widely believed to be unsolvable. Many civil rights and school desegregation groups fall into this category. Third, a group will have significant impact if it is not based primarily in the schools, but turns its attention to specific school issues that touch on the larger purposes of the group. The NAACP and the League of Women Voters are the most notable examples of this type of group.

Of course not all groups of the same type are equally successful in affecting school policy. There are clues within the testimony about what skills and operational characteristics will enhance the performance of a citizens' group. We were able to identify many aspects of citizen groups that indicate they will be important variables affecting the impact the group will have on the school policy-making process.

In Minneapolis the Reverend Peterson pointed out that "People who are articulate, who can speak and verbalize their needs and concerns, like myself, can get things out of the systems or the society, but the people who do not have those kinds of abilities just don't, you know, get the response (M., p. 43)." This theme was echoed in Portland where an advisory group member accounted for the relative success of his group: "One thing about Irvington, it does have a heck of a lot of politically savvy people in it . . . . There are a number of political figures in that community, both black and white. It does help. There are a lot of professional-type people who know how to work the system (P., p. 168)." These witnesses were typical in their recognition that political, organizational, and verbal skills are unequally distributed in our society and that having these skills is quite important to success in political processes. In Atlanta the director of the Southern Regional Council affirmed his belief that school councils are essential to the improvement of public education: "Self-organization is a very effective instrument . . . . But I also recognize that there are many committees where the leadership for self-organization has simply not been there (A., III, p. 157)." This observation is vital, for it points us toward a clear public responsibility for nurturing leadership among citizens who are to be involved in school policy making.

A group will have significant impact if it can get organized and stay organized over a period of a few years, according to the testimony. In Atlanta an advisory council chairman said: "We have found that for many of the school officials to be responsive to our concerns . . . we're going to [have to] be continually vigilant in . . . pointing things out (A., I, p. 71)." Later he commented: "One of the cardinal rules, it seems to me, is even though you disagree with . . . officials, why you continue to talk with them; and you continue dialogue. It seems to me essential, never do you want to get yourself in a position where you cannot continue dialogue with the folks who are responsible for the operation of your school (A., I, p. 74)." The member of the Portland advisory group quoted above indicated that one technique for successful action "is persistence in going or calling a meeting with [the officials] . . . coming in all the time, in other words, you just don't give up . . . . Be sure you can go back again and again (P., pp. 166, 167)." Other witnesses indicated that the first year of a group is usually devoted to organizational matters. Effective influence comes after the organization becomes routine.

The legal grounding of citizen participation is extremely important. Groups whose role is entirely advisory are dependent upon school officials' being interested in their advice. Title I or Model Cities advisory groups can at least prevent the schools from getting federal funds and are in a somewhat stronger position. When funds are cut off, however, it is children who suffer. These groups, therefore, pay a high price for doing their jobs. The director of the Southern Regional Council insisted: "You not only must have the advisory committee that has the functions of monitoring the system in relation to issues, but it must also be a committee that cannot be arbitrarily abolished by the local system. It needs to have some legislative roots. It needs some method of selection that is not subject to the control of the local administration or the local board (A., III, pp. 152-153)."

Others testified that control of policy can only be achieved through an adversary relationship. As the president of the PTA in San Francisco put it, "There are those who say we ought to become the parents' union. Perhaps we ought to drop the T in PTA, and then we could get into that position of getting into that creative tension with others who have a role. We should be in an adversary position (L.A., Fri., p. 146)." The president of AFT in San Francisco concurred that parents should attempt to form a union and bargain collectively with school districts (L.A., Fri., p. 122).

Citizens who represent substantial social and business interests clearly have the advantage over those who are poor or even middle class. A representative of the business-oriented Schools for the City group in Portland reported that "Several of us meet once a month informally with [the superintendent] in unstructured settings of sitting around his office and talking about whatever comes to our mind or his mind. These meetings have proved very helpful (P., p. 121)." He added: "Partly because we do have a direct access to the superintendent, we can tell him about particular problems and sometimes receive rather immediate attention (P., p. 122)."

Those groups, whether citizens, teachers, or others, who put full-time lobbyists or advocates into the field are more likely to get what they want, particularly at the state level. One Oregon legislator summed up the role of the lobbyist in education: "The lobbyists are reliable; they are respected, and you know who they represent, and you know when you ask them that you will get factual material and that they will try to present their side. [Some] lobbyists are . . . the

School Boards Association . . . the teachers' union, the OEA . . . the community colleges . . . (P., p. 150)."

But the professional educators still constitute the most important groups influencing policy, and those who ally with them are much more likely to succeed. A spokeswoman for a Minnesota legislator put it this way: "Without the support of major professional educational lobby groups or the administration of a school board of a major city, it is virtually impossible for a citizen to get a piece of controversial legislation passed (M., p. 177)."

4

THE PUBLIC HEARINGS: THE UNDERLYING CONCEPTS OF GOVERNANCE AND POLICY MAKING

In the two preceding chapters central issues have been identified that are important for shaping school policy. Cutting across these issues was concern with the underlying concepts related to the basis for school governance and policy making.

Fundamental Tensions on Educational Goals

Although the witnesses did not reveal equally their biases on the question of the purpose or goals of schooling, it was possible to identify three fundamental polar tensions on educational goals: between "equal" and "quality" as the chief goal in the provision of educational services; between service to "each child" and service to communities; between the development of skill or character.

These three tensions are, of course, not logical polarities. It would be *theoretically* possible to develop a school system that would aim equally at all six of these goals at the same time. In the practical, everyday world of finite resources, complex policy-making processes, and limited time, however, witnesses were convinced that there is a definite need to choose one rather than the other option on at least one and frequently all three of these competing demands.

Tensions between "Equal" and "Quality" Education

The tendency of witnesses to emphasize the need for either equal educational opportunity or quality education was the most pervasively and intensely separated among the witnesses' testimony on the goals of schooling. Those who focus on equal educational opportunity have significantly different attitudes about school governance than those who focus on the quality of the services. Naturally witnesses representing minority groups and those who are economically disadvantaged were most acutely aware of the lack of equity, while students of all ethnic groups, parents, and some teachers were most likely to focus on the inadequacy of existing school programs to provide quality education in our major cities. When witnesses concentrated on the simultaneous pursuit of equity and excellence they demonstrated the complexity and difficulty of striking a proper balance between these goals. Teachers tend to believe that quality is a matter of professional concern, which should be handled by unilateral professional decision making, while equity is a matter of funding and should be handled by state-level policy makers. Parents, on the other hand, tend to feel that equity is a matter of the sensitivity of the staff to cultural differences and should be handled through community control of staffing. They are inclined to think that quality is a matter of intense commitment rather than technical proficiency and is more likely to result if parents are more intimately involved in the decisions about programs. The courts have intervened extensively over the last two decades in an effort to increase equity, but are recently being presented with what amounts to suits challenging the quality of school programs. Minority groups express an increasing conviction that there should be increased emphasis on the quality of schools in the ghettos and barrios because there has been so little progress toward achieving the goal of desegregation during the last twenty years.

Tensions between Service to Children and Service to the Community

The second polar tension, between servicing the needs of individual students or serving the purposes of the community, is a less intense but still widespread source of divergence among witnesses. The needs of the community include such goals as "transmitting the culture," providing "democratic experiences," ensuring effective "citizenship skills," putting people in the "socioeconomic mainstream" so as to reduce the burden of poverty on the economy, promoting the economic development or healthy social stability of a community through the preparation of skilled workers and educated citizens, and solving pressing social problems like drug abuse, race prejudice, or immorality through the effective socialization of children. Services demanded for students include responding to individual "learning styles" and providing "individualization" programs, meeting the special needs of handicapped or other disadvantaged individuals, giving students "job skills," and providing for the needs of "self-actualization" or "critical thinking" of students.

As the Commission examined the differences between witnesses who focused on serving individual students and those who emphasized serving community purposes, it discovered that the ideas of alternative schools or alternative educational experiences are closely associated with an effort to find new ways to merge these often conflicting goals. There is a widespread feeling that schools are constantly forced to reject either the needs of students or those of the community. References to alternative education almost invariably carry with them the witnesses' conviction that new educational patterns can and must be found that do not produce alienation of students while continuing to serve adequately the public purposes of schooling.

Those who focus on meeting students' needs are interested in "individualization" of school programs when they choose the excellence end of the excellence-equity polarity, while the idea of "compensatory" and "remedial" or other special services is the focus of those who opt for the goal of equity as well as the goal of service to individual students.

An emphasis on the community service side of the second polarity leads those interested in equal opportunity to be more concerned with organization and administration of the schools through such matters as desegregation and alternative program planning. Those who combine an interest in excellence of education with the community service goals focus on particular programs that they want from the schools, such as teaching democratic values.

Tension between the Development of Skill or Character

The third tension is between those who want the schools to focus on specific subjects, such as reading and mathematics or job-related skills, and those who would emphasize cultural or character formation among the students. Among the first group, there was a dominant interest in the accountability of the professional staff, while among the second group there was a much broader interest in the responsiveness of the schools to the input of citizens.

Beneath the Tensions

The hearings forcefully demonstrated that beneath the specific tensions over educational goals education has become a necessity more than just an opportunity in modern urban society. It has become a means to ensure against economic or psychological disaster in the country's urban centers. It seems to perform for the city dweller the same function that the right to homestead property did in an earlier period. While the frontiers were open it was always possible to imagine moving west and starting over again. With the frontier gone, the economic and personal flexibility resulting from an adequate education is the major hope of citizens. Most of the witnesses testifying at the hearings believe that schooling is their frontier for opportunity.

Another underlying dilemma of educational governance is that there is often a difference in perspective between the technical judgments of professional educators about what is an educationally sound program and the citizens' and students' concerns for culturally and personally responsive programs. The professional educator asserts a professional point of view for the "reasonable" course of action in building school programs. For students and parents, however, education frequently seems much more a matter of what is meaningful and relevant to their future success and does not have a clear-cut "right" and "wrong" way of proceeding.

The claims of educators to expertise in the technology of education are spread throughout the testimony. Sometimes the claims were presented defensively in statements such as one by Atlanta's superintendent: "We cannot say that we want you to improve, say the reading achievement by, say, so many percentage points; and then in the next breath say 'you must do it exactly this way' (A., II, p. 18)." At other times the assertion of expertise was presented in a less defensive manner and simply reflected a commitment to the idea that there are effective and ineffective ways of getting the educational job accomplished.

Lay people, as a woman in Portland said, tend to believe that "one of the greatest threats to education is the validity that certain so-called experts have achieved. They have a much greater validity than space experts (P., pp. 153-154)."

In the past, educators have been in control of this conflict. They have been writing the legislative agendas, influencing policy making of school boards, and mobilizing citizen support for education at the local school level. A strong hint of change, is, however, to be found in the hearings: legislators have begun to take the counsel of citizens and to be less heavily influenced by professional views; school boards have begun to preempt professionals in more areas; and citizen groups are seeking to circumvent professional dominance. Furthermore, the separation between teachers and administrators is being reflected in divergent professional judgments about what sort of educational practices really are effective.

This separation between administrators and teachers has made possible a new perspective on the clash of laymen and professionals over the proper basis for policy making. The split demonstrates both a technical principle and an organizational principle for decision making by professional educators. Administrators use an organizational principle, making policy in order to produce an orderly and manageable school system. Teachers use a technical principle, making their demands on policy in order to secure the freedom necessary to practice the skilled craft of teaching.

For some students and parents, the principle of choice is vital. They want to choose their educational experiences or at least to feel that they would have chosen them if given an alternative. For other citizens, however, the basic principle of policy is the democratic one of the greatest good for the greatest number. Hence many citizens and many parents are willing to have children in schools because "it is good for them" at least as often as because "they want to be there."

One central problem for school governance, then, is to build a structure in which the principles of policy making will be properly balanced and will simultaneously produce the orderliness needed for management, the professional craftsmanship of skilled teachers, the democratic choices of the public, and the opportunity for students and their families to choose meaningful education. Each of these guideposts of effective policy must be recognized if we are to have effective schools.

One of the recurring themes in the testimony, particularly in Atlanta, was that citizens' involvement in school policy making tends to be through either ephemeral, crisis-oriented groups that spring up suddenly to deal with a special problem and then fade away just as quickly or co-opted groups that wind up as simply "public relations" groups and serve only as mechanisms for presenting the views of professional educators to the community. The hearings confirmed prevailing theories that lasting groups must have two essential characteristics: an enterprise or purpose that is ongoing and not oriented to immediate problem solving alone; and a formal structure that provides rules for members to follow. Normally these two characteristics are complementary so that formal structures and rules are developed to help the members of the group coordinate their activities.

One problem with groups that seek to influence school policy is that when they take "educating our children" as their goal they quickly find that they are either closely aligned with the regular school organization that has this as its purpose or they are in direct competition and conflict with the schools because they do not believe that schools are working properly. If they become aligned with the schools, they are easily co-opted by school professionals who, after all, are devoting their entire lives to the business of education. When, on the other hand, citizens' groups are carefully structured so as to be independent of the regular school organization, it becomes difficult for them to maintain a clearly definable sense of group enterprise. The testimony shows that the most effective ongoing citizens' groups are those whose purposes are not limited to education, such as the Urban League, the NAACP, and the League of Women Voters. These groups are valued by professional educators who want their support and who therefore tend to respond to their wishes.

Another important set of concepts used regularly in the public testimony was participation and representation. The term "participation" was used to point to a quality of citizen involvement with schools characterized by a free and open give-and-take among citizens and between citizens and educators. Those who urge participation of citizens in schools expect that it will improve the level of service by having citizens' opinions integrated into the planning of programs and also will reduce citizens' alienation and hostility by giving them a chance to feel the sense of participation.

The term "representation," on the other hand, was used to refer to a formally structured relationship among various groups interested in school policy. The most frequent references to representation came in the discussions of the relationships between teachers and the schools and in discussions of the relationships between school board members and school district voters. It is clear from these discussions that representation does not necessarily involve either free and open discussions or any feeling of closeness to the policy process. A person is represented in policy when his interests are taken into account as policy decisions are being made.

Unfortunately, the urge for power on the part of some citizens is incompatible with the desire for participation (as opposed to representation) in policy formulation. Power is a conflict-based concept and assumes the formation of coalitions among allies, with these coalitions represented at the points where decisions are made. A formal legislative body is ideally suited to managing power-based conflicts without destructive consequences. Participation, however, is a concept that entails communal, warm, and open access and includes mutuality and trust among participants. It can only be developed among those who have the patience, commitment, interpersonal skills, and basic respect required to gain the attention and cooperation of other possible participants. Though participation is fairly easy to generate among members of groups who belong to the same social class and ethnic subculture, across class and ethnic barriers it is extremely difficult to achieve and requires an unusually high degree of commitment and patience. The resolution of major questions relating to educational policy requires a careful structuring of representational processes so that intergroup conflicts can be easily handled without precluding the warm and open participation so vital to the conduct of education.

Conflict Management and Public Policy for the Schools

If the hearings demonstrated anything, it is that making decisions regarding school policy is not a scientific process. "Very few major decisions in the public sphere have clear-cut answers," an aide to Atlanta's Mayor Maynard Jackson reminded the Commission. "It's a matter of making judgments among competing factors (A., III, p. 170)."

One way to view the testimony is in the context of five basic propositions that are the cornerstones of democratic government.

Proposition 1: In a democratic society an important function of the governance structure is the control and resolution of conflict.

When one school board member in Atlanta remarked, "People think that if you don't agree with them every time, you're against them (A., II, p. 46)," she was putting her finger on a central fact of both personal and political life. Since disagreements are inevitable in any society that provides even the most rudimentary of personal liberties, people will always be experiencing this feeling that others are "against them." Conflict is endemic to a democratic process. Keeping conflicts moving toward resolution and away from open warfare is an essential task of government.

Proposition 2: The system of governance can operate once the main conflicts are identified, that is, once real issues have been raised and defined.

This defining of the important issues that need attention is the most fundamental of all political activities. We cannot agree on a policy until we have defined the questions. A member of a parents' council in Minneapolis recognized this when she said, "What it amounts to is, you have to know why you want something and you have to participate in deciding how you intend to get it (M., p. 129)." In Portland, another member of an advisory committee put the same point this way: "Focus down on the most important issues; otherwise the administrators will burn you out. If you go for everything, go for broke, you're dead . . . you can't use up all your energy . . . you must be able to get together with the community and say these are the goals we are going to shoot at and then go after them (P., p. 167)."

This parent understood that defining the issue involves both the identification of goals and the setting of priorities concerning these goals. A legislator in Oregon described what happens when there is no clear definition: "I think the apathy isn't really that people don't care. I think apathy comes when they walk into things and find themselves in something so complex they just back away (P., p. 50)."

Once the issue has been clearly defined, much of the flexibility is taken away from a public body because its choices for action become greatly restricted. One school board member in Atlanta insisted that change will come if people will only make very specific demands on public officials and then, "Don't let them forget. You've got to have an answer. If you've got to go back every month until you get an answer. And if you don't like that answer keep going back 'til you get the other answer (A., II, p. 41)."

Narrowing the definition of the conflict to the point that it requires "an answer" makes it quite clear whose interests will be served by each choice among the various policy options.

Proposition 3: Once an issue has been clearly defined, there are several important ways to manage or resolve it.

First, the conflict may be traced to democratic "first principles," to "constitutional guarantees," or to some other important ideological foundation which shows that one way of resolving the conflict is more legitimate than another. The superintendent of schools in Portland used this approach to limit conflict over what powers could be given to school advisory councils by insisting that, "The board of education is charged by Oregon law to carry out certain responsibilities, and I don't believe it can delegate them [to advisory councils] (P., p. 95)."

A second way is to strike a compromise among conflicting interests, all of which may have some legitimacy. A representative of a teachers' organization in San Francisco testified: "It is the AFT position that we don't want to run the schools. As a matter of fact, we don't want to make policy. We believe that is the job of school management . . . . We represent teachers to see that their *procedural* rights are protected [italics added] (L.A., Fri., pp. 126-127)."

He was proposing a compromise in which teachers' powers would not conflict directly with administrative powers in school management.

A third way is simply to suppress a growing conflict in favor of another that is said to be more important. One example of this approach was offered by the director of the Heart of the Earth Survival School in Minneapolis (an alternative school focusing on the Indian population), who said: "[The students] can . . . run the school the way they want it run as long as I feel that it's an intelligent decision. When I no longer feel that it's an intelligent decision, then I make the decision (M., I, p. 70)." In this situation the conflict over choices and decisions was simply suppressed, and students' actions were judged on the basis of their "intelligence."

A fourth strategy for conflict resolution—combining several issues so that the resulting package will attract the combined support of diverse groups—is illustrated in the testimony of a state senator in Florida. He emphasized that recent school governance legislation in that state provided for a "program of educational financing and assessment and citizen involvement [which] was seen as a unified package . . . people who were interested in additional funds . . . saw the interrelationship [between finance and citizen participation] (A., III, p. 100)."

Finally, of course, conflicts can be managed by sheer power: one group deprives others of participation in policy making. The hearings were heavily laden with accusations of abuse of this sort of power by one group or another.

Proposition 4: One objective of public policy is to provide for a balance of power among all those parties with equally legitimate interests in the outcome of a conflict.

Governance structures are themselves political resources that sharply affect the outcome of political conflicts. The question of who has access to the power of government and how that access is managed is crucial. The vice-president of the Portland school board, a man with considerable national experience in collective bargaining, insisted that there are serious problems in balancing teachers' interests with those of school managers and the public. He suggested that there be a "third chair" at the bargaining table for citizens. Such an arrangement would require new legislation and would be an effort to solve this conflict by redistributing the legal power held by each of the parties with legitimate interest in the negotiation of teachers' contracts.

In the hearings, many such proposals were made for reallocating the balance of power among the various parties in the public school policy-making process.

Proposition 5: Another objective of public policy is to make the various legitimate interests more interdependent.

Since governance structures are important in helping people reach their goals, these goals should be combined in such a way that the conflicting parties find mutual interest in cooperation. This not only brings immediate satisfaction; it also builds confidence in the governing body. One witness at the hearing in St. Louis discussed this sort of strategy when she said that citizens "believe citizen participation is a must if schools are to survive and maintain a good balance in decision making for schools. Neither total professional control nor total lay control will be good for education (S.L., p. 277)." She continued: "most parents and citizens believe that there is too little participation. Most administrators think that there is an appropriate amount . . . . We believe that, to be effective, citizen participation will require a reallocation of power (S.L., p. 278)."

The Commission heard a number of proposals for policy changes that would build a web of interdependency among all the legitimate participants in school policy making. In one way or another they were all aimed at making sure no one person or group could make policy without the full consultation and participation of other persons or groups.

5

THE EROSION OF LAY CONTROL

James W. Guthrie   University of California, Berkeley
Diana K. Thomason   University of California, Berkeley
Patricia A. Craig   Stanford Research Institute

The question "Who governs America's schools?" evokes the image of the five blind men attempting to describe an elephant, each from a vastly different tactile perspective of the animal's anatomy. The "correct" answer to the question of governance also depends heavily upon one's vantage point, upon whether the observer is a parent, pupil, teacher, taxpayer, school administrator, or employer. The purpose of this chapter is to unravel some of the complexities of educational governance and to account for the varying perceptions of who controls the schools. This analysis begins with an interpretation of the historical development of control of the public school, moves to a discussion of the present-day balance of political power over schools, and concludes with a description of the possibilities of governmental reform.

It is difficult to conduct an objective analysis of a topic such as government which is saturated with concerns related to values. When all the rhetoric is stripped away, the primary function of government is the authoritative allocation of values. The rules of government determine in a substantial way the distribution of important items such as wealth, material goods, and ideas. In short, a discussion of government is a discussion of power; an analysis of school governance is, in effect, an analysis of who has power over schools. It is almost inevitable that the outcome of such an analysis will be affected by views of "Who *should* have power over schools?"

Conventional wisdom and democratic ideology hold that the social services crucial to the public's welfare and survival should be subject to the public's will. Schooling is no exception, and this chapter begins with the assumption that the ultimate authority to control public schools should rest with the public. The mechanisms for exercising such control must be delicately balanced because education also involves such crucial issues as academic freedom, censorship, and professional autonomy. Despite such complexities the prime thesis of this chapter is that the public's ability to control public schools has undergone a substantial dilution, and reforms are needed to redress the imbalance.

Colonial School Governance: The English Heritage

The educational system in England at the time of America's colonization reflected both the class structure of the mother country and the assumption of the household as the primary agent of education.[1] Tudor social policy throughout the sixteenth century emphasized the role of the family as the systematic educator of the child. The Royal Injunctions of Henry VIII (1536), for example, required fathers, mothers, masters, and governors to "bestow their children and servants, even from their childhood, either to learning, or to some other honest exercise, occupation or husbandry."[2] In addition to the family, by the sixteenth century the apprenticeship system had also developed as an important mode of education and training. In 1563 the Statute of Artificers codified apprenticeship practices and procedures, explicitly defining the responsibilities of master and apprentice during the seven-year training period. The act also made service in an apprenticeship or trade compulsory for all persons not otherwise employed.

During the seventeenth century in England there was continued expansion of family responsibility for education. It was, however, also a time of developing educational institutions. With an increasingly complex political and economic system, and an expanding merchant class, the need for schools and colleges began clearly to emerge. It should be remembered that these institutions did not comprise a single, hierarchical system. Rather, as a reflection of seventeenth-century social class arrangements, schools provided a separate system of education for the lower and upper strata. Though few in number, "vernacular" schools were established to provide basic skills in reading, writing, and mathematics for the lower classes. They were concerned chiefly with the preparation of clerks and artisans. "Dame schools," or private schools conducted in the homes of literate women, also were a common means of instructing children in basic reading and mathematics.

"Latin grammar schools," providing humanistic education and preparation for study in the universities for the middle and upper classes, became widespread during this period. The mercantile class, which by now was benefiting from England's role in world trade, began to contribute unprecedented amounts of money to schools. There was increasing recognition of the fact that the family alone could not perform the task of educating for a complex society. It has been estimated that by 1600 there were 361 schools of this kind, one for every 12,500 people,[3] and that 50 percent of the male population in London was literate.[4] The universities, Cambridge and Oxford, were increasingly attended by the upper class and provided classical education for medicine, law, and theology. These institutions were largely controlled by the church, the guilds, or by private ventures. With the Reformation, the traditional church monopoly over schooling was disrupted, and most seventeenth-century school governing boards included laymen with neither clerical nor teaching responsibilities.[5] Support for schools came largely through tuition payments by students, although a tradition of private endowments and philanthropy contributed significantly. The state encouraged education, but vested authority in the individual and in families to select the purpose, place, and method of instruction. There was neither state support nor control of educational institutions.

Permanent British settlements in North America began at Jamestown, Virginia, in 1607. During the first half of the seventeenth century, in keeping with their English heritage, the colonists made the church and family primarily responsible for education. Early colonists at Jamestown, and later at Plymouth, provided little in the way of formal schooling; religious preaching and catechizing were the forms of education most widely practiced.

The first American educational ordinances were enacted by the Massachusetts colonial legislature, then called the General Court, in 1642. These statutes reaffirmed the family's primary responsibility for providing the ability to read and vocational training for children. They also established a public responsibility for education. If a household failed to provide for a child's education, the town's selectmen were required to remove the child from the home and place him or her in a suitable apprenticeship situation. Similar compulsory education laws subsequently were enacted by all the New England and Middle Atlantic colonies except Rhode Island.

The Puritans of the Massachusetts Bay colony were particularly concerned with preserving social stability and institutions in the wilderness of the New World. As one colonist expressed it, "We in this country, being far removed from the more cultivated parts of the world, had need to use utmost care and diligence to keep up learning and all helps to education among us, lest degeneracy, barbarism, ignorance and irreligion do by degrees break in upon us."[6] The earlier compulsory education statutes prescribed minimum standards, but did not prescribe schools. It became apparent, however, that formal instruction would be needed to provide the amount and kind of education deemed necessary by the Puritan leadership. Thus, beginning in 1635, a number of the towns in Massachusetts and other New England colonies established schools. It was at this time that Harvard College was authorized by the Massachusetts legislature, less than a decade after the settlement of the colony. By 1647 eleven of the sixty towns in New England had voluntarily established, managed, and supported town schools.[7]

In 1647 the Massachusetts General Court enacted the first legislation relating to schools. This act required all towns of fifty families to provide a teacher of reading and writing and those of one hundred families to provide a Latin grammar school. This legislation became known as the "Old Deluder Satan" act, and its explicit purpose was to ensure that everyone in the Bible Commonwealth be able to read and understand the principles of religion and the capital laws. The impact of this legislation, even though a fine was prescribed for noncompliance, was not as dramatic or universal as its framers had hoped. Cremin reports that, in the first decade, all of the eight larger towns complied. However, only a third of the fifty-family towns made provision for hiring a teacher. Thereafter, as towns attained the size requiring a school, the legislation appears to have been largely ignored.[8] While it is difficult to estimate the number of formally established schools during the early colonial period, it is clear that education went on everywhere in the community, not only in schoolrooms, and that children were taught by anyone and everyone, not only by schoolmasters.

Historians disagree on the essential purpose of the establishment of schools, the extent to which they were made available, and the influence of New England traditions upon later educational developments in the nation. Elwood P. Cubberley represents the point of view that traces our present system of universal, free, public schools directly to the New England Puritans. Cubberley saw in this early legislation "the cornerstone of our American state school systems."[9] Other historians, however, have seen early educational legislation in New England as part of the whole body of laws employed by the Puritans to give effect to their ideas about religion, government, and social classes. Schools were established as an agency of social control and direction to ensure that all children remained orthodox in the Puritan faith. Thus, these historians argued, the beginnings of a tradition of free, universal, secular education cannot be found in the early Puritan example.[10]

In their early schools, Puritans sought to reproduce the educational institutions and traditions of England: the dame and petty schools, the Latin grammar schools, and Harvard College, based on the model of Emmanuel College. The colonists, however, found it difficult to support their schools in the English manner, which was through royal grants, endowments, and church and guild sponsorship. Owing to lack of capital in the New World, they found it necessary to supplement endowments, investments, and tuition fees by various types of aid from the towns, including taxes levied on all households. Although incidental to their intent, this represented what David Tyack refers to as a "cautious new departure in 'public' financing and control of schools."[11]

This early legislation left towns free to decide the method of support for their schools: public land set aside as an endowment, private subscription, tuition charged those able to pay, or taxes levied on all property. The most common method was some form of public support, with the remaining cost prorated among parents of students who could afford to pay.

During the colonial period laws were enacted that established the authority of the legislature to determine whether towns should be required to maintain schools, the kinds of schools, length of terms, means of support and control, and qualifications of teachers. In so doing, the Massachusetts General Court established the principle that education is a function of the state. Deliberately, however, the legislature emphasized the town as the unit of local school administration. Town meetings, comprised of those who had the right of local suffrage, were the source of local authority. Decisions concerning schools, whether to have a school or pay a fine, determining the method of support, and hiring of a teacher, were made in open town meetings. It must be remembered, of course, that for early Puritans the church and state were the same, and church membership was the primary requirement for suffrage. The objectives of education, content of instruction, means of support, and the system of administration and control all reflected, therefore, the prevailing view that education was to serve the requirements of institutionalized religion.

As towns grew in size and complexity, matters relating to education were increasingly delegated to town selectmen, elected town officers. In 1692 the Massachusetts General Court granted to selectmen the power to supervise schools and employ teachers. The selectmen, in turn, began to delegate educational responsibilities to special school committees comprised initially of their own members and later expanded to include other people.

In 1789 the Massachusetts General Court established by law many of the actual practices that had developed in the state. With respect to control and supervision of schools, the law stated: "And it shall be the duty of the minister or ministers of the gospel and the selectmen (or other such persons as shall be specially chosen by each town or district for that purpose) of the several towns or districts, to use their influence and best endeavors, that the youth of their respective towns and districts, do regularly attend the schools appointed . . . and once in every six months at least . . . to visit and inspect the several schools in their respective towns and districts . . . ."[12] This law placed responsibility for certification of teachers with the selectmen, rather than town ministers and preachers; it gave legal recognition to the school committee as an official group charged solely with control and maintenance of local schools; and it officially recognized the district as a level of community organization involved with the establishment and control of schools.

By the end of the seventeenth century the population of the once closely knit New England townships had begun to disperse to more rural areas. This movement, brought about largely by increases in population, elimination of the threat of Indians, and removal of the legal requirement of church attendance, signaled the beginning of a separation of civil authority from church authority.

In the outlying settlements parents found it difficult to send children to the town school. Thus, they began to employ their own teachers and resisted taxation for the support of town schools. The decrease in revenue was noticeable, and townspeople frequently found it impossible to maintain a school from their own tuition. The initial response was a compromise: the moving school. An itinerant schoolmaster shifted from one community to another, remaining a few weeks or months depending upon the tax proceeds each settlement had paid into the town school treasury. A complete circuit could take from one to three years.[13] The moving school was a characteristic feature of the New England colonies until 1725, when district schools began to be established. The circuit riding schoolmaster eventually proved unsatisfactory. Outlying districts began to demand their quota of town taxes to employ their own schoolmaster and to maintain their own schools. This development marked not only a beginning of decentralization of school control, but also a functional separation of school and municipal administration.

Following the Revolution most New England states adopted the district form of organization, and powers of the local school district grew in the following three decades. The legislation of 1789 in Massachusetts that authorized district organization did not delegate revenue-raising authority to the districts. It was not until 1800 that the power to tax was granted local districts. This was accompanied by the power to form a district "prudential" committee certified by the town committee to select teachers and raise money for the building and maintenance of schoolhouses.

The act of 1826 in Massachusetts made compulsory the maintenance of school committees for all towns. This legislation required the selection of a committee that would not be part of the regular town government, but would have a special function of school governance. It also established the principle of lay control; nowhere did it mention ministerial, professional, or educational standards for membership on the committee. "By the end of the second decade of the nineteenth century," Cremin asserts, "Massachusetts had virtually accepted the principle of community control for publicly supported common schools."[14] Throughout the colonial and early national period, laws in Maine, Vermont, New Hampshire, and Connecticut followed the example set by Massachusetts.

The southern colonies showed regional variations in the control of public education. With the successful cultivation and sale of tobacco in 1612, Virginia quickly became a land of small farms sprinkled along the waterways that provided transportation and communication links. It was not until late in the seventeenth century, with the introduction of large numbers of slaves, that the plantation economy developed. In the absence of a need for communal activities, southern towns did not develop in the early colonial period. The dispersal of population prevented development of educational institutions, and early settlers in the South continued the English tradition of familial responsibility for education.

The southern colonies also differed from their New England counterparts in that they were settled by a greater diversity of religious groups, many of whom were seeking economic gain rather than the founding of a new social order. Thus, although the Anglican Church was established by law, the settlers had little or no interest in promoting religious or cultural conformity. Neither the church nor schools, therefore, developed as major institutions of social control.

The only early legislation in the southern colonies with respect to education concerned the children of paupers and orphans, for whom, as was the case in England, apprenticeship was required. There were no laws requiring the establishment of schools or providing for their support. Such legislation as existed, therefore, encouraged rather than required the founding of charity schools for the poor or tuition schools for a limited number of children.[15]

The tradition of private and religious philanthropy marked the early educational efforts of the southern colonies. In England the Anglican Church established the Society for the Propagation of the Gospel in Foreign Parts, which sent missionaries to most of the American colonies. The schools they established provided instruction

in reading, writing, and arithmetic, as well as religion, to the poor
throughout the South. Other religious groups also established schools
for the instruction of their own children. During the eighteenth century endowed free and tuition schools, such as Syms and Eaton, as
well as a number of private academies also were founded.

Plantation owners, who had amassed huge holdings at the beginning of the eighteenth century, employed tutors for their children.
Wealthy families also sent their sons, and sometimes daughters, to
England to be educated. They often lived in a semiapprentice relationship with a wealthy mercantile family in London to learn a business and to acquire cultural, religious, and moral training. Others
were sent to the schools and universities in England, Scotland, and
the Continent. By and large, the social, economic, and religious traditions of the South placed full responsibility for providing training
and education directly upon the family. A sharp differentiation in
the provision of education arose, therefore, between the upper and
lower economic strata. The rich had tutors or attended private
schools, the poor had limited access to philanthropic charity schools,
and children of the rural poor had almost no formal educational
opportunities.

The populations of the Middle Atlantic colonies, New Netherland
(New York), New Jersey, Pennsylvania, and Delaware were characterized by a high degree of ethnic, cultural, and religious diversity.
Although the political and religious history of these individual colonies differs, each of them evolved a similar pattern for the provision
of education. With the close historical association between church
and school, proliferation of religious sects prevented any one group
from establishing common schools, as the Puritans did in Massachusetts.

These colonies, although more densely settled than their southern
counterparts, shared with the latter a tradition of private provision of
education through family or church and philanthropic schooling for
the poor. Public support for instruction of paupers was accepted, at
least in principle. For example, the Pennsylvania Constitution of
1789-1790 required the establishment of a school for the indigent in
each county, to be supported by public funds. It is not clear whether
many schools were actually operated; the stigma of pauperism everywhere prevented large numbers of the poor from attending charity
schools.

By far the most common means of acquiring education was through private instruction, either at home by family or tutors, or in the many private schools that developed during the eighteenth century. The phenomenon of the private school, precursor of the academy movement at the end of the century, burgeoned in the more metropolitan trading centers of New York, Philadelphia, and Boston. These schools offered instruction in more practical fields than were traditionally available in classical Latin grammar schools of the time. They provided training in subjects useful for trade, navigation, and business. An example of the type of instruction offered is found in an advertisement from *The Boston News-Letter,* March 14-21, 1708: "Opposite the Mitre Tavern in Fish-Street near to Scarlets-Warff, Boston, are taught Writing, Arithmetick in all its parts; And also Geometry, Trigonometry, Plain and Sphaerical Surveying, Dialling, Gauging, Navigation, Astronomy; the projection of the Sphaer, and the use of Mathematical Instruments: by Owen Harris who Teaches it at easie Rates, and as speedy as may be."[16]

Following the colonial period the rich western lands were opened for settlement, and large numbers of persons moved from the original thirteen states and Europe to the expansive western territories. By 1820 the number of inhabitants of this area had increased to 2,500,000, representing a fourth of the population of the United States.[17] The new residents came from New England, the Middle Atlantic states, and the upper South, and all brought with them their own traditions of educational sponsorship and control: public, private, and philanthropic. The New England tradition of public education exerted, nevertheless, a strong influence over federal policy for the new territories. Following the pattern of settlement in New England, land in the territories was sold in townships. The Ordinances of 1785 and 1787 also reserved the sixteenth section of each township for the "maintenance of public schools within said Township," thereby establishing in each new state a tradition favoring public support for education.[18]

Ninteenth-Century Development of the Common School

During the period from the American Revolution to the 1830s the pattern of schooling remained heterogeneous, reflecting the colonial patterns of educational support, control, and ideology. A number of changes were occurring, however, in the political and social life of the new nation that would ultimately have a profound effect on education. For example, the U.S. began to undergo rapid industrial expansion. This triggered urbanization, extreme poverty, and the unregulated use of child labor in factories. Large numbers of immigrants came from Europe and Ireland. There was a widespread democratization of politics, which led to extension of the franchise to most white males and culminated in the election of Andrew Jackson in 1828. The process of defining an American culture provoked the rise of a self-conscious nationalism. Lastly, there was a substantial liberalization of Christianity with an emphasis on the dignity of man and the possibility of man's perfectibility.[19]

One outcome of these trends was a major reform movement, humanitarian in nature and led by the upper and middle class and the intellectual community. It was during this era that education, for the first time, was offered as a panacea for society's ills. It was argued that a system of free, high-quality common schools could preserve American democratic institutions, inculcate patriotism and spiritual and moral virtue, and increase productivity.

One of these idealistic groups, the short-lived Workingmen's parties begun in 1828, gave educational reform top priority. These organizations, composed of craftsmen in nearly every city of the nation, regarded it as essential "that an open school and competent teachers for every child . . . should be established, and those who supervise them should be chosen by the people."[20] Such groups saw education as a means of bettering their social and economic lot and for realizing the promise of Jacksonian Democracy.

Despite efforts of groups such as the Workingmen's parties, it was not the working class that ultimately effected school reform. Leaders of the free school movement were predominantly men of influence in the community who had careers in fields other than education. Horace Mann, for example, resigned as president of the Massachusetts State Senate to become secretary to the first Massachusetts State Board of Education. The historian Michael Katz comments that the mid-nineteenth-century reform movement "represented a degree of participation in public education by lay communal leaders perhaps never again equaled."[21] This is not to imply, however, that the common school movement was motivated by a desire to increase local participation in the control of education. On the contrary, reformers of the 1820s and 1830s sought greater centralization in the supervision of education through the state and town school committees.[22]

Until the nineteenth century the prevailing administrative system in New England consisted of towns divided into districts, each maintaining and managing its own school through a local school committee. These schools were supported by local taxes, aided by funds from the town school committee, and received revenue from a state school fund.

Local control of the decentralized district system had resulted in a general degeneration of the public schools by the second decade of the nineteenth century. Many of the districts were lax in providing public schools, being either unwilling or unable to tax themselves for the needed funds. Worse yet, as was common in rural areas, the population was apathetic about or even hostile to education. Professional schoolmen condemned the district system as fostering administration based on provincial interests and appointment of unqualified teachers and as encouraging what was alleged to be pedagogically unsound, the one-room school. James Carter, an educational lobbyist in Massachusetts and a contemporary of Mann, wrote in an essay published in a Boston newspaper in 1824:

If the policy of the legislature, in regard to free schools, for the last twenty years be not changed, the situation, which had been the glory of New England, will, in twenty years more, be extinct. If the State continues to relieve themselves of the trouble of providing for the whole people, and to shift the responsibilities upon the towns, and the towns upon the districts, and the districts upon the individuals, each will take care of himself and his own family as he is able . . . . The rich will, as a class, have much better instruction than they now have, while the poor will have much worse or none at all.[23]

Through the efforts of Carter and, later, Mann, the Massachusetts legislature established a State Board of Education, created the office of State Superintendent of Schools, and established a state normal school for preparation of teachers. The legislature also reduced the powers of local districts by making town school committees responsible for certification and supervision of teachers, required towns of a specified size to maintain a high school, and, finally, in 1852, passed the nation's first compulsory school attendance law.

While the task of the reformers in New England was to expand the tradition of publicly supported and controlled schools, the efforts in other areas were directed more at securing public control of private institutions supported by public funds. In the early nineteenth century there were no clear distinctions between many social institutions we now regard as "public" or "private," including schools. States liberally subsidized private academies and colleges, while towns and cities contributed to the support of private charity schools. These institutions were controlled by self-perpetuating governing boards.

New York City represents an example of private, philanthropic, and charity school development in eastern cities. The Free School Society operated from 1805 until 1853 as a chartered philanthropic organization of wealthy Protestant laymen to provide basic education for indigent children. After 1815 the Society received state school funds as well as special grants from the state legislature. In 1826 legislation transformed the Society into a quasi-public agency, transferred its property to the city, and opened the schools to all children, regardless of economic level. Also at this time the name was changed to the Public School Society, with the mayor and city council serving on the board of trustees.

The flood of Irish immigrants of the 1830s resulted in a clash between the Protestant school system and the Catholic poor. Catholics petitioned for their share of the common school funds in 1840, triggering a storm of controversy. The Society opposed public aid to sectarian schools, but the fiery Bishop Hughes was able to build a case against the highly centralized corporation that controlled the public schools. The result was legislation in 1842 placing control over the Society's schools in the elected board of education.[24]

The public schools of New York City were organized into seventeen local areas, or wards, controlled by a locally elected board of education. Each ward was empowered to select its own personnel, determine curriculum, and purchase books, supplies, and services from vendors. The central board was composed of two commissioners elected from each of the seventeen wards. Diane Ravitch, in her history of the New York City schools, quotes an early observer-historian of the era: "[the victory of the ward schools] was based on a DIRECT AND IMMEDIATE APPEAL TO THE PEOPLE. No body of men, no matter what their character or social standing, were placed between them and their children. If they have one intent, in this land of *self-government,* they should jealously guard, and keep as closely as possible under their control, surely it is the selection of

those into whose hands is committed that most sacred and responsible trust, the education of their offspring."[25]

The common school movement was carried throughout the western states by crusading reformers, as well as by New Englanders who
settled in these areas. In most states of the West the rugged individ-
ualism of the frontier, scattered population patterns, and economic
hardships mitigated against establishment of a tax-supported system
of common schools. The settlers, however, shared traditions of learning, and the egalitarianism of the frontier aided in establishing the
concept of schools untainted by the stigma of pauperism. Thus, by
1865, all of the states outside the South had achieved, or at least
began to establish, universal, free, and tax-supported public schools.

The South, by the 1830s, had come to view itself as culturally distinct from the rest of the nation. The pattern of education that had
emerged by 1850 reflected the political and social structure of the
rural, two-class plantation system. Public provision of education for
the poor and the black was almost entirely absent. However, the
South had more private academies than New England or the Middle
Atlantic states, and Virginia had more colleges and college graduates
than Massachusetts.[26] Education of the white aristocracy was gen-
erously supported. It was not until after the Civil War that the common school tradition began to be established.

In summary, during the first hundred years of American settlement, control over education was vested primarily in the family. Parents or guardians were responsible for providing moral, spiritual,
vocational, and academic training. The earliest laws relating to education were derived from the tradition of English poor laws, making
basic literacy and vocational training compulsory. The interest of the
community in legislating compulsory education was twofold. First, the
small, interdependent communities were barely able to survive economically in the wilderness of the New World. They simply could not
afford an unproductive indigent class. Further, the task of building a
self-sufficient social and economic culture required the transmission of
skills and knowledge to each person. Second, the Puritans came to the
New World with a spiritual mission. Their intent was to establish a Bible
Commonwealth, a government based upon and dedicated to the Puritan view of man and God. Because their religion was intellectual,
requiring intimate knowledge and study of Scripture, it was essential
to the ecclesiastical mission that all children be at least literate.

New England laws requiring establishment of schools did not remove control and responsibility from parents for the education of their children. These laws were an attempt to encourage communal effort in the provision of schooling, as education was recognized as an interest of the community. The control of these schools, where they existed, rested with the voters of the community through the town meeting. Since a requirement for suffrage was membership in the Puritan congregation, school control was, in effect, a prerogative of the church.

The connection between churches and schools was very close throughout the seventeenth and eighteenth centuries, and secularism was an issue in the mid-nineteenth-century movement to expand the common school. In many of the colonies, and the western territories as well, it was often a religious sect that established schools for the training of its own children and the children of the poor. Gradually, however, the movement in New England was away from domination by the church. School authority was transferred from the congregation as the voting franchise was extended to all propertied citizens. Subsequently, the role of the clergy in supervision of the schools diminished. A separate lay committee, chosen by the elected officials of each town, became directly responsible for maintaining the school.

Prior to 1800 control of education did not undergo parallel development in other regions of the country. The traditions of private and philanthropic provision of education again left control essentially in the hands of individual families, who could select from a variety of arrangements, according to their means. For the poor this meant, of course, no schools at all in many areas. By the 1830s, however, the control of education became a nationwide issue. Rapid industrialization, urbanization, and a concomitant influx of immigrants altered the fabric of social, economic, and political life. Schooling came to be seen by middle-class reformers of the day as a vehicle for assimilating immigrants and coping with the vicious results of urban poverty.

If the schools were to serve a function of socialization and equalization thrust on them by early nineteenth-century reformers, then complete discretion could no longer be granted to local communities and individuals. It was argued that the larger body politic had to assume responsibility for providing schools for all, to assure their quality, and eventually to require attendance. The New England states, through effective leadership and legislation, initiated establishment of a system of free, tax-supported common schools. By 1865 all the states outside the South had enacted similar legislation.

The tradition of the district system was retained. Legislation placed direct control of and responsibility for schools at the district level, while at the same time strengthening the supervisory powers of the town school committee. The district system, in effect, acknowledged and reinforced the tradition of local control of education. Simultaneously, state legislation firmly established the state's interest in and legal responsibility for education. The state was to decide whether to establish a school, how it should be financed, and who should attend it. Local discretion remained over determination of the level of school support, hiring of teachers, and decisions concerning methods of instruction.

As common schools spread, important decisions were no longer made by religious leaders in the community, but over time devolved on economic and political leaders. In a relatively homogeneous community, such as a small New England village or an urban ghetto, these leaders could be assumed to have more or less reflected the desires and interests of the community as a whole. With increasing diversity of class and culture in the mid-nineteenth century, however, lay leadership in heterogeneous districts tended to reflect the interests of the dominant social class. The leaders of the common school movement were outspoken in their goals for education, among which were the inculcation of the values and traditions of the white, Protestant, middle and upper classes. Mann was greatly concerned with the threat to social harmony and stability inherent in the heterogeneity of the population and expansion of the lower classes. He proposed schooling as necessary to instill a common code of morality, based on nonsectarian Protestantism, and respect for American political traditions. His chief concern in this regard was for the urban poor and immigrants.

The inherent conflict between the will of the majority and the rights of the minority has persisted throughout the history of public schools. The ultimate establishment of common schools as nonsectarian (though most often Protestant in fact) and the retention of the ideology of lay control over the affairs of the local school reflect this tension. The local majority could not, in theory, use public schools to inculcate its religious views, but control was not given over either to the state or to experts.

Thus, by the close of the nineteenth century, the ideological and legal framework for governance of America's schools had been established. Education was a public function, rooted in state statute, but administered primarily by local officials. School districts served as the primary unit of management. Each district had a governing board, members of which were neither church officials nor educational experts. They were, ideally, to represent the general public in making educational policy, but in fact they sometimes reflected the views of a social and economic elite. Regardless of their social standing, they usually were in frequent, face-to-face contact with their constituents. Schools were expected to perform a number of lofty miracles, but the governmental mechanisms for their control were rooted in a myriad of down-to-earth practicalities, lay supremacy, local autonomy, and public support.

Twentieth-Century School Governance: The Erosion of Lay Control

In 1900 the locus of school governance was still embedded in the local community. The national population had grown to 72,000,000; there were nearly 110,000 local school districts with an average of five members per school board, that is, one board member for every 138 citizens.[27] Such a ratio provided an opportunity for residents of a community to have close contact with local school board members, and disagreements over schools could be settled on a personal basis much in the same fashion as in colonial times.

The School Consolidation Movement

Since 1900 the population of the U.S. has grown dramatically, and there has been a continuing effort by state legislatures to consolidate small school districts into larger units. This has meant that the ratio of representative to constituents has changed markedly. Today the number of operating school districts has dropped to less than 17,000 while the national population has increased to more than 210,000,000. One school board member now represents roughly 2,470 people (see Figure 5-1).[28] An obvious consequence is that the individual citizen is less able than before personally to interact with

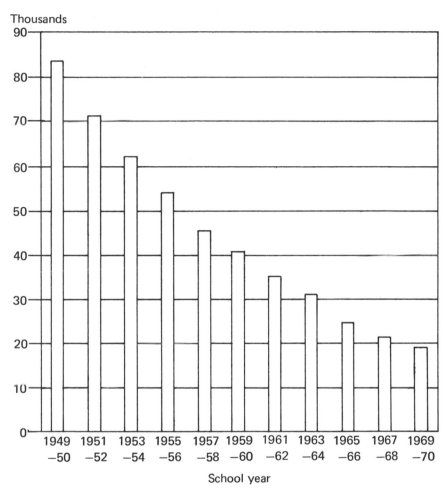

Figure 5-1
*Decline of school districts in the United States
during the period 1949-1950 to 1969-1970
(from U.S. Office of Education,* A Century of U.S. School Statistics
*[Washington, D.C.: Department of Health, Education, and Welfare,
1974])*

the board member and thus have direct influence upon school policy. This may account for the growing reliance upon pressure groups and lobbying activity to influence public policy decisions. This imbalance between boards and those they represent has contributed to serious erosion of the layman's role in matters of school policy, an increase in the power of professional educators, and greater uniformity among schools. Many present-day school districts are large, sprawling, and frustratingly bureaucratic. This is particularly distressing since schools frequently touch citizens more directly than any other level of government. Many people may never have direct association with city or state officials; even when it may be necessary to have contact with municipal government, such as with policemen, firemen, the city council, planning commission or other agency, such contact is limited in both time and scope. Schooling, on the other hand, is intimately tied to the daily routine of virtually all citizens during an extended period of their lives, usually as students and parents of students. Yet, a governmental gap between a citizen's ability to express his or her desires about schools and actual school practices has been developing since approximately 1900.

Efforts to Depoliticize Education

Another trend beginning at the turn of this century that has tended to exclude laymen from policy decisions about schools has been the effort to separate schools from the political process. The call for "depoliticization" grew out of the rampant governmental corruption occurring around 1900. Richard Hofstadter vividly characterizes the era of machine politics and bossism:

The urban boss, a dealer in public privileges who could also command public support, became a more powerful figure. With him came that train of evils which so much preoccupied the liberal muckraking mind: the bartering of franchises, the building of tight urban political machines, the marshaling of hundreds of thousands of ignorant voters, the exacerbation of poverty and slums, the absence or excessive cost of municipal services, the cooperation between politics and "commercialized vice"—in short, the entire system of underground government and squalor . . . .[29]

Education was no exception to the rule of scandal in government. City schools were administered primarily by ward-based school boards. These bodies were dominated by the same ward bosses and partisan political machines as were municipal governmental services.

Teachers frequently owed their jobs to a political operator. If they were not a member of or did not support the "right" party, they sometimes lost their teaching posts. Similarly, contracts for supplies, school construction, and building maintenance were frequently accompanied by illegal rebates and kickbacks to board members. Being a school director was widely viewed as a relatively unimportant political position useful only as a stepping-stone to higher office. Reformers of the period viewed the political ills and corruption characterizing all schools as a consequence of an excess of democracy. Power was said to be too widely dispersed and fragmented. First, the ward-based school board system provided a source of spoils and patronage to local politicians, to the detriment of schools. Ward-elected board members advanced parochial interests and practiced logrolling rather than considering the needs of the children and the school system as a whole. Second, the more centralized high school boards could not possibly work as one body, and so decision making was conducted by numerous subcommittees, leading to inefficiency, fragmentation of authority, and difficulty in fixing responsibility.[30]

Proposals for reforming the governance of city school systems centered on radical reorganization of the board of education. There should be but one board for the entire city, and it should be small, elected at large in special nonpartisan elections, and then it should rely on professional educators to deal with the complexity of actual school administration. By centralizing the boards in large cities and by reducing the size of their membership, reformers hoped to make their actions more highly visible and, thereby, more subject to public scrutiny. Also, it was hoped that the high visibility and reduced opportunity for tangible political rewards would make the position less attractive to politicians and more enticing to public-spirited citizens.

By 1900 most of the older cities had abolished ward or community school boards.[31] In the following years they continued to reduce the size of the central board, until, in 1917, the average size of school boards in cities above 100,000 population had declined to ten members.[32]

Several historians have seen the entire municipal reform movement in terms of a struggle for control of the cities between the lower and middle classes, many of whom were immigrants, and the economic and social elite.[33] Ravitch points out that 92 of 104 members of a

New York school reform group in 1896 were listed in the Social Register.[34] Further, George S. Counts, surveying centralized boards of education, found them to be largely composed of business and professional elites who had succeeded in capturing control of the city schools while ostensibly reforming them.[35] In a study of the composition of school boards in 104 large cities, another researcher found that of 967 board members, 433 were businessmen, 333 were professionals, 87 were workers, and the remainder were either retired businessmen or wives of businessmen.[36]

In addition to attempting to centralize big-city boards of education, and populate them with nonpartisan elites, early twentieth-century reformers brought about a number of other changes aimed at removing schools from the mainstream of the political process. For example, school boards in many cities, particularly smaller ones, were provided with independent taxing power. By being able to provide their own resources, it was argued, they would no longer be dependent on municipal politicians, "the worst kind." Today 85 percent of the school boards in the U.S. enjoy taxing power. This is known as fiscal independence and is defended strenuously by professional educators as crucial in order to keep education politically untarnished.

Other depoliticizing effects came in the form of separate school board elections and laws prohibiting elective school officers from being partisan. The result, mostly unintended, of the effort to separate schools and politics was to create a public perception that politics was dirty and should not be permitted to soil little children and the decisions about their education. The public began to delegate more control of education to fewer elected officers and to participate less in the selection of those officers.

The Beginning of Bureaucracy

The reduction in elected officials, when coupled with the growth in the size of school systems, both because of district consolidation and population increases, almost inevitably triggered another reform: the burgeoning of professional school administrators. Many cities added administrative and supervisory personnel, under the direction of the superintendent, to relieve the board members of the duties of direct school management and supervision. In 1890 the president of the Chicago board of education in an address to board members expressed this new view of the responsibility of the board: "[the more you refrain] from handling details in business departments, but content yourselves with laying down general lines of work and policy, and holding the proper subordinate responsible for results, the better it will be for the school system and you."[37]

Although it is true that many smaller towns and cities throughout the country have followed the model of the big cities, Katz has proposed that "whether a given locality is more democratic or more bureaucratic [in the governance of its schools] depends upon its size. In smaller communities, direct board involvement with the schools is easier, whereas in large cities the very scale of the operation, by preventing intimate board involvement, fosters bureaucratic control at all levels. It is one of the paradoxes of American education that democratic localism remains, even within cities, in the official administrative ideology, while bureaucracy remains the practice."[38]

Thus, depoliticizing and centralizing control of city school systems served to reduce the number of lay participants in educational decision making, to create a professional school bureaucracy, and to establish the expanded role of the superintendent.

Professional Administration and the Dilution of Lay Control

It was against the backdrop of "underground government" that the Progressive movement pushed its "cult of efficiency." Within this milieu of reform both the city manager and the professional school superintendent emerged. The goal was to remove "politics" from the administration of both city government and schools. One consequence of removing party politics from the policy-making process was, however, simply to make politics less visible and, thus, less public. Policy decisions concerning schools are, in fact, tightly tied to the political process, and the pervasive belief over the past fifty or sixty years that education had become apolitical was simply a myth. The effect has been that the layman, notably boards of education, have become more dependent upon the professional rather than upon the public for making school policy.

Prior to 1900 there were no "professionals" in education: "Laymen ran the schools the way they wanted to run them, delegating to schoolmen only the more esoteric problems of curriculum and supervision. Most personnel, maintenance, and business matters were handled by lay boards without professional consultation."[39]

As the business of schools increased, school board members acquired too much responsibility, serving without pay to tend to day-to-day details. The task of visiting schools and evaluating teachers became impossible for individual board members as districts continued to grow in size. Consequently, schools began to seek full-time employees to oversee the operation of the schools. In most cases these positions were filled by former teachers. There was, however, no systematic development of the role of these early "superintendents," and the office "depended upon the expectations of boards."[40] In one study of the early expectations of superintendents it was found that the Baltimore school board wanted to find someone to "scrutinize carefully the books which were to be adopted rather than have the decisions made by laymen who might succumb to the influence of friends and book agents."[41] In San Francisco the new superintendent was "instructed to rent or otherwise obtain an adequate number of buildings for school houses and to prepare them for operation."[42] Other districts were interested in finding someone who would be able to communicate with teachers.

It was expected, in theory, that the local superintendent would implement policy that was determined and mandated by the board. The superintendent was not expected to be an educator but a caretaker: keeping records, supervising the building of schools, allocating supplies. In the time since the inception and spread of the office, the professional superintendent has, in fact, come to exercise strong control over the preparation and presentation of the budget. The superintendent has the option of suggesting policy alternatives, and he has control over the flow of information to the school board and the public. "The superintendent often defines issues, proposes alternatives, provides technical ammunition for his supporters, and in the end implements or evades the decisions arrived at."[43]

The school board member and the general public have frequently been awed by the professional who claims vast expert knowledge. Teachers' colleges and much of the educational literature have fostered the claim of educational expertise on the part of both administrators and teachers. Educators frequently have convinced the public that most matters related to the school are far too esoteric for laymen to understand.

The comparison is often made between education and professions such as medicine and engineering. It is argued that one would not presume to suggest to a surgeon or physician that the patient be consulted regarding proper treatment. Nor would a layman question an engineer's assessment of structural stress in the design of a bridge. These matters, it is stated, clearly require professional competence. The educator contends that the same professional skills are necessary in order to make decisions in education. There is, however, at least one important difference between educators, physicians, and engineers. Schools are, after all, public agencies. If one is not happy with the way in which a doctor handles a medical case or with the engineer's design, one is usually free to choose another doctor or engineer. This is not generally true if one is unhappy with the quality of a particular public school. In most communities, because of attendance regulations and district boundaries, changes in public schools cannot be made except at great expense and sacrifice to most parents, and private schools are financially prohibitive for the average family. In addition, doctors and engineers depend upon quantitative analysis or a relatively large body of scientific knowledge as a basis for their decisions, and these decisions normally require a minimum number of value judgments. It is difficult for educators to sustain an argument in favor of expertise when, in many cases, educational decisions are qualitative, and a teacher or other professional educator has only a modest claim to the truth over the opinions of other members of society.

Professional influence is not confined to intradistrict governance. Professionalization is a centralizing influence at the state level as well. Organizations of teachers and administrators lobby to have written into the state education code as law their standards for certification, their beliefs about program scope and curriculum, and their policies on hiring, firing, tenure, and salaries. Professionals, mostly administrators who have served at the local level, compose the staffs of state education departments and promulgate regulations in the process of administering state codes. The centripetal force exerted by educators can be seen even at the federal level; national associations seek to influence federal aid policies, and teachers write for textbook publishers with a national audience.[44]

The Era of Efficiency

Closely coupled with the coming of professional administrators was the effort to model education after business. This movement strengthened the hand of the professional at the expense of citizens. Frederick Taylor, in *The Principles of Scientific Management,* published in 1911, set forth his approach to industrial management based upon detailed analysis of factors affecting productivity.[45] He was concerned especially with waste and efficiency in industry, and he advocated procedures for increasing the productivity of industrial workers. It must be noted that the reorganization of the governance structure in city school systems was largely accomplished before the burgeoning of the efficiency movement in education. While the progressive reformers were certainly interested in increasing the efficiency of public services, the adoption of the principles of scientific management in school administration occurred after most of the school board reorganizations at the turn of the century.[46] The movement to apply engineering efficiency methods and criteria to education was directed at the internal organization and processes of schools and school districts.

Many professors of school administration adopted and disseminated the concepts and language of the efficiency experts and assisted in creating the role of superintendent as business manager. Among these leaders were Ellwood P. Cubberley of Stanford, George Strayer of Teachers College, Columbia, Edward C. Elliot of Wisconsin, Paul Harris of Howard, Franklin Bobbitt of the University of Chicago, and Leonard Ayres of the Russell Sage Foundation. Cubberley, for example, in his widely used text on school administration, said: "Our schools are, in a sense, factories in which the raw products [children] are to be shaped and fashioned into products to meet the various demands of life . . . . This demands good tools, specialized machinery, continuous measurement of production to see if it is according to specifications, the elimination of waste in manufacturing, and a large variety in the output."[47]

Some of the practical outcomes of the efficiency movement have passed into the category of historical quirks, but many of the developments have been longer lasting. What the progressives of the era referred to as "science" was actually collection of data. Enormous amounts of statistics were collected about many social institutions, and education was no exception. Beginning in about 1910, the school survey movement was begun, with outside "experts" hired by school districts across the country to collect data for boards of education. These study teams were almost always composed of profes-

sors and other professional educators. A great many "scientific" reforms took place at their insistence, some of which have subsequently been shown not to be very scientific or efficient.

Centralizing Effects of Court Decisions

Another force lending momentum to the centralization of educational decisions is the increasingly litigious nature of American society. Since the late 1950s individuals have turned increasingly to the
courts, rather than to the legislative process, in order to settle questions of social policy. Thus, the courts have become more frequent
participants in educational policy making. Such increased litigation
of educational issues portends a diminished role for local decision-
making bodies as well as state legislatures.

Courts have already issued decisions directing school boards in
matters such as the regulation of student conduct and discipline;
personnel compensation and dismissal; and types of examinations
that may be given to children. Courts also are being asked to interpret negotiated contracts between districts and teachers' organizations.

Many court decisions, it may be argued, have probably provoked
badly needed and long-awaited reforms that school boards and other
legislative bodies have not been willing to make on their own initiative. Nevertheless, the long-range effect may be the further diminu-
tion of the direct role of the public and may, perhaps, eventually
lead to a loss of desire to participate. While such decisions may serve
to ameliorate intolerable social and political conditions, there exists
the likelihood that litigation will begin to serve an immediate political end, an end not intended to be served nor one the courts are
equipped to serve. In a reapportionment case in 1964, U.S. Supreme
Court Justice Harlan reflected upon such a consequence in his dissenting opinion. He wrote:

What is done today saps the political process. The promise of judicial intervention in matters of this sort cannot but encourage popular inertia in efforts of
political reform through the political process, with the inevitable result that the
process itself is weakened . . . the vitality of our political system, on which in the
last analysis all else depends, is weakened by reliance on the Judiciary for political reform; in time a complacent body politic may result.[48]

A careful reading of the majority opinion in the school finance
case heard by the U.S. Supreme Court in 1973 indicates a movement

of the Court toward possible judicial restraint in matters of local taste. The tenor of the *Rodriguez* opinion tends to support the concept of political and social diversity articulated earlier in this chapter. In Justice Powell's opinion he wrote:

the question regarding the most effective relationship between state boards of education and local school boards, in terms of their respective responsibilities and degrees of control, is now undergoing searching re-examination. The ultimate wisdom as to these and related problems of education is not likely to be defined for all time even by the scholars who now so earnestly debate the issues. In such circumstances, the judiciary is well advised to refrain from interposing on the States inflexible constitutional restraints that could circumscribe or handicap the continued research and experimentation so vital to finding even partial solutions to educational problems and to keeping abreast of ever-changing conditions.[49]

In his closing remarks Justice Powell continued: "The consideration and initiation of fundamental reforms with respect to state taxation and education are matters reserved for the legislative processes of the various States . . . ."

The Court was, at the same time, careful to make clear that the decision was not to be interpreted as favoring present arrangements of state financing: "We hardly need add that this Court's action today is not to be viewed as placing its judicial imprimatur on the status quo. The need is apparent for reform in tax systems which may well have relied too long and too heavily on the local property tax . . . . These matters merit the continued attention of the scholars who already have contributed much by their challenges. But the ultimate solutions must come from the lawmakers and from the democratic pressures of those who elect them."[50] Thus, in the *Rodriguez* decision the onus of reform has been placed upon the states. While it is true that the process of change will be much slower on a state-to-state basis than would have been true given a reverse decision, reform is not impossible. State courts in California, Connecticut, and New Jersey have acted favorably in similar cases. Even so, intervention of the courts may have serious policy implications. Decisions made by state legislatures under court mandate may produce different outcomes than the result of publicly articulated political demands.

Demands of Teachers for Increased Decision-Making Power

The growth of teachers' organizations may be seen as a centralizing tendency in that associations unite teachers across individual school districts, states, and at the national level. This increases the influence of teachers in state capitals and Washington and adds to the salience of educational issues at these higher levels. It has been asserted, in fact, that united, well-financed teachers' organizations, using highly paid and trained professional negotiators, will so overpower local school boards in the bargaining process that negotiations will graduately shift to the state level. Aside from such speculation, however, the significance here of "teacher power" is its effect upon lay control. Teachers too want a share of the decision-making power beyond the classroom; they want to be major participants in the governance of education.

Since 1940 the work force of teachers has tripled from slightly over 1,000,000 to nearly 3,000,000 in 1971.[51] A somewhat surprising concomitant has been the growth of teachers' organizations based on the trade-union model and the increased politicization of teachers. It has been estimated that by 1980 membership in the two national teachers' organizations (National Education Association and American Federation of Teachers) could reach 3,500,000, and their ability to generate funds, through dues and other assessments, could attain the somewhat staggering annual level of $500,000,000.[52] Over the past fifteen years the two national associations have grown substantially closer ideologically and more active politically.[53] A movement to merge the two organizations, which quietly began in 1969, has continued to gather momentum. On June 5, 1972, the New York State Teachers Association (NEA) voted to merge with the United Teachers of New York (AFT). This merger now makes the teachers' organization in New York the largest state organization of public employees in the nation. Similar negotiations are under way in other states.

Teachers have used these professional organizations to consolidate their power in order to influence local decision making. Even though statutes in virtually every state forbid use of strikes by public employees, teachers' associations have successfully withheld or threatened to withhold their labor in order to improve their working conditions and financial benefits. The overall effectiveness of these tactics can be illustrated by relating strike activities with increases in salaries and the number of negotiated agreements that have been signed.

Between 1955 and 1966 there were only thirty-five strikes by teachers throughout the United States. During only a one-year period, 1967-1968, however, there were 114 strikes, affecting 21 states, involving 163,000 teachers, and causing the loss of 1,400,000 days of teaching. During the following year the number of strikes increased to 131 with a loss in teaching almost doubled, reaching 2,400,000 teaching days. Paralleling the mushrooming of strike activities has been the growth in the number of negotiated agreements. Between the first period of significant strike action (1966-1968), the number of signed contracts increased by 44.5 percent.[54]

The primary aim of these strikes has been a concern for working conditions and salary increases. There is some evidence to suggest, however, that such strike activities have, at least in the short run, been detrimental to students. Tests given in New York City during the school year 1969-1970 indicated that students had regressed two months in reading ability during the previous school year.

The public may have been sympathetic initially to teachers' demands for salary increases. In the 1960s their gains in pay outstripped other indicators of economic growth. During the period 1952-1968, while teachers' salaries increased by 128.6 percent, per capita personal income rose by only 94.7 percent, and the average earnings per employee increased by only 94.1 percent. Even in terms of the adjusted dollars of 1970-1971, teachers were well ahead of all other occupational categories; their salaries increased by 36 percent in adjusted dollars compared to an increase of only 24 percent for all other full-time industrial employees. (See Table 5-1.) These gains have been eroded slightly by the economic decline of the mid-1970s.

The stereotype of the modern teacher has radically changed from that of the colonial teacher who was described by Willard Elsbree as "unclassifiable":

He was a God-fearing clergyman, he was an unmitigated rogue; he was amply paid, he was accorded a bare pittance; he made teaching a life career, he used it merely as a stepping stone; he was a classical scholar, he was all but illiterate; he was licensed by bishop or colonial governor, he was certified only by his own pretensions; he was a cultured gentleman, he was a crude-mannered yokel; he ranked with the cream of society, he was regarded as a menial. In short, he was neither a type nor a personality, but a statistical distribution represented by a skewed curve.[55]

Today's teacher is often labeled "militant." The consequence of militant tactics has been that school boards have been forced to share decision-making power over matters which, in the past, have been almost entirely within the scope of laymen. Matters that have already

Table 5-1

*Average annual salary of instructional staff in public elementary
and secondary day schools and average annual earnings of
full-time employees in all industries in adjusted dollars,
United States, 1959-1960 to 1972-1973
(1972-1973 purchasing power)*

School year	Salary per member of instructional staff	Earnings per full-time employee
1959-1960	7,539	6,749
1961-1962	8,115	7,016
1963-1964	8,657	7,454
1965-1966	9,297	7,826
1967-1968	9,922	8,109
1969-1970	10,020	8,313
1971-1972	10,508	8,635
1972-1973	10,608	8,874

Source: National Center for Educational Statistics, *Digest of Educational Statistics, 1973 edition* (Washington, D.C.: Government Printing Office, 1974), 48.

been negotiated by teachers include size of classes, transfers of teachers within districts, assignment to nonclassroom duties, teachers' hours, and pupil-teacher ratios. In addition, teachers are continuing to ask for increased participation in matters such as curriculum development and selection of textbooks and subject material.

An additional consequence of these bargaining techniques is that the strikes and boycotts have blunted the teachers' claims to professional status and damaged their public image as "socializers" of the young. Part of the role of teacher is that of inculcating the ideals of democracy, fair play, respect for authority, and obedience to legitimate rules. As one school administrator asked: "How can youngsters have respect for their teachers nowadays when teachers are threatening to strike and are actually going on strike? There is a growing trend for members of our society to obey only those laws, rules, codes, with which they are in agreement. Tragic is the only word that can be applied to teachers who violated the 'no strike' provision . . . . How can we expect students to obey the laws when the teachers don't?"[56]

Most of all, such activities force boards to share power. Albert

Shanker, president of the New York City United Federation of Teachers (AFT), phrased it bluntly: "Power is taken from someone. Teachers, as one of society's powerless groups, are now starting to take power from supervisors and school boards. This is causing and will continue to cause a realignment of power relationships."[57] Yet, in the Newark strike of 1970, the community, without success, urged the board to stand firm against teachers' demands and insisted that "the community should be able to determine who will administer its schools, who will teach in the schools, and what will be taught."[58] Thus the conflict over who should govern escalates.

Countervailing Reform Movements

By the beginning of the second half of the twentieth century, the historical forces and events described to this point—consolidation of school districts, attempts at depoliticization, growth of professional administration, burgeoning bureaucratization, increasing litigation, and unionization of teachers—had combined to dilute dramatically public control over the schools. This loss of power benefited professional educators who had gradually come to dominate the policy-making process for schools.

It has usually been the case throughout history that such a dramatic shift of power triggers a countermovement; education is no exception. Efforts to restore citizen control have taken a number of forms. A few examples, primarily the "community control movement" and efforts to gain an elusive "accountability," will be reviewed. For reasons we shall describe later, however, as of 1975 none of these attempts at reform appears successful in redressing the balance of power.

Decentralization and Community Control

Beginning in the late 1960s parents and neighborhood residents in large cities sporadically demanded an increased voice in school affairs. The ultimate extension of demands to participate is a desire to control, that is, to break up big-city school systems into small, neighborhood districts governed by locally elected boards with authority over programs, curriculum, personnel, and expenditures.

A distinction is frequently made between decentralization and "community control." The former is often thought of as purely administrative; professionals in the field, rather than in the central office, would be in charge. Community control, in contrast, implies political change with a redistribution of power from central boards and central offices to neighborhood parents and citizens. In a sense, however, the distinction made between administrative and political change is based upon a false dualism since administration, being the implementation and execution of decisions made by elected leaders, is always political.

At issue, then, in any plan to reduce the scale of educational governance, whether referred to as decentralization or community control, is the question of the authority to make and implement policy. Thus, the ultimate aim of the advocates of both decentralization and community control is to remove the authority from central boards and staff who are seen as too remote and bureaucratized to meet the varied needs of individual communities. Advocates of decentralization suggest, therefore, that, if professionals are freed from the constraints of the central office, several positive outcomes will result: schools will become more responsive to local needs; they will reflect the special characteristics of the community; and local residents will have greater access to decision makers. If true community control were established, residents, through their elected representatives, would choose staffs and policies that would reflect the educational goals of the neighborhood.

As has been pointed out, in the twentieth century the major impetus has been to centralize educational governance, to increase the power of the state in order to ensure minimal standards and oversee programs, and to strengthen the authority of central city boards and superintendents at the expense of ward-based, politically controlled boards. It is possible that the current pressure to decentralize is simply the next phase in a cyclic process brought about by a reaction to excessive centralization.[59]

On the other hand, advocates of community control point to specific incidents and events in the 1960s as antecedents to the drive for decentralization. They cite the well-publicized failure of city school systems to educate children in the ghetto, lags in reading scores, and high dropout rates. Some also trace the demand for decentralization to the failure of integration in big cities. One of the rationales for integration was based on the suggestion in the Coleman Report that blacks, in integrated settings, have higher achievement

rates than blacks in segregated institutions.[60] This rationale was interpreted by some black groups as racist; to suggest that blacks could
only achieve in the presence of whites was considered an insult. As it
became clear that desegregation was not proceeding "with all deliberate speed," either because of an absence of will, fervent opposition
to bussing, or the fact that the populations of many schools in large
cities were already overwhelmingly black, thus making integration
physically impossible within city boundaries, community control was
seen as a possible answer. If schools were not to be integrated, if children were not to be bussed, if neighborhood schools were to continue as the mainstay of the system, then at least schools should be
controlled by neighborhood parents and residents. It was argued that
only local neighborhoods could suggest the kind of education most
relevant for their children.

Another reason often given for the rise of the movement for community control is the "participatory ethos" of the 1960s. Demonstrations, marches, and community action programs stimulated the
interest of citizens in the idea of direct political participation and, to
some extent, helped them develop skills necessary for involvement.
Nevertheless, whatever its antecedents, by the end of the decade
decentralization was on the agenda of several cities and ultimately
became reality in both New York and Detroit. In neither city, however, was a plan enacted that provided for complete community
control; central boards still retained powers of review and exclusive
control over some areas, such as high schools in New York City. In
both cities teachers' unions, fearing a purge of white, middle-class
teachers, lobbied to restrict hiring, firing, and rights of transfer of the
community districts.

It is difficult to evaluate the effects of decentralization and community control since existing plans in cities such as New York,
Detroit, and Los Angeles involve only partial transfers of authority
to local boards. It is possible, however, to analyze the concept and
the claims of its advocates. Laudatory as the concept of citizen participation may be, the creation of smaller districts is no guarantee of
increased interest and activity on the part of local citizens. One has
only to look at the tendency for boards, even in the smallest districts, to defer to professionals, in order to realize that citizen involvement will not result automatically from a reduction in size or
from structural reform.

Accountability

Also by the 1960s the increasing costs of providing educational services,[61] when combined with the erosion of citizen control, prompted another kind of effort to restore public control over schools. This effort, known generally as the "accountability" movement, implicitly admitted that professional educators dominated local school policy making. Accountability said, in effect, that laymen have little hope of recapturing control over the process of schooling, but, by gaining control over the "product," it might be possible for them to reassert their rightful authority. Thus, the proponents of accountability attempted primarily in state legislatures to impose quality control standards upon local school districts.

As with many fashionable labels, "accountability" is an imprecise term that has different connotations depending upon the audiences involved. It has served as a semantic umbrella under which have clustered school administrators, state and local budget officials, legislators, organizations of taxpayers, and a number of informed laymen, all of whom desire better information as to what they receive for the school dollars they spend. For example, because of the prodding of Governor Rockefeller, New York established an Office of Education Performance Review to conduct studies on school efficiency. Under Daniel Klepak, the first director of that office, reports have been issued on topics such as administrators' salaries and the training and performance of teachers. The Legislative Analyst Office in California added an entire new unit to conduct evaluations of educational programs. In 1972 Florida enacted a list of "accountability" statutes aimed at making school dollars more productive.

In California, as in many other states, attempts to evaluate schooling tumble out of the legislative hopper ad nauseam. The bills are seldom thoughtful and the mechanisms for accountability embedded in them are usually unrelated to each other. The fact that they are enacted is a triumph of faith over experience because to date none of them has had a significant impact on that state's mammoth public school system. In 1967, for example, the legislature mandated that every school district in the state install a Program Planning and Performance Budgeting System. This legislation was subsequently rescinded when it became evident that such measures were impracticable, not to mention terribly unpopular with teachers' organizations.[62] The legislature, apparently learning little from its PPBS experience, subsequently produced the Stull Act which mandates local assessment of teaching performance. As if that were insufficient, the Assembly and Senate established a Joint Education Committee on Goals and Objectives to promulgate statewide local citizens' meetings intended to develop statements of school purposes. Presumably these are to provide a base against which school performance can be measured.

The most widely used tactic of accountability has been statewide testing programs. According to a joint publication of the Education Commission of the States and the Educational Testing Service, thirty states had a form of a statewide testing program in 1972.[63] The system established in Michigan in 1971 is, in some ways, the most famous, or infamous, example of statewide testing as a procedure of accountability. The legislature approved, and the state Education Department administers, a statewide system of "criterion-referenced" tests.[64] Districts characterized by high concentrations of children who score low on the tests are accorded added state funds for compensatory education programs. Unless such pupils exhibit gains in achievement in subsequent years, however, the added funding is reduced or withdrawn. This plan, whatever its virtues, and there appear to be several, has created substantial controversy. Opponents allege that the idea is a fascist plot to permit the state to dictate learning objectives. Yet others complain that the withdrawal of funds from "nonperforming" districts is most harmful to the very children the program was designed to help. Opponents also assert that the program encourages cheating and misrepresentation of students' performance and displaces important but difficult to measure school goals in such areas as literature and health.[65]

The private sector has not been neglected in attempts to install plans of educational accountability. Many of the models proposed for assessing school performance, and much of the accompanying technical jargon, are adapted from industry and business, usually without attempting to modify them for the purposes of the public sector. Indeed, "accountability" is a generic term usually associated with private enterprise. The technical-industrial model includes schemes such as Management by Objectives (MBO), Program Performance Budgeting Systems (PPBS), systems analysis, Program Evaluation and Review Technique (PERT), performance contracting,

educational production function analysis, Competency Based Teacher Education (CBTE), and "learner verification," all of which have
their analogues in efforts to understand and maximize output in
manufacturing organizations. Despite the best intentions of school
boards, administrators, teachers, and the public, none of these technical-industrial schemes has succeeded significantly in providing
policy makers and clients with the information they desire about
what does and what does not work in schools. Further, these techniques have steadfastly failed to relate dollar costs to school effectiveness. Policy makers at all levels of government are as ignorant
today as they were a decade ago about what school programs will
provide the most "educational bang for the taxpayer's buck." Worse
yet, in many ways these technical models of accountability have
been counterproductive because they have fostered false hopes and
thereafter provoked unnecessary cynicism and bitterness among educators and laymen alike.

What is wrong with the present accountability model? Why does it
not work?[66] The primary answer is that the strategy being pursued in
most states is premised on a number of invalid assumptions. The first
incorrect assumption of the industrial-type accountability model is
that there is widespread agreement on goals for pupils' learning; without such goals there is nothing against which to assess whether or not
schools are succeeding. Disagreement over the purposes of public
schooling has, however, been a fact of life from the first days of the
republic and has increased ever since as patterns of immigration and
geographical expansion forged a pluralist system of values. Objectives
for schools are nowhere clear or simple. Gallup polls and university
surveys repeatedly document the varying, and frequently conflicting,
expectations held for public schools. This is not new to those individuals who have run for public office and have tried to listen to the
electorate's voice on educational matters.

In the absence of consensus concerning school goals, typically a
compromise of either of two sorts is struck by policy makers. One
route is, in effect, to have no goals for schools or to have them stated
at such a high level of abstraction as to render them vapid, plati-
tudinous, and, most important, immeasurable. The second route is to
try to accommodate all tastes by having a multitude of objectives to
be accomplished.

The second invalid premise of the present industrial accountability model is the existence of a measurement technology capable of determining school output. It is true that psychologists have contributed greatly toward measuring school outcomes, but the problem still defies solution. One factor is that the traditional testing strategy, so-called norm-referenced testing, is geared to ranking those who take the test on a continuum. Tests are deliberately constructed to discriminate among students. Easy questions, those which almost everyone can answer, and difficult items, those which no one can answer, are eliminated. The only remaining questions distribute those who take the test over a range of scores from low to high. Thus, scores on norm-referenced tests represent a ranking, how one student stands relative to another. Such scores do not necessarily convey information as to how much the student has learned. Indeed, as norm-referenced tests are made, and items are discarded because they fail to discriminate, the tests become increasingly abstract, more like general intelligence tests (IQ tests), and may have less and less to do with what a pupil has been exposed to in school.

An answer to this problem is to employ what are now called criterion-referenced tests, which focus on the subject matter to be mastered and pay little or no attention to the ranking of students. The difficulty connected with criterion-referenced tests is that someone or some group has to decide what is to be tested. The necessity for this decision triggers the previously referred to disagreement about the purposes of schooling. Where criterion-referenced tests have been proposed on a wide scale they have prompted substantial conflict. Early efforts to launch the National Assessment of Education Progress drew threats of boycott from professional school administrators, and similar efforts by the Michigan State Education Department provoked accusations of a fascist plot to dictate control of the schools from the state level.

Thus, norm-referenced tests are politically acceptable but technically shortsighted; criterion-referenced tests are technically adequate but politically troublesome. Until a compromise is achieved, the industrial accountability model is severely handicapped.

A third false assumption in accountability efforts is that there exists a sufficiently developed pedagogy to prescribe the means by which the achievement level of any given student can be elevated from point A to point B. The best available example of this fallacy is the legislative attempts in many states to implement Competency

Based Teacher Education (CBTE). This system asserts the existence of a known set of teacher behaviors which, if used, will make a student learn a specified increment of subject matter. In order to receive credentials, a prospective teacher must exhibit mastery of the "scientifically proven" teaching behavior. The problem is that no large body of scientifically proven teacher behavior exists. We may someday accumulate a body of information about successful teaching and have a scientific base for schooling. Today, however, good teaching is still weighted heavily toward being an art, with wide variation from individual to individual. To mandate that a teacher adhere to a rigid list of "instructional behaviors" is likely to hinder the learning of as many pupils as it helps. Consequently, it is impossible to evaluate a teacher on grounds that he or she did or did not follow the correct pedagogical procedure. This stands in vivid contrast to most manufacturing endeavors where it is possible to deduce and thereafter standardize the most efficient production process to maximize output.

A fourth assumption embedded in the technical accountability model is that it is possible to separate important out-of-school learning factors from the effects of schooling. In order to be fair to educators, an accountability strategy must partial out or control for influences on learning over which the school has little or no control. In this regard, one of the strongest held findings in social science is that the social environment of the home and neighborhood affects a student's performance in school. Similarly, genetically endowed intellectual ability is logically thought to be a heavy determinant of a child's performance. Herein lies the rub. The techniques of social science for holding out-of-school learning influences neutral are highly inadequate. We do not have easily gathered measures of a child's social background, and conventional intelligence tests appear badly contaminated by environmental factors, not the least of which may be schooling itself.

Another problem with many conventional accountability schemes has been their inability accurately to measure school inputs. If we are ever to identify the elements of a successful educational program and to be able to assess whether or not it is cost effective, it is necessary to specify its components. For example, if schools have an effect upon the performance of students, presumably it comes about in large measure through the behavior of teachers and other school personnel. Many famous studies of the effectiveness of schooling, the Coleman Report among them, have not, however, included measures of teachers' behavior. They have, rather, relied upon proxy measures such as a teacher's age, education, and level and years of experience. Crucial errors in measurement have, moreover, appeared in some of the proxies. For example, the original Coleman Report used a district-wide expenditure average as a measure of the dollar resources spent per pupil. As many readers will quickly realize, amounts spent per pupil throughout a district vary widely; expenditures for students in secondary schools are generally half again higher than for those in elementary schools.

Reliance upon the technical-industrial accountability model is not only proving to be a disappointment, but, over time, it is also likely to be counterproductive. Continued neglect of important value considerations, invalid assumptions regarding the science of schooling, and insensitivity to political realities are transforming previous supporters into opponents and further alienating many professional educators.

This rather glum view of the accountability movement, however, should not be taken as an argument that no instrument of measuring the achievement of students is possible. States might find it in their interest to develop examinations that assess the degree of achievement on at least two dimensions: reading and mathematics. If state legislatures desired, they might include other fields in the tests, such as music, science, literature, civics, foreign languages, and history. Inclusion of the two prime areas of basic skills is, however, almost an absolute necessity.

An assumption here is that, despite the diversity of tastes for schooling and the public's general inability to achieve consensus on specific educational objectives, there is widespread acceptance of reading and computing as minimal learning components for every child. Individuals may disagree on the relative significance of these skills, but it is difficult to identify a rational point of view that holds that they are of no importance. It is, consequently, highly probable that an annual statewide assessment of children's achievement on these two dimensions will be acceptable.

Other than to stipulate that the tests be criterion-referenced, there is no necessity for specifying a single best method of establishing a statewide testing scheme. It is not necessary to test every child every year. By selecting a relatively small sample at each grade level from each school, it would be possible to assess the degree to which students were gaining in achievement. It is important, however, that the sample be sufficient to generalize about each grade level at each school. To sample in larger aggregates would suffice only to tell us how a district or state is performing; these units are too large to permit accurate identification of which pupils are learning and which are not.

Beyond decentralization, accountability, and community control there exist dozens of suggestions for restoring public control over schools. Third-party negotiations whereby parents, citizens, and students are included in the bargaining process between the school board and teachers is increasingly proposed as a scheme to buttress the power of laymen.[67] The idea of an ombudsperson in each district to represent the interests of parents and students is periodically put forward. Educational "juries" to adjudicate grievances of parents and students against a school district have also been suggested.

Perhaps the ultimate "weapon" in the reformers' arsenal is the so-called voucher plan, which would transform parents into the basic unit of educational decision making. By providing households with chits redeemable for educational services at schools of their choice, education would be regulated by the mechanism of the market. Schools, in attempting to obtain parents' "business," would heed the kind and quality of schooling the public desires. Schools failing the test of competition would be forced out of business. Those that succeed would prosper in the sense that they would survive.

Voucher plans have not been widely tried in lower education, though they have been used extensively at the postsecondary level in the form of the GI Bill. The only systematic effort to assess the consequences of vouchers for elementary and secondary schools still in progress is at Alum Rock, California.

Conclusion: A Community of Interests

We adhere in general to the principle that government decision-making discretion should rest with the smallest jurisdiction possible. Because of the wide range of values and tastes throughout our population, individual preferences would seem most likely to be maximized in the smaller governmental units of a multitiered federal hierarchy. For a decision to be elevated to a higher level, there must exist a compelling reason. Simply translated, this means that school decisions should take place whenever possible at the school site. This is the arena in which the greatest amount of interaction takes place between those who deliver instructional services and those intended to benefit from them. Also, judging from studies of the relationship between size of governmental jurisdiction and electoral participation, smaller units facilitate increased expression of constituents concerning educational preferences. School districts are presently the prime level for decisions regarding school governance, and accommodation with political reality probably will demand that this condition persist for some time to come. Thus, regardless of whether it is the school site or the school district, as many policy decisions as possible should be taken at the lowest level.

When one examines the situation closely, however, he finds several compelling reasons for state intervention or state-level decision making about schools. First, if left totally to their own discretion, lower-level decision-making units, whether they be families, schools, or school districts, might underinvest in schooling to the detriment of both the child and the larger society. A local school board, for example, might have an extraordinarily pessimistic view regarding the utility of schooling or might simply be too ignorant to care about the quality of instruction. Consequently, children under their jurisdiction might grow up illiterate or unversed in the responsibilities of citizenship. In addition to the sufferings visited on the children themselves, their ignorance would be a handicap to the state. The point is that in a period of extraordinary social and economic interdependence, society must protect itself from the risk that a governmental subunit will shirk its educational responsibilities.

A further consequence of intolerably low educational quality at local levels is the damage inflicted upon the individual student. It is usually the case that both school officials and parents are sufficiently concerned to see that each student learns in accord with his or her capabilities. The state must, however, have a means by which to protect children in those exceptional instances where parents and local school officials tolerate situations likely to be damaging, physically or psychologically, to the child.

Beyond its concern for minimal standards of instructional quality and students' learning, the state also has an interest in assuring the larger population that school resources are utilized in a manner both legal and efficient. Even when generated from local property taxes, school funds are legally state revenues. As such, they are subject to state accounting standards. Moreover, because some portion of the revenues for almost every school district is generated outside its geographic boundaries, the state has an interest in seeing that these general funds are not "wasted" in financially extravagant or outrageously inefficient ways.

Balanced against these and other state concerns are the substantial views of local school clients that their voice be heard regarding educational purposes and practices. If we had a society of extraordinary homogeneity, this might not be a concern. However, the United States represents a complicated mixture of values and tastes with regard to schooling. If such diversity is to be protected, whether it be the school district, the school, the classroom, or the individual pupil, above state minimums, room must remain for choice.

The welfare of the client is, in principle, of paramount concern to professionals. Each client must be assessed separately, and the optimum mix of services prescribed. Thus, individuals engaged in professional endeavors argue that they should have discretion to decide what is the best possible treatment. Because the professional practices and skills involved are learned from a lengthy process of study and apprenticeship, it is only another professional or group of professionals who are capable of judging the individual practitioner's performance. Laymen, presumably, would not have sufficient expertise to assess whether or not an engineer, physician, lawyer, or pilot had performed correctly. In short, in order to ensure that "treatment" of the client is appropriate and of the highest order, the professional must be allowed substantial personal authority and discretion, subject only to review by peers. In that education aspires to be a profession, teachers and other school practitioners argue that they should be permitted similar autonomy.

At least two circumstances mitigate against unfettered professional autonomy for educators. First, unlike many professional services offered in the private sector, public schools have close to a monopoly. A dissatisfied parent or student has only a small margin for changing school districts, schools, or teachers. Thus, as with many other monopolies, there are reasonable grounds for "regulation" by the larger society. A second reason for lay control over professional educators stems from the socially sensitive nature of the school's functions. Schools are commonly held responsible for transmitting values from one generation to the next. In order to maintain society and ensure social cohesion, it is necessary that the values being handed down are consistent with those held by the wider society. The lay public must, consequently, have within its power the authority, rewards, and punishments to accomplish this end. To paraphrase Talleyrand, "Schooling is too important to be left to educators." Public schools must be governed by the public.

Notes

1. Lawrence Cremin, *American Education: The Colonial Experience, 1607-1786* (New York: Harper and Row, 1970), 122.

2. *Visitation Articles and Injunctions of the Period of the Reformation,* ed. Walter Howard Frere and William McClure Kennedy, Alcuin Club Collections (London: Longman's, Green & Co., 1910), II, 7-8, cited *ibid.*

3. Howard Brown, *Elizabethan Schooldays: An Account of the English Grammar Schools in the Second Half of the Sixteenth Century* (Oxford: Basil Blackwell, 1933), 7.

4. Lawrence Stone, "The Educational Revolution in England, 1560-1640," *Past and Present* (July 1964), 41-80.

5. Cremin, *American Education,* 171.

6. Johnathan Mitchell, *A Model for the Maintaining of Students and Fellows of Choice Abilities at the Colledge in Cambridge* (about 1663), Publications of the Colonial Society of Massachusetts, XXXI (1935), 311, cited *ibid.,* 176.

7. Marcus Jernegan, *Laboring and Dependent Classes in Colonial America 1607-1783* (Chicago: University of Chicago Press, 1931), 82.

8. Cremin, *American Education,* 182.

9. Elwood P. Cubberley, *The History of Education* (Boston: Houghton Mifflin, 1920), 366.

10. See, for example, Merle Curti, *The Social Ideas of American Educators* (New York: Charles Scribner's Sons, 1935), 4-5; and Charles A. Beard and Mary R. Beard, *The Rise of American Civilization* (New York: Macmillan, 1972), I, 179.

11. *Turning Points in American Educational History,* ed. David B. Tyack (Waltham, Mass.: Blaisdell, 1967).

12. *The Acts and Resolves, Public and Private, of the Province of Massachusetts Bay,* Vol. I, Acts of 1789, Chap. XIX, cited in Lawrence Cremin, *The American Common School* (New York: Teachers College, Columbia University, 1951), 130.

13. See Newton Edwards and Herman Richey, *The School in the American Social Order* (Boston: Houghton Mifflin, 1947), 110 ff.

14. Cremin, *The American Common School,* 136-137.

15. Edwards and Richey, *The School in the American Social Order,* 190 ff.

16. *The Boston News-Letter*, March 14-21, 1708, as quoted in Robert Seybolt, *Private Schools of Colonial Boston* (Cambridge, Mass.: Harvard University Press, 1935), 11.

17. Edwards and Richey, *The School in the American Social Order*, 214.

18. Cremin, *The American Common School*, 88-90.

19. *Ibid.*, 1 ff.

20. Frederick M. Binder, *The Age of the Common School, 1830-1865* (New York: John Wiley and Sons, 1974), 33.

21. Michael Katz, *The Irony of Early School Reform* (Boston: Beacon Press, 1968), 36.

22. Binder, *The Age of the Common School*.

23. James G. Carter, *Essays upon Popular Education*, 1824-5, cited in Cremin, *The American Common School*, 139-140.

24. Diane Ravitch, *The Great School Wars, New York City, 1805-1973* (New York: Basic Books, 1974).

25. Thomas Boese, *Public Education in the City of New York* (New York: Harper Bros., 1869), 71, cited *ibid.*, 84.

26. Binder, *The Age of the Common School*, 141.

27. *A Century of U.S. School Statistics* (Washington, D.C.: Department of Health, Education, and Welfare, 1974).

28. These figures are, of course, rough approximations. There still exist a few school districts in the U.S. with more school board members than pupils. At the opposite extreme is New York City with more than a million constituents for each central district board member.

29. Richard Hofstadter, *The Age of Reform* (New York: Vintage Books, 1955), 175.

30. For example, in 1890 the Baltimore Board of Education had twenty-six standing committees, and the Chicago board in 1885 had seventy committees. Charles Reeves, *School Boards* (New York: Prentice-Hall, 1954), 24-25.

31. Joseph M. Cronin, *The Control of Urban Schools* (New York: Free Press, 1973), 9.

32. Reeves, *School Boards*, 27.

33. See, for example, Cronin, *The Control of Urban Schools*; Michael Katz, *Class, Bureaucracy and Schools* (New York: Praeger, 1971); and Samuel Hayes, "The Politics of Reform in Municipal Government in the Progressive Era," *Pacific Northwest Quarterly* (October 1964), 157-169.

34. Ravitch, *The Great School Wars*, 145.

35. George S. Counts, *The Social Composition of Boards of Education* (Chicago: University of Chicago Press, 1927).

36. Cited in Theodore Reller, *Development of the City Superintendency of Schools* (Boston: the Author, 1935), 266.

37. Quoted in Raymond Callahan, *Education and the Cult of Efficiency* (Chicago: University of Chicago Press), 150.

38. Katz, *Class, Bureaucracy and Schools*, 49.

39. Cronin, *The Control of Urban Schools*, 9-10.

40. Ralph B. Kimbrough, *Political Power and Educational Decision Making* (Chicago: Rand McNally, 1964), 52.

41. *Ibid.*

42. *Ibid.*

43. Frederick M. Wirt and Michael W. Kirst, *The Political Web of American Schools* (Boston: Little, Brown, 1972), 92.

44. The tendency toward growing state-level participation in education is described in James W. Guthrie and Paula H. Skene, "The Escalation of Pedagogical Politics," *Phi Delta Kappan* 54 (February 1973), 386-389, republished as "Local Control Gives Way," *Compact* 8 (March-April 1974), 17-20.

45. Cronin, *The Control of Urban Schools*, 103.

46. *Ibid.*, 109.

47. Elwood P. Cubberley, *Public School Administration* (Boston, 1916), 337-338, cited in Callahan, *Education and the Cult of Efficiency*, 97.

48. *Wesberry* v. *Sanders*, 376 U.S. 1 (1964).

49. *San Antonio School District et al.* v. *Rodriguez et al.*, U.S. 71-1332 (March 1973 slip opinion), 39.

50. *Ibid.*, 54.

51. See National Center for Educational Statistics, *Digest of Educational Statistics, 1972 edition* (Washington, D.C.: Government Printing Office, 1973).

52. Myron Lieberman, "The Union Merger Movement: Will 3,500,000 Teachers Put It All Together?" *Saturday Review* (June 24, 1972), 53.

53. During 1972 the NEA spent well over $200,000 in state elections, and the AFT sponsored an active campaign to dump President Nixon.

54. Compiled from National Education Association, Research Division, *Negotiation Research Digest*, 1955-1969.

55. Willard S. Elsbree, *The American Teacher; Evolution of a Professional in a Democracy* (New York: American Book Company, 1939), 123.

56. Michigan Department of Education, Lansing, Michigan, "Educational and Moral Values in Michigan," May 1968, 13.

57. Albert Shanker, "Where We Stand," New York AFT.

58. *Washington Post*, February 23, 1970, A-3.

59. A point well made by Herbert Kaufmann, in "Administrative Decentralization and Political Power," *Public Administration Review* 29 (Jan.-Feb. 1969), 3-15.

60. James S. Coleman *et al.*, *Equal Educational Opportunity* (Washington, D.C.: Government Printing Office, 1966).

61. For example, even when adjusted for inflation, average annual cost per pupil in the nation increased fivefold between 1940 and 1970. *A Century of U.S. School Statistics*.

62. Michael Kirst, "The Rise and Fall of PPBS in California," *Phi Delta Kappan* (April 1975), 535-539.

63. Educational Testing Service, *State Educational Assessment Programs*, revised edition (Princeton, N.J.: Educational Testing Service, 1973), 1.

64. The term will be explained in a later section of this chapter.

65. The exchange in the June and September 1974 issues of the *Phi Delta*

Kappan nicely illustrates the controversy surrounding the Michigan effort at accountability.

66. This question is pursued more fully in James W. Guthrie, "The Political Economy of School Productivity," to appear in a forthcoming volume on education and social science edited by John McDermott. A discussion also appears in Lawrence C. Pierce, Walter I. Garms, James W. Guthrie, and Michael W. Kirst, *State School Finance Alternatives* (Eugene: University of Oregon, 1975), 97-98, 99-100.

67. In 1974 the California legislature enacted a statute to mandate portions of such a strategy.

6

TEACHERS' ORGANIZATIONS AND BARGAINING: POWER IMBALANCE IN THE PUBLIC SPHERE

Lawrence Pierce   University of Oregon

Collective bargaining has produced a dramatic change in the governance of American schools. The dominance of professional administrators is being challenged by teachers who insist that they be given a larger voice in the operation of schools. The familiar theories for administering schools no longer seem adequate. Unity of command, hierarchical organization charts, leadership training, and public relations are giving way to negotiated contracts that specify the rights and obligations of teachers and administrators in much greater detail than ever before. Teachers are rapidly gaining control over many aspects of school operations.

Many educators believe collective bargaining will destroy the public school system as it exists today.[1] They warn that school boards will be emasculated if the strength of teachers' organizations continues to increase, and the little control the public now has over schools through its elected representatives will be lost. Teachers will demand and receive a larger and larger share of the educational dollar, leaving little for program improvement or innovation.[2] The public will lose confidence in the schools and become increasingly unwilling to vote the funds needed to maintain quality public education. Teachers' demands for higher salaries and the subsequent loss of public support will doom schools to mediocrity.

This gloomy picture is bewildering to businessmen and labor leaders. Management and labor in the private sector have learned over the past forty years to negotiate the terms and conditions of employment to the mutual benefit of both sides. Business managers have not been brought to their knees by collective bargaining. Consequently, no one in private industry seriously questions the right of employees to have a voice in matters relating to their employment.

In public education, however, collective bargaining threatens to upset a pattern of governance in which decision making has become a virtual monopoly of the school superintendent and his staff.[3] Beginning around the turn of the century, reformers reorganized school government to eliminate politics from education. It was argued that education was too important to be tampered with except by professional educators. To protect them from political interference, small school districts were consolidated into larger independent school districts separate from city councils and other units of local government. Separate rules and procedures were established for the election of school board members; to emphasize the distinction between school board elections and "political" elections, the former were typically nonpartisan and were held in off years. School board members generally served without pay and without the staff or resources needed to develop policy alternatives to those presented by the superintendent and his staff.[4]

At the same time reformers were weakening the legislative side of school governance, they were pushing for a more businesslike and professional administrative structure in schools. School boards would continue to set broad policy, but they were not to interfere with the administration of schools. Professional managers would run schools efficiently without interference from school board members or the public.

As school districts became larger and the number of teachers and administrative personnel increased, an administrative bureaucracy developed which put several layers of organization between school boards and the classroom. Teachers were cut off from contact with the school board and the public and were increasingly told how to manage their classrooms by business managers, administrative assistants, subject-matter coordinators, and department heads. While still considering themselves professionals, teachers actually were left with little control over their teaching activities. As Professor Guthrie points out:

Bureaucracy and bigness have not only reduced the potency of public policy makers, but also severely curtailed teachers' feelings of efficacy. As school systems grew and came under the dominance of expert managers, teachers lost their ability to communicate freely with their employers, school trustees, or even with the superintendent and his staff. The frustration was heightened as city schools became more populated by children from low-income households and minority groups whose backgrounds and values were frequently at odds with those of middle-class teachers. Under such circumstances, teacher alienation became more real and more intense.[5]

By the 1960s control of schools was firmly in the hands of school administrators, but the domination of professional managers created as many problems as it was supposed to correct. Parents and citizens became dissatisfied because they found the public schools too bureaucratic and unresponsive to their demands and preferences. School boards also seemed impotent to produce the kind of changes they wanted. At the same time, teachers became dissatisfied with being treated more like hourly employees than professional educators. Many students were "turned off" because the traditional educational program seemed irrelevant to their problems in the present and their plans for the future.

The first real challenge to the hegemony of the educational bureaucracy was the demand for greater citizen participation in educational choices. School districts reacted to this demand by setting up alternative schools and citizens' advisory councils. Because of limited participation by parents and the reluctance of administrators to give the councils any real power, however, this movement did little to break administrators' control over the schools.

It was not until teachers began to organize and use collective bargaining to gain more control over educational policy that the monopoly of the school administrators began to crumble. The greatest contribution of collective bargaining to American education is that it is forcing everyone concerned with public education to reconsider who should control American schools.

There are, of course, many problems with the way collective bargaining is currently being conducted in public education. This chapter discusses some of these problems and suggests ways of restructuring the process of negotiation to achieve better the goals of public education. The main point of this chapter, however, is that there is nothing to fear from collective bargaining if it is carried out in a reasonable manner. With an appropriate institutional arrangement, in fact, it can be an important force for the improvement of American public education.

In a democracy everyone should have the right to participate in decisions affecting the conditions of their employment. Collective bargaining is a process in which the employer and the employee determine the terms of employment. It is immaterial whether the employer is public or private; the right to control one's working conditions is fundamental. State governments have, in fact, been criticized for requiring private employers to engage in collective bargaining while at the same time refusing to implement a similar procedure for their own employees.[6]

Furthermore, students can learn how problems are solved in democratic political institutions by observing teachers and administrators resolving disputes via negotiations. It is unreasonable to expect students to be effective democratic citizens if they only experience nondemocratic decision making in their schools. As one witness commented, "we teach about democracy . . . but we don't teach democracy."[7] Eventually, the process of negotiation should be expanded to include parents and students, as well as teachers and managers. There is no better way to teach about democracy and collective choice than to arrive at the decisions affecting students democratically and collectively.

A third benefit of collective bargaining is that it is likely to improve the quality of teaching by increasing teachers' commitment to their profession. It is no wonder teachers lack commitment, when they have little to say about what is taught or how it is taught. If we allow them to negotiate what goes on in the classroom as well as how much they are paid, they will take their professionalism more seriously.

Finally, collective bargaining is already forcing school districts to develop more effective management.[8] If the first experiences with collective bargaining have revealed anything, it has been the inability of management to bargain effectively. Because of collective bargaining, school districts are being forced to develop lists of educational priorities, hire good negotiators, develop better budgeting procedures, and explain more fully to the public what is being accomplished in the schools.

In summary, collective bargaining is a potential model of democratic decision making, which, in itself, can be an important learning experience for students. It can, in addition, help teachers create the professional environment that is important for effective teaching. And it can force more effective public management of the schools.

The major problem now is that wholesale adoption of the bargaining model from the private sector has given teachers a disproportionate amount of power in the negotiations process. Bargaining can only be effective if both sides are relatively equal in strength. Both sides must recognize that they have something to gain and something to lose if there is to be a fair resolution of differences. School boards have never had much power to influence important educational decisions. Now they find themselves with a formidable opponent and inadequate resources to bargain effectively.

One strategy for restoring balance between school managers and teachers is to seek legislation limiting the scope of collective negotiations.[9] This would ensure continued dominance by superintendents and some balance between school boards and teachers. Another strategy is to increase the bargaining power of school boards so that they can effectively represent the public and meet teachers at the bargaining table on an equal footing.

The argument presented here is that collective bargaining is a good thing and should be substantially expanded to include parents and students, as well as management and teachers. To make collective bargaining work for the benefit of the public, however, a new balance of power must be achieved between the public's representatives and the representatives of the teachers. This can only be done by revitalizing the legislative side of school governance. State legislatures should take a more active role in educational policy making. They should establish rules for collective bargaining without favoring either side and should establish a strong administrative body to ensure compliance with the collective bargaining laws.

At the district level, school boards must be strengthened so that they can bargain effectively. They must be able to hire competent negotiators, to involve the public if the public interest is at stake, and to go to strike without outside intervention. Laws must make it clear that both sides have something to lose if they fail to seek agreement on disputed issues. Finally, there should be a local school council with the authority to determine collectively the school program. Final settlement of district-level contracts would be contingent upon resolution of contracts for individual schools.

Collective Bargaining in Public Education

Until recently most public employees have been prohibited by law from bargaining with management. This has not meant that management enjoyed unilateral control over decisions affecting public employees, although they certainly had more power than the employees. Nevertheless, public management has been restricted by a number of forces.

Conditions of employment in the public sector have been influenced by a variety of market forces. Because public agencies must hire their employees competitively, management has been forced to maintain near parity with private wages in order to attract scarce labor skills. This is particularly true of skills that could easily be moved into jobs in the private sector.

Public workers have at times resorted to strikes and slowdowns to gain concessions from their employers, usually escaping the penalties for such illegal activities. As early as 1816 employees in a naval shipyard went on strike for a shortened workday and gained provisions similar to those in private shipyards.[10] In addition, some government employers have customarily allowed employee input into decision-making processes, although none of these influences involved direct bargaining. Clearly, though, unilateral decision making by public management did not exist even before the advent of formal arrangements for legal bargaining.

Collective bargaining in the public sector first took place in formerly private organizations that were taken over by the government. State legislation guaranteed bargaining rights that had been gained in the private sector by mass-transit workers, public-utility employees, and hospital workers.[11] Bargaining agreements reached in the private sector were transferred to the public sector nearly intact, except that compulsory binding arbitration was often substituted for the right to strike. Although these contracts negotiated in the mid-1940s are of historical interest, their importance in the development of collective bargaining laws is limited. The enabling statutes applied only to those employees whose firms had operated in the private sector and not to other public employees in the same industry who had never worked in the private sector. There was no philosophical or political desire to expand the bargaining rights of public employees; collective bargaining relations developed in the private sector were merely maintained in the public sector.

The Development of Collective Bargaining in Public Education

Meaningful legislation giving public employees a voice in determining the conditions of their employment was first enacted in the 1960s. Prior to 1962 only Alaska and New Hampshire had statutes that allowed local governments to negotiate with groups representing public employees.[12] The New Hampshire law of 1955 and Alaska law of 1959 did not require or ensure bargaining; local governments were merely allowed to negotiate under specified conditions.

In 1962 Wisconsin enacted a statute requiring local governments to bargain in good faith with employee groups and also set up administrative machinery to enforce the law.[13] The Wisconsin Public Employee Relations Board was charged with determination of appropriate bargaining units, prevention of prohibited practices, fact-finding, and mediation of disputes (when agreed to by both parties). No procedure was defined, however, for the final resolution of deadlocks.

A great surge of state legislation requiring collective bargaining occurred about 1965.[14] Of the eight laws enacted at that time, six had specific provisions for public school teachers. Massachusetts and Michigan passed comprehensive legislation for all state and local government employees. While most of the 1965 legislation was patterned after the Wisconsin statute, the Michigan law added provisions to produce bargaining from more equal bases of power. Specifically, the Michigan Employment Relations Commission was allowed to mediate disputes upon the insistence of either party, and the commission was given considerable power over the prohibition of unfair labor practices. Though the Michigan statute did not allow strikes or compulsory binding arbitration instigated by employees, this law was the first strong collective bargaining act.

Early state legislation allowed, or more often required, local governments to meet and confer with employees about conditions of employment. Special provisions were often included for teachers, firemen, and police, as evidenced by the six statutes of 1965 relating specifically to teachers. Although the legislation required "negotiation," "bargaining," or "collective bargaining," the absence of defined unfair practices and the lack of neutral administrative machinery and balanced procedures concerning impasse continued to give employers the upper hand in negotiations. Some meaningful negotiation was carried out, but only under the guarded discretion of the managers of the public enterprise.[15]

These early statutes provided impetus for the development of stronger collective bargaining laws and for increased participation by employees in the negotiation process. Conflicts were now being aired in a public forum, and the employees could appeal to public opinion. Teachers gained access to information not previously available. What is most important, citizens learned that negotiations between public employees and their employers could be conducted with few disruptions of public service.

More meaningful statutes regarding negotiations have developed in two different ways. Some states, like Oregon and Massachusetts, have changed their regulations in light of experiences within the state. As a result of this approach, teachers in Oregon may legally strike, and Massachusetts allows instigation of binding arbitration by either party after other remedies have failed. In other cases, states like Iowa have strengthened and adopted existing statutes from other states. Iowa's first public bargaining law, enacted in 1974, is one of the stronger state laws.

The incidence of effective negotiation has been aided by several types of legislation related to bargaining. State administrative agencies often serve to oversee public employee bargaining. As neutral third parties, these agencies may be called into disputes to define and enforce the rules of the negotiation. Many state laws became more powerful when provisions requiring bargaining in good faith and prohibiting unfair labor practices were included. Successful negotiations also became more prevalent when fact-finding and mediation were required, with the recommendations made binding in some instances. In a few states legislative provisions permitting public employees to strike and allowing either side to force compulsory binding arbitration have been added. Each of these provisions has created more balanced negotiations. Though legislative developments have not been smooth or all-encompassing, the growth of bargaining by public employees has brought about a steady increase in the power and influence of employee groups.

Developments in the Last Decade

The increased militancy of public employees in the last decade contrasts with the decline in solidarity within and between labor unions in the private sector.[16] The comfortable standard of living achieved by many union members has weakened support for traditional bread-and-butter issues. As workers have attained more property they have become more conservative and concerned with maintaining their possessions. Many union members are unwilling to respect the picket lines of those they feel are making exorbitant demands. These interunion squabbles have led to disregard for the picket line, the once sacred symbol of solidarity. Public employees (especially teachers) have shown an increase in solidarity. The conflict between the National Education Association (NEA) and the American Federation of Teachers (AFT) over the propriety of collective bargaining has disappeared.[17] The picket lines of teachers have proved impenetrable. Indeed, no case comes to mind where a teachers' strike was broken by the infiltration of nonmember teachers.

Several social and cultural factors account for the increased militancy of teachers. Public demonstrations, nurtured by the civil rights movement and proven in the Viet Nam era, have shown that peaceful marches can be an effective force and that picketing need not be confined to working-class groups.

A decade ago the need for teachers far exceeded the supply, and so teachers had little need for written job security. As declining enrollments have turned the tables, teachers have looked to formal negotiated agreements to ensure their employment. In addition, teachers have enviously watched as the bargaining rights of federal employees continue to grow. Other public employees have carried out highly visible, though generally illegal, strikes and gained profitable contracts.

Other influences have changed the nature of the work force of teachers and teachers' relationships with their employers. The teacher corps is becoming increasingly masculine, and male educators, who are usually their family's main wage earner, are more committed to union efforts. School district consolidation has concentrated the teachers, which has increased the distance between each teacher and his school board and superintendent and has also facilitated the organizational efforts of unions.

Competition between the NEA and the AFT has increased the militancy of each organization's leadership, as each group attempts to offer more lucrative proposals to potential members.[18] The NEA, the larger of the two groups, switched its position in the mid-1960s and now advocates strong collective bargaining statutes. Collective bargaining is no longer viewed as unprofessional by either organization, or by most teachers.

The gains of teachers in New York City under the Taylor Law effectively demonstrated the power of a strong union. The AFT, with considerable financial and organizational assistance from the AFL-CIO, struck the nation's largest school system and came away the winner. The high visibility of this strike and its settlement added further impetus to the drive among teachers for greater bargaining rights.

The most important recent activity of teachers' organizations is their effort to influence legislative outcomes. Not only do the NEA and AFT have large membership lists, but their financial resources are tremendous. Helen Wise, president of the NEA, announced in the spring of 1974 that over $5,000,000 was being sought for use in the November campaigns. "We got our feet wet in 1972," said Dr. Wise. "We learned the process well; our skills are sharpened now, and we will work for our goals across the nation . . . ."[19] The educational organizations have also continued their political efforts during legislative sessions. During the 1973 session of the Oregon legislature, the NEA and its Oregon affiliate were the largest single spender among lobbyists. When organizations with the perceived legitimacy of teachers' groups wield this much power, their political clout is massive.

Finally, some of the early arguments against bargaining by public employees are eroding. Governmental bodies that had forced private firms to bargain faced the incongruous situation in which their own employees did not have the right to bargain collectively. As government, especially at the state and local levels, has increasingly taken over traditional functions of the private sector, arguments concerning state sovereignty and the inviolability of governmental services have been reexamined.

The Legal Structure of Collective Bargaining in Public Education

Legal provisions for the conduct of public collective bargaining have come almost exclusively from state governments. The legislatures of thirty-seven states have passed some sort of laws regulating the bargaining of public employees, though statutes vary considerably.[20] Altogether, twenty-seven states provide for exclusive representation of nonsupervisory personnel by an employee group, and mediation or fact-finding are mandatory in twenty-three states. A strong state administrative agency oversees negotiations of public employees in twenty-two states, while twenty-two states prohibit certain unfair labor practices and provide some means of enforcement. In addition to the above provisions, seven states have impasse procedures that allow teachers' organizations to go on strike or force compulsory binding arbitration.[21] It is obvious that the legal status of collective bargaining for teachers has come a long way since 1965.

The extent of collective bargaining now reaches far beyond the legal specifications provided by statutes. Contractual agreements have been reached in many cases where no statutory requirements are specified, and some school boards have set up bargaining procedures more favorable to teachers than the law requires. What is most important, the range of bargaining issues extends far beyond what is specified in the statutes. These extensions of bargaining beyond the legal requirements are not violations for the most part, but rather cover matters not prohibited or procedures not specified by law. As a result, collective bargaining in the states far exceeds that required by law.

The bargaining of federal employees has been covered by executive orders since President Kennedy issued Executive Order 10988 in 1962.[22] This administrative order required federal agencies to negotiate with public employees' groups, but allowed the agency to designate the appropriate bargaining unit. Impasse procedures were negotiable. In 1969 President Nixon issued Executive Order 11491 which specified procedures to be used under the earlier order.[23] Order 11491 designated the Federal Labor Relations Council to administer and interpret bargaining regulations and allowed the Assistant Secretary of Labor for Labor-Management Relations to determine appropriate bargaining units and supervise the accompanying elections. It also required formal recognition of bargaining units, increased the scope of negotiable subjects, and specified the Federal Mediation and Conciliation Service to assist in resolving disputes occurring in the negotiations.

As administrative fiats, executive orders are subject to change at the whim of succeeding Presidents. Although bills have been introduced to replace the system of executive orders, Congress has mainly focused on creating public collective bargaining laws applicable to state and local governments.[24] The House of Representatives held hearings in 1972 to consider possible federal legislation to regulate negotiations of public employees at the state level. Additional hearings on the matter were held by the House Special Subcommittee on Labor and the Senate Labor Subcommittee during the Ninety-third Congress.

The legislation introduced thus far has followed two general patterns. One bill, introduced by Congressman Frank Thompson in the House and Senator Harrison A. Williams, Jr., in the Senate, eliminates the prohibition against application of the National Labor Relations Act to state and local governments. Under this bill public employees would have the same rights as workers in the private sector. The second approach being considered provides for creation of a National Public Employment Relations Commission. Sponsored in the House by Congressman William Clay and in the Senate by Senator Williams, these companion bills ensure the rights of employees' groups in an agency shop. This second approach has received much greater consideration in the hearings thus far.

When the Ninety-third Congress ended, none of these bills had been reported out of their respective subcommittees, but the repeated introduction of such measures by powerful legislators and the increase in interest generated by the hearings suggest growing support for a federal bill of this type.

The likelihood of further collective bargaining legislation at the state and federal levels portends more comprehensive and extensive statutes providing greater influence for public employees. Public employees everywhere are demanding more rights, largely as a result of the lucrative settlements and power gained by employees under stronger bargaining laws. These demands are backed by tremendous political resources. The NEA has over one million members, and the American Federation of State and Municipal Employees has twice that number. What is more important, these organizations of public employees have large financial resources; the NEA, for example, spends millions of dollars a year for lobbying and for the support of sympathetic candidates. The political muscle is evident.

Public support for greater collective bargaining also may be increasing. As citizens are inconvenienced by strikes of public employees, sentiment shifts in favor of a more reasonable means of settling grievances. Rapid development of state legislation providing mechanisms for collective bargaining by public employees is bound to continue. The shape of this growth will determine the equity of negotiations for both public employees and the public they serve.

Summary

Collective bargaining has emerged in public education for a variety of reasons. The growing bureaucratic power of school administrators undermined the professionalism of teachers and their control over the classroom. Teachers were increasingly frustrated by the problems that have beset urban schools in the last two decades. Forced integration and emigration to the suburbs left cities with fewer students overall and more minority and low-income children who were harder to teach. Afraid for their jobs and unhappy with their teaching situation, teachers were ready to be organized.

Unions were, at the same time, looking for new groups of workers to organize. Unionism was on the decline in the private sector, partly because industrial work is becoming increasingly capital-intensive. Education, on the other hand, is highly labor-intensive. When the belief that educators were professionals and above unionization began to crumble in the 1960s, the unions were ready to move in.

It was logical that those encouraging collective bargaining for teachers would look to the private sector for their model. The unions that organized teachers were familiar with the private bargaining model, and it had served industrial workers well. Wages and working conditions in the private sector had improved steadily under union organization. Also, since administrative procedures in schools were patterned after business practices, it was appropriate to use bargaining procedures that would be familiar to management. The private model of collective bargaining was adopted, therefore, to deal with a recalcitrant administrative bureaucracy that had adopted the management practices of the private sector.

Since no one disputes the right of teachers to organize if it is in their interest to do so, collective bargaining is likely to remain an integral part of the decision-making process in public schools. The reason collective bargaining is still controversial is that it has raised important questions about who should govern public education. Over the past decade, collective bargaining has definitely shifted some of the control of schools from school boards and school administrators to the teachers. Teachers are not asking only to share in decisions over salaries and fringe benefits. They are asking, in some states receiving, the right to determine collectively the size of classes, transfers of teachers within districts, pupil-teacher ratios, class content, and other important areas of educational policy.

This shift in decision-making power to teachers' organizations has further diminished the power of school boards and the public's ability to express its preferences regarding school policy. The adoption of the private-sector model of collective bargaining has raised questions about the role of various groups in the formulation of educational policy. What is the proper balance among the public, school boards, school administrators, teachers, and students in educational decision making? Do the present collective bargaining laws establish this balance? Does the wholesale adoption of the private-sector model facilitate the cooperation and compromise necessary to accomplish the public purpose in education? If power has shifted too much toward teachers, how should the proper balance be restored?

The next section will attempt to answer these questions by examining the appropriateness of the private-sector bargaining model in public-sector negotiations.

The Appropriateness of the Private Bargaining Model in Public Education

Most collective bargaining laws enacted by state legislatures across the country are modeled after the private-sector bargaining model. The question is whether this form of collective bargaining is appropriate in public education. Is decision making in the public sector sufficiently different from the private sector that different arrangements are needed to settle disputes between management and labor? In answering this question we must keep the welfare of the public in mind. Does this particular form of collective bargaining serve the public interest? If not, why? And how could collective bargaining be carried out to the mutual benefit of all interested parties?

Assumptions Underlying the Private-Sector Bargaining Model

In discussing the applicability of the private-sector bargaining model, we must look both at what collective bargaining involves and at the institutional assumptions underlying it.[25] Collective bargaining is a process by which employees negotiate with employers over the terms and conditions of their employment. Wage settlements clearly affect the price of goods or services, since labor costs are an important component of production costs. In education, where 70 to 80 percent of total costs are salaries and personnel benefits, settlements resulting from collective bargaining are closely related to the price of education.

Besides affecting the tax price of education, collective bargaining also has important implications for educational policy. In situations where teachers' unions negotiate on questions of size of classes and transfers of personnel, for instance, the impact is direct. But even when negotiations are limited to economic issues, the fact that 70 to 80 percent of a school's budget is absorbed by teachers' salaries means that many program alternatives hinge on the final wage settlement.

The private-sector bargaining model is based on several important assumptions about the relationship between the parties at the bargaining table and the final consumers of the goods and services produced.[26] The model assumes, specifically, that the bargaining behavior of both employers and employees is constrained by the behavior of consumers in the marketplace.

In the private sector, a change in the price of an organization's services owing to collective bargaining may lead to a variety of responses. The consumer may pay the higher price, realizing that it may be spread over a number of months or years. He may, on the other hand, postpone buying the product because it is too costly. Or he may choose another brand or a cheaper substitute. The fact that the consumer has the choice of buying or not buying places a constraint on the bargaining strategies of both management and labor. Because employers want to maximize profits, they attempt to hold down costs as much as possible. Unions are also faced with a similar constraint.

A price rise of [the] product relative to others will result in a decrease in the number of units of the product sold. This in turn will result in a cutback in employment. And an increase in price would be dictated by an increase in labor cost relative to output, at least in most situations. Thus, the union is faced with some sort of rough trade-off between, on the one hand, larger benefits for some employees and unemployment for others, and on the other hand, smaller benefits and more employment.[27]

Consumers, in other words, have an important role in collective bargaining in the private sector. Since employers want to maximize profit, and employee representatives are concerned about the continued employment of their members, both sides must anticipate the likely response of consumers.

The role of the consumers is not so clear in the economics of public-sector bargaining. In the first place, it is often difficult to identify the ultimate consumer of many public goods. There are, of course, some obvious beneficiaries of most public programs. In education, the students (and, indirectly, their parents) are primary recipients of educational services. Less direct consumers include the firms and governmental agencies that take advantage of a labor force trained by schools. Other citizens benefit to the extent that democratic government is improved by an educated electorate or by virtue of the psychic satisfactions of helping to educate children.

But even when the ultimate consumers of education can be clearly identified, there is no direct link to indicate the consumer's reaction to an increase in the tax price of public goods resulting from a negotiated settlement. In public education students usually do not have the option of changing schools, postponing schooling, or consuming a smaller quantity of education. Management and union representatives are constrained in negotiations on economic matters only by the withdrawal of public support in elections concerning budgets or by public protests.

Collective bargaining may also lead to a change in the quality of services being provided. This is particularly troublesome when it occurs in education, since there is little recourse for dissatisfied students, parents, or members of the public. The reason for this lies in the differences between private- and public-sector decision making, and again it raises questions about the applicability of the private-sector model to collective bargaining in the public sector.

Let us assume for a moment that the performance of an organization in the private sector begins to deteriorate. The lapse in performance may result from changes in the situation related to demand and supply that faces the organization, in which case it cannot be helped. But even if the poor performance results from inefficient management or unreasonable labor demands, we are not too worried. Consumers simply quit buying the inferior goods or services and switch to another product. In a competitive market economy one firm's loss is another firm's gain. Competing firms absorb the market share of the faltering firm, hire its employees, and thus reestablish market efficiency. As with changes in the price of a product, changes in quality are dealt with by the marketplace, as individuals exercise their right to buy or not to buy a product.

This is, of course, a simplistic notion of the self-correcting market process in the private sector. In a complex industrial society many factors limit consumers' ability to control market behavior.[28] Where production is controlled by monopolistic or oligopolistic firms, consumers may have little or no choice between alternative goods and services. Large segments of private activity are, nevertheless, constantly monitored by cost-conscious and quality-conscious consumers.

In public education, as in most activities in the public sector, consumers have few choices in responding to the performance of public organizations. Because of the compulsory nature of public education and its reliance on taxation for revenues, there are few market choices that can reverse a process of decline. If parents are dissatisfied with the quality of educational services, for instance, they usually cannot move their children to other schools without substantial costs. Nor can they express their dissatisfaction by withholding taxes for schools. Public schools receive tax support even when they are closed by strikes. The only feasible recourse for dissatisfied citizens is to complain to the school board or anyone else who will listen. Many parents feel that the impact of such complaints is extremely low.

Although market competition serves as an effective constraint on collective bargaining in the private sector, it fails to restrict public management or labor because of the virtual monopoly enjoyed by most public services and the separation between the processes of raising revenue and distributing products. The direct link between consumers and producers in the private market is replaced by uncertainty over who the final consumers of public goods are and how their preferences are communicated.

There is another important difference between private- and public-sector decision making that makes collective bargaining in the two sectors dissimilar. If the parties involved in private-sector bargaining cannot reach a settlement, labor will strike or management will lock out the employees. The result is economic hardship for both sides: the employer loses sales and profits, and a prolonged strike may force the company out of business; workers lose wages. Both parties suffer as a result of their inability to reach agreement. Consumers are also inconvenienced, but only to the extent that they may have to wait to purchase a particular product.

A strike against a public agency, however, has little or no effect upon the agency's continued income. Some states withhold state aid if schools are not open a specified number of days, but generally taxes will be collected and apportioned to an agency despite the curtailment of its services. A strike by public employees, therefore, must be aimed at the consumers of public services rather than at management.[29] By withholding public services the unions put pressure on consumers. While consumers may do without cars or new housing for some time, the loss of mail delivery, electric power, schools, or police protection creates an immediate hardship. Since clients usually cannot purchase public services elsewhere, they can only apply political pressure on their elected representatives or the managers of the public agency to settle the strike and restore service.

Strikes in the public sector are also less likely to lead to economic losses for the employees than in the private sector. Knowing that most public services are essential for the health and safety of a community, public employees do not need to fear a long period without wages. The fear of lost wages is even less among teachers since most states require schools to be in session for a minimum number of days each year. Any wages lost because of a strike are almost always made up by adding additional days of work throughout the year or at the end of the year.

Strikes in the public sector are, therefore, distinctly more political than in the private sector. Their purpose is not to create economic hardship, since neither public management nor public employees are likely to lose income or wages, but to inconvenience the consumers of public services and create political pressures for a quick settlement. To the extent that public employees substitute political pressures for economic pressures, the private-sector model may have to be altered to allow management the same access as labor to political processes. At this point, however, the elimination of politics from the management of public education and restrictions on the use of politics in collective bargaining work to the distinct disadvantage of management in public collective bargaining.

It should be pointed out that the motivations of management in

the two sectors are different. Private employers are primarily concerned with profits; thus labor demands that threaten long-term profits are unacceptable. Sometimes a strike or lockout is in the company's best interest. Private employers are under no compulsion to
remain in business and may, if it is to their economic benefit, close
their plants and cease operations. Managers of public agencies try at
all cost, however, to maintain or expand services. School boards, for
example, do not have the option of closing schools; they are required
by law to operate the schools as best they can. A strike against a
public agency is likely to be seen as a failure by the agency to perform its mission.

In summary, the private-sector model of collective bargaining assumes that consumers constrain the demands of both employers and
employees by their decisions to buy or not to buy the goods or services of an organization. This constraint works relatively well in the
private sector, but the absence of market choices and the separation
of tax revenues from the consumption of public services make the
market constraint ineffective in most situations in the public sector.

The private-sector model assumes, furthermore, that failure to
reach agreement will result in costs to both employers and employees. The employer will lose profits, and the employees will lose
wages. Both of these results are less likely to occur in the public
sector. The income of public agencies is generally unaffected if a
strike occurs, while public employees know the chance of a long and
costly strike is slight because a strike is usually unacceptable politically. And so, instead of producing economic pressure for a settlement, strikes in the public sector are designed to create political pressure for a settlement.

Finally, the private-sector model assumes that both employers and
employees are free to withhold their services if an agreement is not
reached. Employers can refuse to hire workers, and workers can refuse to work. This assumption does not apply in the public sector.
Management is obligated by law (as are employees, in many states)
and expected by the public to provide public services. The reluctance
of management to accept a strike weakens its bargaining position.

Public Control of Educational Decisions

We began this section by asking whether the private-sector model
of collective bargaining is appropriate in the public sector. The

answer comes down to a question of control—in this case the control of public education. In the private sector, control is shared by employers, employees, and consumers. Consumers' control via the marketplace is essential if collective bargaining in the private sector is to benefit the public as well as management and labor.

Though consumers' control through the marketplace is lacking or severely weakened in public-sector bargaining, neither management nor labor stands to lose much by a strike of public employees. The only way citizens can affect the outcome of collective bargaining is to "kick up a fuss," and so they must use political channels to confront management with their demands or complaints.

The need for public "input" or "citizen participation" is gradually being accepted in public-sector decision making—except in the area of negotiations by employees. In most states with collective bargaining statutes, the public is explicitly excluded from sessions devoted to negotiations. Open meeting laws usually exempt personnel negotiations. And most collective bargaining laws make public disclosure of bargaining positions or strategies an unfair labor practice.

The argument developed here is simple. For collective bargaining to serve the public interest, the public must have some control over the outcome of the bargaining process. Since citizens cannot influence the outcome through the marketplace, they must assert their control by directly participating in the negotiation process. Direct participation would require substantial changes in the present collective bargaining process. Rather than running negotiations as in the private sector, public negotiations need to be more political. Teachers and teachers' unions will object strongly to this notion, as will many school administrators. As one administrator commented, "I think it is just almost universal agreement that bargaining is best conducted in private."[30]

It must be pointed out that teachers have been instrumental in reintroducing politics to school government. If teachers can use collective bargaining (which is the essence of the political process) to determine their wages and working conditions, why should the public not use political channels to influence public collective bargaining?

In an important book entitled *Exit, Voice, and Loyalty*, Albert Hirschman distinguishes between two processes for influencing the performance of an organization.[31] When customers stop buying an organization's product or some members leave the organization, management is impelled to try to correct the faults that led customers and members to leave. This is called the "exit option."

Another possibility is for customers or members to express their dissatisfaction directly to management or anyone else who will listen. This is the voice option.[32] Hirschman says:

> Its breakup into the two contrasting, though not mutually exclusive, categories of exit and voice would be suspiciously neat if it did not faithfully reflect a more fundamental schism: that between economics and politics. Exit belongs to the former realm, voice to the latter. The customer who, dissatisfied with the product of one firm, shifts to that of another, uses the market to defend his welfare or to improve his position, and he also sets in motion market forces which may induce recovery on the part of the firm that has declined in comparative performance. This is the sort of mechanism economics thrives on. It is neat—one either exits or one does not; it is impersonal—any face-to-face confrontations between customer and firm with its imponderable and unpredictable elements is avoided and success and failure of the organization are communicated to it by a set of statistics; and it is indirect—any recovery on the part of the declining firm comes by courtesy of the Invisible Hand, as an unintended by-product of the customer's decision to shift. In all these respects, voice is just the opposite of exit. It is a far more "messy" concept because it can be graduated, all the way from faint grumbling to violent protest; it implies articulation of one's critical opinions rather than a private, "secret" vote in the anonymity of a supermarket; and finally, it is direct and straightforward rather than roundabout. Voice is political action *par excellence*.[33]

As will be argued later, opportunities for parents and students to choose among competing educational programs should be expanded. For the most part, however, public concern about education will have to be expressed directly through the voice option, rather than indirectly through the exit option. Hirschman defines voice as "any attempt at all to change, rather than to escape from, an objectionable state of affairs, whether through individual or collective petition to the management directly in charge, through appeal to a higher authority with the intention of forcing a change in management, or through various types of actions and protests, including those that are meant to mobilize public opinion."[34] Voice is nothing more than making demands on the political system. It is commonplace in most political institutions, but truncated and suspect in education.

It is now appropriate to examine how voice may affect the behavior of educational decision makers.[35] The likelihood of a satisfactory response by educational management to a citizen's complaint depends on the strength of the protest. Not everyone adversely affected by a particular action need complain, however, for voice to be effective. It is probably best, in fact, if the complaint is expressed mildly at first. This gives management time to respond to the pressure being brought upon it. Failure to respond will arouse those citizens to complain who at first were content to wait for others to do so.

One problem with this analysis, of course, is the apparent apathy of most citizens toward education. It is even difficult to get the public involved in something as simple as voting in school elections. What conditions may encourage citizens to express their views on educational policy?

In the first place the client must decide to remain in a particular educational system. If a parent chooses to move to another district he or she will be unable to complain. For those parents who must remain, the only hope is to express their complaint. But even those who can move to another district or send their children to private schools may decide to stay and fight it out, if they think the public schools will improve or respond to their complaints in a satisfactory way. An assessment of this decision is made by Edward Banfield in his study of public policy. "The effort an interested party makes to put its case before the decision-maker will be in proportion to the advantage to be gained from a favorable outcome multiplied by the probability of influencing the decision."[36]

Besides considering whether attempts to influence decisions are likely to succeed, the individual must also weigh the costs of getting involved. He must weigh the opportunity costs of not moving to a better school system, as well as the organizational costs—time, money, and energy—required to change the decisions of an organization.[37] Participating in collective choices is always more costly than making an individual choice. And organizational costs increase as more people become involved in a group and the more decisions the group attempts to influence. Before getting involved, an individual will not only consider the likelihood of a favorable result from his efforts, but also whether the likely benefits outweigh the organizational costs of involvement.

This formulation helps explain the difficulty central-city school systems have in keeping students and getting the public involved in solving district problems. Since these school systems are big and

cumbersome, individuals perceive that their chances of achieving
desired changes are very small. There are, furthermore, so many
problems in the cities that the cost of becoming involved with the
schools is likely to be greater than the expected overall benefit.[38]
Size and the difficulty of getting things done further discourage
urban residents from taking part in educational decision making and
probably account for some of the flight to the suburbs that occurs in
most cities.

The implications of this analysis are clear. In a complex urban
environment the costs of trying to correct the faults of schools are
higher for many people than the costs of moving to a suburban
school district. On the other hand, urban schools are increasingly
important, particularly for ethnic and racial minorities who do not
have the option of moving. If schools are going to be responsive to
the needs of these citizens, political mechanisms must be developed
to permit them to voice their preferences. "Once voice is recognized
as a mechanism with considerable usefulness for maintaining performance, institutions can be designed in such a way that the cost of
individual and collective action would be decreased. Or, in some
situations, the rewards for successful action might be increased for
those who had initiated it."[39]

There have already been some attempts in public education to
develop new channels for the public to communicate complaints
easily and effectively. Voting, of course, is one of the least costly
ways of getting the input of citizens. But, because voting has its limitations, school districts have turned to other mechanisms to encourage public involvement. Decentralization of large urban school districts reduces the bureaucratic barriers between citizens and decision
makers and thus facilitates better communications. Citizens' advisory
committees and ombudsmen also open up channels for citizen participation.

Since collective bargaining involves many decisions of concern to
the public—decisions affecting their taxes and the schooling of their
children—the process should be opened up to greater public participation. As was suggested earlier, teachers have a right to negotiate
the terms and conditions of their employment. But the public also
has a right to participate in public decisions affecting their lives.
Since citizens cannot influence public-sector collective bargaining in
the marketplace, their only option is to influence collective bargaining decisions through direct participation.

The final section of this chapter will outline a number of possible ways to increase public access to the collective bargaining process. First, though, we must consider some of the procedural and substantive problems of the current collective bargaining process in public education.

Problem Areas in Negotiations by Teachers

Finding ways to restore public control of educational governance (particularly collective bargaining) requires an understanding of the problems of the current collective bargaining process. Collective bargaining per se is not at issue. Teachers have a legitimate right in a democracy to participate in negotiations concerning the conditions of their employment, although observers disagree on what the rights of public employees should include. For the purpose of this discussion, it is assumed that the right to negotiate applies at least to all issues affecting the welfare of teachers: salaries, fringe benefits, working schedules, grievance procedures, tenure, extra pay for extra work, and so forth.

One major question regarding negotiations by teachers is whether the scope of negotiations should extend beyond economic issues. Nationwide teachers' organizations are pushing to extend collective bargaining to cover not only economic issues but also the mission of school districts and how the mission is to be carried out.[40] Although labor and management in the private sector fought bitter battles over the scope of bargaining issues in the 1930s and 1940s, labor never asked for control over decisions concerning products and pricing. What was produced and when or how it was produced were considered inherently managerial decisions. Many unions of public employees have also limited their demands to basically economic issues. In public education, however, teachers are actively gaining control over many areas of decision making affecting educational policy.

The scope of bargaining issues in public employment has traditionally been linked to the notion of sovereignty.[41] At both the federal and local levels, it has been successfully argued that government service is public in character and is responsible to the people. Only elected representatives of the people can, therefore, have the final say on decisions affecting the provision of public service. In most places this doctrine of government sovereignty is still protected. Successive negotiation laws have, however, gradually added to the areas of government decision making that can be shared with employees' groups. It was once felt that even questions of wages and working conditions were ultimately the responsibility of elected officials; now most aspects of school governance are covered under rules set out in collective bargaining agreements.

Various groups have called for legislation to limit the scope of negotiations to economic matters. These efforts have usually failed because teachers' unions have too much political clout. In Oregon, for instance, the school boards association decided not to press for limitations on the scope of bargaining because there simply is not enough support in the legislature for such a measure. There seems, in fact, to be a growing movement among state legislatures to extend the coverage of collective bargaining rights to more issues.

Recently this issue has been taken up by the courts. On January 22, 1975, the Parents Union for Public Schools in Philadelphia filed suit in the Philadelphia Court of Pleas against the Board of Education of the School District of Philadelphia and others, charging that the school board has unlawfully delegated educational policy-making authority and responsibility to nonpublic bodies (a teachers' organization and a nonadvisory joint committee). The suit claims that decisions affecting pay for extracurricular activities, procedures for transferring teachers to effect racial balance, goals for the standards and performance of teachers, programs for retarded educables, accountability, and the progress and educational skills of pupils have been delegated to groups that are not elected by or responsible to the public. The outcome of this case may profoundly influence teachers' bargaining throughout the country.

Except for the legal arguments over the divisibility of sovereign powers, the issue of the scope of negotiations raises the most fundamental political issue. Why should a public employee living in a democracy have fewer rights concerning the condition of his employment than an employee in the private sector?[42] A strong case can be made that public employees should have the same rights as private employees. An even stronger case can be made that the education of children is likely to improve if teachers, who work with children every day, are permitted to participate in decisions affecting the educational program. The issue, then, is not whether teachers have something to contribute in the making of educational policy. Most people would say they do. The issue is whether teachers should monopolize the policy-making process, particularly at the expense of the public.

It is true that collective bargaining in the private sector is conducted privately. In the private sector, however, the public is not compelled to live with the decisions of management and labor. If people do not like the result, they simply quit buying the product. In public education parents and students do not have that option. Since they must live with the results of a collective bargaining agreement, they should have the right to influence that agreement.

A second problem concerns the role of outsiders in collective bargaining. As the scope of negotiations has expanded, the role of fact-finding, mediation, and, in some cases, arbitration has also expanded. These functions are frequently performed by lawyers or professional negotiators who have no direct connection with the school district. Furthermore, teachers' groups frequently go outside the district to put political pressure on management to settle a dispute. Particularly worrisome is the behavior of state officials in threatened strikes of teachers. Twice in early 1975 the governor of Oregon intervened at the last minute to avert a threatened strike by teachers. In both cases pressure was successfully applied to cause school boards to increase their offer and break the stalemate. As Imundo has said, "Continuance of this system of circumvention will not facilitate meaningful collective bargaining at the local levels where agreements have to be implemented."[43]

The role of the state should be to establish rules of collective bargaining that favor neither side in the negotiations. Final decisions should be left to the negotiators and the citizens of the district. Teachers have little incentive to settle if they believe the governor or some other outsider will come in and pressure the school board to make concessions on disputed issues.

The policy of keeping teachers' negotiations secret is particularly troublesome to those concerned about public control of schools. Under most recent collective bargaining laws, teachers' negotiations are not only exempt from state laws regarding open meetings, but the negotiating parties are forbidden to reveal the positions or strategies of either side. Publication of information about the negotiations is considered an unfair labor practice and is specifically prohibited.

Frequently in large school districts the teachers' negotiation team is headed by a professional negotiator from the state teachers' organization, and the school board's team is led by a hired negotiator. School board members usually do not have time to follow the proceedings, and members of the press and public are not permitted to sit in on the sessions. Secrecy is supposed to ensure that serious bargaining will take place. It also means, unfortunately, that items of critical importance to the public may be negotiated away by people who are not accountable to the public.[44]

Under present procedures there is no right of communications either during or after negotiations. The school board cannot explain to the public or the teachers its position on the issues being discussed. Those most concerned with the outcome—teachers, parents, students, and taxpayers—frequently have no idea what is being negotiated or what is being traded away for something else. Nor is there any information about what actually transpired during negotiations. How can negotiators be accountable to the public when the public is excluded from participation and no records of the negotiations are available?

Another problem with current collective bargaining laws is the lack of control the management team has over the resources at issue in the negotiations. In the private sector, management can live up to an agreement to pay higher wages by increasing the price of its products, increasing efficiency, or reducing profits. None of these options is available to governmental agencies.

Increased teachers' salaries have to come from taxes, but most legislative bodies, including school boards, cannot simply raise taxes. The demands of teachers must be weighed against the demands of every other group making a claim on government and the general desire to keep taxes from rising. Increasing efficiency is a more realistic option when an organization produces goods rather than a service like education. And government cannot absorb increased costs by reducing profits because government does not make a profit. School boards frequently set aside funds to cover contingencies such as unexpected labor settlements, but knowledge of a contingency fund is likely to lead to even higher labor demands.

The problem is that school boards must negotiate about resources they do not have and are unsure of obtaining. They must, at the same time, fear a strike and the reaction of the public should there be one. Both of these uncertainties encourage management to make concessions on educational policy in return for a salary package that can be supported.

Current collective bargaining procedures are closely tied to several important substantive issues. First, many teachers are demanding that a minimum percentage of the budget be allocated for instructional programs. Since the major part of the money for instructional programs goes to pay salaries, this would give teachers' salaries priority above all other items in the budget. The school board may want to increase salaries, but to do so may mean giving up a new program or deferring necessary capital improvement or maintenance. At some point school managers will not be able to forgo other priority items to pay higher salaries without seriously weakening the educational program.

A second substantive problem is in the area of personnel practices. School boards are quickly losing control of many decisions related to the hiring, placement, evaluation, assignment, and firing of staff. Many of these personnel decisions have important policy implications. For example, the question of maximum pupil-teacher ratio is increasingly being raised by teachers in negotiations. If management agrees to negotiate on this issue they will lose a large degree of flexibility concerning programs.[45] Another example is the use of teachers' aides and parents in the classroom. Teachers often argue that all classroom activities are the teacher's work. But negotiations on this one item will directly affect staffing patterns such as team teaching and differentiated staffing, as well as the use of resource centers, libraries, teaching machines, and other tools for providing better education.

Weakened control over the budget and over staffing patterns has removed much of management's flexibility in providing educational services. These restrictions become even more critical when the district is confronted with controversial problems, such as bussing to achieve racial balance or providing services for physically and emotionally handicapped children. The ability to respond effectively to problems is being taken away from school boards at the bargaining table.

Thus far only problems concerning collective bargaining practices have been discussed. Many states do not, of course, have collective bargaining laws, and so the government's tenacious grip on the doctrine of sovereignty remains strong enough to prevent meaningful collective bargaining. Indications are that teachers' unions will continue their efforts to pass more collective bargaining laws and expand the scope of issues covered under the present laws.

The problem is to find the right balance between the teachers' right to negotiate the terms of their employment and management's responsibility to be responsive to public demands. For years management had a disproportionate amount of power in educational decision making; now the balance of power has shifted in states with collective bargaining laws. Teachers' newly won bargaining rights, coupled with the public's inability to exercise any real control over education, have left teachers in a decidedly stronger position than educational management.

To protect the public interest, new mechanisms must be developed to equalize the bargaining relationship in education. This cannot be done (as is frequently suggested) by taking rights away from teachers. Having gained a position of power, teachers will be reluctant to give it up. It can only be done by revitalizing the legislative powers of school boards and by increasing public control of education through direct citizen participation in the collective bargaining process. The final section of this chapter discusses some possible ways to accomplish that goal.

Reforming Collective Bargaining in Public Education

The essential need today is to establish a pattern of educational governance that creates a new balance of power among those responsible for educational policy. Schools are too important to leave most policy and administrative decisions in the hands of school administrators alone. For this reason, the emergence of teachers as a powerful voice in school governance should be applauded, and additional steps should be taken to bring teachers fully into the decision-making structure of schools.

By the same token, steps must also be taken to increase substantially the influence of the public on educational decision making. Since there is no inherent consumer sovereignty in public education, public control of schools can only be reestablished by revitalizing the legislative process of educational governance and opening up channels for direct citizen participation in school government. To accomplish these purposes, reform of the collective bargaining system must be accompanied by reform of the system of educational governance.

State-Level Reform

To make collective bargaining more responsive to the public, a number of changes are required at the state level. First, states that do not have collective bargaining laws should enact laws guaranteeing the right of teachers to organize and to negotiate with management on matters relating to the welfare of teachers. Teachers are already negotiating in many school districts throughout the country where negotiations are not permitted by state law. Governments that continue to resist collective bargaining efforts can expect defiance from teachers and resulting administrative problems at the district level.

In establishing a mechanism for collective bargaining, states should institute basic ground rules for bargaining without giving a preponderant advantage to either side. These rules must be carefully designed to provide each side with incentives to reach agreement. There must not be binding arbitration, since both sides must recognize they have something to gain and something to lose from the bargaining process.

Besides giving teachers the right to negotiate, states should strengthen the ability of school boards to negotiate. Laws that constrain school boards from negotiating effectively should be eliminated or revised. Current laws related to the tenure of teachers, for instance, make it difficult for boards to fire incompetent teachers or replace unneeded teachers when program priorities change. Employment security is important to everyone. It is clearly an item for negotiation, but its terms should not be mandated by state law.

States should look carefully at certification regulations. Under most present regulations it is extremely difficult to hire noncertificated personnel to work in the classroom. If local conditions warrant it, school boards should be able to experiment with teachers' aides, classroom assistants, and other teaching techniques that are presently constrained by certification requirements. Until some consensus is reached on the attributes of a good teacher, local school districts should have a freer hand in the hiring of personnel.

Laws specifying the length of the school year should also be eliminated or relaxed. Knowing that state funds will be withheld unless children attend school for a certain number of days eliminates much of the risk for striking teachers. Under present law, teachers know that any salary they lose during a strike will be made up at the end of the school year. It is conceivable that school boards might want to use the salary money saved during a strike to develop new programs or invest in new learning aids. Or they might use the money to pay parents and others to keep the schools operating. Even when teachers are not on strike, alternating a week in school with a week of work-study might be highly desirable in some situations. The choice should be made by local districts and not by the state. The point is not that the school year should be shortened, but rather that school boards should be free to adjust its length to meet local conditions.

Suggestions to eliminate certification requirements and regulations requiring a minimum number of school days have been objected to by civil rights groups, particularly in the South. They argue that the relaxation of these requirements will lead to a decline in the quality of education for minorities: school districts might shorten the school year and send the poorest teachers into schools with concentrations of minority children. This concern is justified. Too often minority children have been served poorly when educational policy decisions have been left to local school boards. This problem can probably be better remedied, however, by stronger state legislation guaranteeing student rights. Even now, cases currently before the courts challenge policies regarding the transfer of teachers that discriminate against minorities. The outcomes of similar cases arguing that handicapped and bilingual children are being denied equal educational opportunity may also provide greater protection for minorities than state certification and standards concerning the length of the school year.

States should examine carefully the interaction of new collective bargaining laws and their existing budget laws. There is some evidence that both management and teachers consider the budget laws when they are planning tactics and strategies for bargaining.[46] Knowing that school boards must submit a budget to the people by a certain date has sometimes led teachers' representatives to postpone negotiations on economic matters until the last possible moment. School boards have countered this strategy by going into an election without a final labor settlement and inserting a unilateral "last offer" in the budget, which in turn leads to charges of unfair labor practices, and so on. This is a highly complex problem, and there is not much information on the effects of budget laws on collective bargaining. Attempts should be made, however, to isolate the bargaining process from the budgetary process, to avoid giving an advantage to either side.

The most important reform at the state level is to eliminate laws that prohibit the public from participating in or gaining information about school negotiations. Provisions exempting bargaining sessions from laws concerning open meetings should be removed. Furthermore, regulations prohibiting discussion of contract proposals before, during, or after negotiations should be changed to encourage dissemination of information about the negotiations. A fundamental principle of democracy is that the people should control their institutions, but public control is impossible if meetings are held behind closed doors.

Public control of education requires greater citizen participation in the bargaining process. Perhaps strengthening local school boards and opening bargaining sessions to the public will be enough to provide adequate protection of the public interest. Public response should be watched carefully, however, and, if necessary, direct citizen involvement in some form of tripartite bargaining should be considered.

Once a fair and open legal framework has been established, the state should stay out of local negotiations. Intervention by state legislators or members of the governor's staff interferes with a process designed to force school board members and teachers to reach agreement. If a local strike occurs it is unlikely to do any great damage. Without outside intervention, those involved in the negotiations will have to resolve the differences that led to the strike. The state's major responsibility regarding collective bargaining in public education is to establish a set of rules that is fair to all sides and guarantees adequate public access and influence. Once that framework is established, state officials should stay out of local disputes. They should, however, carefully monitor the collective bargaining law to see that local districts comply with it and to ensure that it works properly.

Detailed information on collective bargaining settlements should be collected and made available to state legislators. If specific provisions of the law are creating problems, they should be changed to neutralize their effects. The ultimate goal is to equalize the power of school boards, teachers, and the public so that settlements can be negotiated that are responsive to local tastes and interests.

School District Reform

At the school district level, the greatest need is to revitalize the legislative powers of school boards. Today school boards are extremely weak. They are constrained by restrictive state regulations and prohibitions, and they lack the fiscal resources needed to bargain in good faith or to implement program priorities. What is more important, they are cut off politically from the public whose support they need to run the schools effectively.

In order to make school boards more responsive, members should be elected from single-member districts. Every citizen should know his school board representative so that he can hold that person accountable. It would also be desirable to make school elections partisan. Each voter would have a better idea of candidates' views if they carried a party label and campaigned on a party platform.

To function as an effective legislative body, a school board needs an independent staff so that it can develop its own policies independently of the superintendent and his staff. Particularly in the area of collective bargaining, the board should be able to develop its bargaining demands and strategies without relying on the school administration. Because school administrators are usually former teachers, they often have mixed loyalties when it comes to bargaining. Not only do administrators often sympathize with teachers; their salaries are frequently keyed to the settlements won by teachers. For the school board to represent effectively the public's interest, therefore, it needs its own sources of information and a staff to analyze alternatives.

If there is to be a change from administrative government in schools to legislative government, then the school board should assume the responsibility for bargaining with teachers. School administrators may either negotiate a separate agreement with the board or be included in the teachers' agreement. The important point is that if the school board is going to be the major policy-making body at the district level, then it should have the responsibility for negotiations.

The most important reform related to collective bargaining at the district level is to open up the process to the public. After state laws preventing public participation in collective bargaining have been changed, the school board should adopt new procedures to involve the public directly in the negotiations process. One idea is to include lay members on a collective bargaining committee (similar to lay participation on many local budget committees). These public representatives could be selected by the board or by local parents' groups and would help the school board develop its bargaining package. The board might then hold hearings throughout the district to elicit as much public reaction as possible to its proposals, and its position should then be given wide distribution among teachers, students, parents, and the general community.

The actual negotiations between the school board and teachers' representatives should also be open to the public, and direct participation by the public should be considered. If the board decides to hire a professional negotiator, then the public may only be observers. But districts should be very careful about outside negotiators. With no direct involvement in the community, professional negotiators may be insensitive to local concerns and indifferent about sacrificing local priorities to obtain a settlement.[47] If at all possible the board should do its own negotiating, with public representatives sitting on its side of the table.

The press should be permitted to cover collective bargaining meetings and disseminate information on their progress. No aspect of the bargaining sessions or the contract proposals should be restricted from public scrutiny.

Opponents of "fishbowl" bargaining say that public collective bargaining sessions will encourage grandstanding and hamper progress toward an agreement. This may occur to some extent. Over time, however, negotiators will learn to bargain in public, just as city councils and legislative committees are learning to function in public under recently enacted laws relating to open meetings. No one argues that democratic decision making is easy. But in a period when public distrust of government is on the rise, the added trust and support that result from open negotiations may well be worth the added cost.

It is possible that public collective bargaining sessions may reduce the difficulty of winning voters' approval of local school budgets. When 70 to 80 percent of the school budget is tied up in salaries, and the public is excluded from any decisions affecting salaries, concerned citizens are left only with their ability to cast negative votes in budget elections. Perhaps the opportunity for direct citizen participation in salary negotiations would eliminate the need for repeated school budget elections. This in turn would reduce the uncertainty of school board negotiators, who must now bargain without knowing whether money will be available to honor the agreements they make.

School Site Reform

In many school districts public control would be enhanced by the establishment of new legislative bodies at each school site. These school councils would have full legislative authority over curriculum, school program budgeting, school progress reports, and personnel evaluation. Many of the questions concerning school programs and staffing that are currently negotiated by the school board could be negotiated between the school council and teachers of each school. Enough budget flexibility would, of course, be needed to permit broad program discretion among individual schools, and final settlement of the district-wide contract would be contingent on settlement of individual school contracts. This reform would directly involve the public in the development of educational policies affecting the local school program.

Conclusion

Collective bargaining in education has raised the fundamental question of who should control public schools. The private-sector collective bargaining model suggests that educational policy should be worked out privately by teachers and school administrators. The major loser in this realignment of powers has been the public, since private citizens are now excluded by law from participating in or gaining information about the negotiations that directly affect the quality of public education.

The changes proposed in this chapter are based on the principle that in a democracy the people should control their institutions. Since the consumers of public education are virtually excluded from exercising any control through the marketplace, they must exercise that control by participating in the decision-making process. The suggestions made here would increase public influence in education by revitalizing the legislative process in school governance at the state, district, and local levels and by opening up new channels for direct public participation in the collective bargaining process.

These suggestions may help to restore proper public influence over educational decision making. But educators should not stop here in their search for new mechanisms that will enable the public to communicate their concerns cheaply and effectively. Efforts should also be made to design educational programs that increase the choices available to students and parents and make educational institutions more responsive to diverse needs and demands. Above all, the guiding principle should be responsiveness to the public. Collective bargaining for teachers challenges the traditional form of administrative government in schools. It will serve education well if it brings about a new balance of power that permits greater participation by the public as well as by teachers.

Notes

1. For a general review of the implications of collective bargaining in the public sector, see Daniel H. Kruger and Charles T. Schmidt, Jr., *Collective Bargaining in the Public Service* (New York: Random House, 1969); Michael H. Moskow, J. Joseph Loewenberg, and Edward Clifford Koziara, *Collective Bargaining in Public Employment* (New York: Random House, 1970); *Perspective in Public Employee Negotiation,* ed. Keith Ocheltree (Chicago: Public Personnel Association, 1969); and Robert T. Woodworth and Richard B. Peterson, *Collective Negotiation for Public and Professional Employees* (Glenview, Ill.: Scott, Foresman, 1969).

2. Robert Ridgley, vice-chairman, Portland School Board, emphasized this point in saying that "there may be no money as a result of bargaining on these issues to put into what you would call instructional improvement, discretionary funds that are given to administrators and teachers in various school buildings to try to improve the quality and delivery of services." Portland hearing of NCCE Commission on Educational Governance, June 1974.

3. See James W. Guthrie, "Public Control of Public Schools: Can We Get It Back?" *Public Affairs Report* 15 (June 1974), No. 3.

4. Harmon Zeigler *et al., Governing American Education* (North Scituate, Mass.: Duxbury Press, 1974).

5. Guthrie, "Public Control of Public Schools," 3.

6. The American Bar Association commented in 1955: "A government which imposes upon other employers certain obligations in dealing with their employees may not in good faith refuse to deal with its own public servants on a reasonably similar . . . basis . . . ." Quoted in Patricia N. Blair, "State Legislative Control over the Conditions of Public Employment: Defining the Scope of Collective Bargaining for State and Municipal Employees," *Vanderbilt Law Review* 26 (January 1973), 6.

7. The witness, Mr. Bill Oberteuffer, a Portland teacher with seventeen years of experience, went on to say, "We teach a kind of fascism in the public schools of this country, I believe, and if a child has a nondemocratic family and goes through twelve years of a nondemocratic public school system and then is ready to vote at eighteen, I don't know what real good preparation he has had. He's

learned about how to vote as far as when to vote, but he hasn't learned how to vote in terms of shared decision making, and I could regale you with case after case of a lack of shared decision making by professionals in the school system." Portland hearing of NCCE Commission on Educational Governance, June 1974.

8. Mr. James Ballard, representative of the San Francisco Federation of Teachers, explained that the teachers' unions favor strong management. ". . . we don't want to make policy. We believe that is the job of school management. That is the reason we advocate strong . . . superintendents, with competent boards, the whole process." San Francisco hearing of NCCE Commission on Educational Governance, October 1974.

9. See Paul Prasow *et al.*, *Scope of Bargaining in the Public Sector—Concepts and Problems* (Washington, D.C.: Government Printing Office, 1972).

10. Moskow, Loewenberg, and Koziara, *Collective Bargaining in Public Employment.*

11. U.S. Department of Labor, Labor Management Services Division, Division of Public Employee Labor Relations, *State Profiles: Current Status of Public Sector Labor Relations* (Washington, D.C.: Government Printing Office, 1971), 13, 29, 73.

12. T. M. Stinnett, Jack H. Kleinmann, and Martha L. Ware, *Professional Negotiations in Public Education* (New York: Macmillan, 1966), 19.

13. *Ibid.*, 265-268.

14. *Ibid.*, 19. The legislation is reproduced on pp. 240-268.

15. See U.S. Department of Labor, *State Profiles*, for evidence of bargaining far in excess of legislative requirements.

16. A. H. Raskin, "Is the Picket Line Obsolete?" *Saturday Review/World* (October 19, 1974), 12-17.

17. Since 1965 the National Education Association has advocated "professional negotiations," reversing a previous position that negotiations were unprofessional. See Stinnett, Kleinmann, and Ware, *Professional Negotiations*, 2.

18. Myron Lieberman and Michael H. Moskow, *Collective Bargaining for Teachers* (Chicago, Rand McNally, 1966), Chap. 2.

19. National Commission on the Reform of Secondary Education-Charles F. Kettering Foundation, *The Reform of Secondary Education: A Report to the Public and the Profession* (New York: McGraw-Hill, 1973), Chap. 5.

20. Doris M. Ross, "State Collective Bargaining Laws Affecting Education," in *A Legislator's Guide to Collective Bargaining in Education*, Research and Information Service, Education Commission of the States, January 10, 1974. See Appendix of this book.

21. The data presented here were taken from research prepared for the Coalition of American Public Employees by NEA's Research Division, entitled "State Negotiations Statutes Covering Teachers Enacted through September 1974."

22. Moskow, Loewenberg, and Koziara, *Collective Bargaining in Public Employment*, 38-56.

23. *Ibid.*, 72-79.

24. Library of Congress, Congressional Research Services, "Labor-Manage-

ment Relations for State and Local Government Employees: Legislative Activity in the 93rd Congress," October 21, 1974.

25. For a useful analysis of the differences between collective bargaining in the public and private sectors, see Patricia A. Craig, "The Applicability of Private Sector Collective Bargaining Models in Public Education: Reopening the Question," unpublished paper, College of Education, University of California, Berkeley.

26. Lieberman and Moskow, *Collective Bargaining for Teachers*, contains a useful discussion of alternative models of collective bargaining.

27. Harry H. Wellington and Ralph K. Winger, Jr., *The Unions and the Cities* (Washington, D.C.: Brookings Institution, 1971), 15.

28. See John K. Galbraith, *The Affluent Society* (Boston: Houghton Mifflin, 1958).

29. Craig, "The Applicability of Private Sector Collective Bargaining Models," 6.

30. Comment made by Thomas Rigby, executive director of the Oregon School Board Association, at Portland hearing of NCCE Commission on Educational Governance, June 1974.

31. Albert O. Hirschman, *Exit, Voice, and Loyalty* (Cambridge, Mass.: Harvard University Press, 1970).

32. *Ibid.*, 4.

33. *Ibid.*, 15-16.

34. *Ibid.*, 30.

35. The following analysis summarizes a number of points made by Hirschman. *Ibid.*, 30-43.

36. Edward C. Banfield, *Political Influence* (New York: Free Press of Glencoe, 1961), 333.

37. James M. Buchanan and Gordon Tullock, *The Calculus of Consent* (Ann Arbor: University of Michigan Press, 1962).

38. Hirschman, *Exit, Voice, and Loyalty*, 40.

39. *Ibid.*, 42.

40. Comment made by Rigby, Portland hearing of NCCE Commission on Educational Governance, June 1974.

41. Louis V. Imundo, Jr., "Some Comparisons between Public Sector and Private Sector Collective Bargaining," *Labor Law Journal* 24 (December 1973), 811.

42. *Ibid.* 812.

43. *Ibid.*, 813.

44. This point was emphasized by Ridgley, Portland hearing of NCCE Commission on Educational Governance, June 1974.

45. *Ibid.*

46. Milton Derber, Ken Jennings, Ian McAndrew, and Martain Wagner, "Bargaining and Budget Making in Illinois Public Institutions," *Industrial and Labor Relations Review* 27 (October 1973), 49-62.

47. Thomas M. Love and George T. Sulzner, "Political Implications of Public Employee Bargaining," *Industrial Relations* (No. 2, 1972), 24.

7

ALTERNATIVE EDUCATIONAL EXPERIENCES: THE DEMAND FOR CHANGE

Mario D. Fantini   State University of New York, New Paltz

About 15 percent of all American families have always had alternatives to public schools. These have included academic prep schools like Andover, Choate, Mt. Hermon, or Northfield; day schools like Collegiate in New York City, the Commonwealth School in Boston, or Horace Mann in New York; religious-affiliated schools like the National Cathedral School in Washington, D.C., St. Paul's in New Hampshire, or Germantown Friends in Philadelphia; progressive independent schools like Walden and the Little Red Schoolhouse in New York City or Fieldston in Riverdale, New York; the Montessori day schools for preschool children. For the masses, however, the only choice was and is a rather uniform public school system.

In the past few years educational options have become available within the public schools at such a rate as to form a major movement in American education. The Center for Options in Public Education at Indiana University confirmed the existence of over 500 alternative schools in 1972-1973. It was estimated that in 1974-1975 there may be 4,000 or more alternative public schools enrolling over 500,000 students, still, however, only about 1 percent of the students in elementary and secondary schools.[1]

A problem arises in defining the "alternative" school or program.

Both within and without public school systems, programs that are nothing but adjuncts to regular schooling are termed alternative. Several school systems throughout the country have recently opened schools to which delinquent, disruptive, emotionally disturbed, or hyperactive students are assigned without choice; more and more these institutions are being labeled alternative schools. Alternative should mean choice, not compulsion; this was the one common characteristic of all the alternative schools described to the Commission on Educational Governance. Whether these schools were part of public school systems or received operating funds from outside sources, students attended them voluntarily.

Nor should alternative be confused with innovative, for in American education very little is new. The vastness of the educational system—public and private—allows for a multiplicity of programs that duplicate each other and similar efforts for decades back. "If somebody figures out something innovative in education in Minneapolis [this year]," the director of an alternative school in Atlanta told the Commission, "we invent the whole thing over somewhere else in 1979."[2]

The Commission, of course, came in touch with only a small number of alternative schools of the many hundreds from coast to coast. These ranged from schools for real and potential teenage dropouts in Atlanta and St. Louis to the Southeast Alternatives Project of the Minneapolis Public Schools to the Heart of the Earth Survival School in Minneapolis, whose very title connotes its meaning to Indian students in that city.

The Commission found little evidence of open warfare between administrators of alternative schools and public school systems, even where the alternative facility had deliberately avoided seeking public funds because of strings that might be attached (as was the case with the Indian school in Minneapolis). Even these independent projects were, in fact, working closely with the public schools, depending upon them for student referrals and developing curricula in the hope they would be adopted by the public schools. "I would like to see programs like [ours] become advisers to public education," said the director of an alternative school in St. Louis. "I would like for us to be an adviser in terms of creating, developing, experimenting."[3]

The alternative schools encountered by the Commission perceived their value in student-centered education, meaningful counseling, closer student-teacher relationships—in short, the avoidance of the "sterile atmosphere" of public schools, in the words of James O'Brien, director of the Heart of the Earth School.[4] These ideas are not new. If Neil Shorthouse, of Peachtree Alternative School in Atlanta, told the Commission that the school practiced the "personal approach to education," in which pupils call their teachers by their first names, and if he said pupils are treated with "genuine love and affection,"[5] he was echoing the organizers of alternative institutions such as Walden School in New York City sixty years ago.

In most cases the spokespersons for alternative schools told the Commission that parents and teachers—there was little mention of students—played key roles in the organization and operation of the schools. In Minneapolis, for example, it was stated that there are advisory councils of parents, faculty, and staff at all five schools in Southeast Alternatives and that parents and faculty serve on screening committees for all new administrative appointments. Three new principals were appointed to the project in three years, and each was recommended by the screening group and accepted by the central school board.[6] "I think we do discuss substantive policy issues, budget review, evaluation review including evaluation of the director. We are bringing up the possibility of evaluating other administrators as well as appointments on all hearing committees and review of individual school governance and a review of our function in governance," said the enthusiastic member of one of the advisory councils.[7]

The Commission found that, in general, the voice of the student was ignored in educational policy making, and this extended across the board from regular school programs to alternative schools. Adults, be they teachers or parents, made most of the decisions in the alternative schools whose operations were described to the Commission. One of the most authoritarian statements of the five hearings came from the director of the Heart of the Earth School in Minneapolis. "I might sound like a tyrant," he said, "but these students can outline their own classes, and they can just as well run the school the way they want it run as long as I feel that it's an intelligent decision."[8]

Because the Commission's hearings were devoted almost exclusively to public school matters, no speakers were heard from the so-called free school movement that began with the civil rights struggles of the early 1960s. As the quest for desegregation gained momentum, boycotts of public schools by parents, teachers, and the community led to the establishment of temporary freedom schools in storefronts and church basements. Teachers, community residents, parents, and college volunteers collaborated to continue the education of black children in the freedom schools.

For many blacks and whites alike, the freedom schools provided a glimpse of alternative programs tailored to their perceived needs, which included sympathetic adults working with children, curriculum specifically geared to the concerns of self-determination of black people, and involvement in the immediate political life of the community. To pursue these educational concerns, those involved departed from established procedures by assuming a flexible stance that advocated expanding the boundaries of schooling to include the community and its resources, establishing smaller educational units to humanize the experience for those involved, and relating educational experience to the life of the community. These ingredients remain prevalent in the current movement for alternative schools.

Another social trend that continues to contribute to alternative education is the so-called counterculture movement. Viewing public schools as repressive and authoritarian institutions reflecting the deteriorating values of the dominant society, members of the counterculture have attempted to sponsor alternative institutions that are free to develop new learning environments that are personally liberating and geared to individual and group life-styles. Participants in this search were quick to embrace the new educational philosophies of A. S. Neill, Ivan Illich, and a host of the so-called romantic education writers, such as Paul Goodman, John Holt, Herbert Kohl, Everett Reimer, and George Dennison. Underlying this philosophy is the central concern with individual freedom. A. S. Neill states his philosophy clearly: "My view is that a child is innately wise and realistic. If left to himself without adult suggestion of any kind, he will develop as far as he is capable of developing." To Illich and Reimer, schools, especially public (but also, perhaps, free schools) get in the way of real education. To them, the best idea, one that maximizes both freedom and individual development, is one that gives each person the right and the means for orchestrating his own distinctive plan.

Allen Graubard, former professor of philosophy at M.I.T., spent three years as a participant-observer of free schools in the United

States; this culminated in his book on the subject, *Free the Children*. Graubard explains that most free schools are dedicated to eliminating all the public school apparatuses that are viewed as oppressive: imposed discipline and punishment, lockstep age gradings, time period divisions, homework, frequent tests, grades and report cards, rigid graded curriculum, standardized classrooms dominated and commanded by one teacher with twenty-five to thirty-five students under his or her power.

Freed from such a structure, these new school alternatives (from nursery to high school) take on diverse forms, all trying to develop self-directed learners, and there is no doubt that the flexible, spontaneous nature of many free schools does provide a refreshing change from the conventionality of traditional schools.

Graubard describes, for instance, one San Diego school that was prompted by financial difficulties to move into a public park. The facilities of the park—grassy grounds, trees, picnic tables, fireplaces, electric outlets, sinks, sports fields—were fully utilized. Graubard, who participated in the school, wrote:

The great virtue of the park has turned out to be its openness, which has greatly improved communication among and between the teachers and students. Everyone can see everyone else; we know where the students are and they know where we are and what we are doing. This has eliminated the need we felt last year for schedules. Furthermore, the teacher, instead of each being sequestered in his or her room, [is] with his or her group of students. The result is that we tend to work more closely together, to plan together and coordinate our efforts much more than we ever did before. We don't, moreover, have to pay the price usually paid by large groups of people together in a big room: noise. The children who want to run can run, the children who want to be noisy can be noisy . . . .[9]

In another new school in Vermont, Graubard reports, "the people involved in the school any given year determine what the curriculum will be." Some of these child-initiated activities included the production of such plays as *Oedipus Rex* and *The Tempest*, the building of a pond, the construction of a bridge across a brook, the preparation of an opera, and dance recitals. Children could study Russian or Chinese or Egyptian writing. If several children were interested in studying something in particular, a course was promptly organized. In another free school the main curriculum during the first few months was "how to make your own school."

In short, many free schools emphasize non-Western culture, community participation, and patterns of governance resembling town meetings.

And yet, despite their diversity and openness (and granted the few exceptional successes and glimpses of exciting learning in many other settings), Graubard concludes that these schools reveal a less than optimistic picture. It is estimated that approximately 200 new free schools have been developed during the past five years. The life span for these schools is now judged to be about two years. The average enrollment of free schools is about thirty-three students, and the turnover rate among both students and teachers is high. Many students, Graubard reports, are just as turned off in free schools as they were in public schools. Most of the free schools are facing fiscal problems despite the tuition being paid and the willingness of many committed teachers to work for subsistence wages.

Why is this? How can a humanistic, learner-centered philosophy so eloquently enunciated by such contemporary writers as Holt, Jonathan Kozol, Kohl, Dennison, Sylvia Ashton-Warner, and Goodman be faced with such problems?

There are several possible reasons that go beyond the gap between rhetoric and performance emphasized in *Free the Children*. For one thing, this youthful activity has attracted many well-intentioned people who, nonetheless, really want to use freedom in learning for their own ends. Some want to use it to "get themselves together" and see free schools as therapeutic communities. Others want to develop an alternative life-style. Still others want to create a counterculture school with a radical political orientation. This mixed bag not only fails to encourage a productive orchestration of the many unglamorous administrative and management tasks necessary to support any new organization, but invites divisiveness and dissipates reform energies.

In brief, those within the free school movement do not agree with each other; it is difficult, for example, to reconcile the differences between those who would pursue the self-centered interests of joy and ecstasy and those who would emphasize political action against social injustices. Also, many of the older students who choose these alternative schools expect too much from them. Free schools, like most schools, cannot hope to deal with youth's deep-rooted problems of alienation and confusion.

For Graubard and the other radical reformers, not only is the likely incremental pace of reform within public schools too slow and too late, but any attempt to incorporate free schools within the system seems virtually predestined to result in a serious compromise with their true value. Structured public schools continue to transmit the dominant culture of American society, a culture that for radical reformers is not worth transmitting. Increasingly, therefore, Graubard sees the mission of free schools becoming more and more political. Ultimately, under the terms of radical reform, what is necessary is the halting of the operation of existing public schools and the substitution of politically oriented free schools—a revolution that clearly has all the odds against it.

The odds are similarly stacked against a revolution brought about by "citizens," as Thomas Robischon, of Antioch College-West, warned the Commission. Speaking for the tiny alternative school movement in the Los Angeles area (1,500 students of a total enrollment of 614,000), Robischon declared:

> To my surprise, and to my disappointment, I have found that it is just not enough to turn a school over to parents and children and a staff, and expect that a lot of differences in the school will result. There are differences, a lot of them good, and enough of them thus far to keep me from giving up all hope. But they represent little basic change, by which I mean vesting control of these schools in those most affected by the decision making. What shift of control there has been has been almost entirely confined to a shift to adult control, not to control by young people. [We are repeatedly told] that something like 60 to 70 percent of Americans are satisfied with their schools. I think I could agree with that. What I disagree with is the idea . . . that the dissatisfied 30 to 40 percent would, if given the power, produce better schools . . . .
>
> A sizable number of adults I have seen in alternative schools, who have passionately and sincerely condemned their regular schools and vowed never to institute their practices in their own alternative schools, have shown in the clutch that there is a big gap between their heads and their guts.[10]

Nevertheless, both the rhetoric and practice of free schools have, in fact and already, begun to stimulate alternatives within the monolithic public schools. This new alternative movement within the public schools can lead to significant achievable reform, reform that does not scrap everything and does not have to impose a new orthodoxy on others. Free schools also have provided the training ground for much of the current leadership necessary for a new alternative reform effort in public schools.

Alternative public schools—by the choice of teachers, students, and parents—appear to be a far more promising and plausible approach to school reform than is the radical conception projected by the push for free schools. Thus, while free schools have not generated a massive radical reform movement, it can be said that they have influenced a progressive change process within public schools. This stimulation alone justifies the existence of free schools and establishes their role in the history of American education.

Another movement stimulating alternative education grows in part out of the British experience (including the years of World War II) that supported the progressive principles of education articulated by John Dewey. This is the currently popular view of education variously called "British infant," "integrated day," "open," or "informal" education.

While not as radical as the alternatives embraced by those in the counterculture, the open classroom has become increasingly prevalent within the public system of education. Such books as *Crisis in the Classroom,* by Charles E. Silberman, helped popularize this philosophy with the general public. Moreover, teachers, school administrators, and professors have embraced it, rekindling a new interest in Dewey and the progressive education movement of the earlier part of this century. While the advocates of the open classroom believe in giving the learner more freedom, they limit this freedom when it comes to determining the common content areas for which the school is responsible, such as the three Rs, sciences, and languages. Open classrooms have become alternatives in which the learner is free to explore these academic areas in a more natural, personal, and experiential way. Teachers are more likely to be resources to the learner in these settings. In other words, there are still schools and classrooms, only now the structure is more informal.

These major movements helped highlight other alternatives that had either been around for years or were recently in operation because of the growing dissatisfaction of consumers. Montessori education, for instance, became an important alternative. In New York City, Harlem Prep and the Street Academy became prominent specimens of schools that took public school casualties and made them successful college-bound students. In Philadelphia, the Parkway School triggered a nationwide awareness of the concept of the city as a classroom.

Alternatives through Vouchers

Recently the crisis in education has been linked to the citizen's pocketbook; in a tightening economy the educational consumers have begun to raise questions. Are the federally supported programs in education working? Did the financial investments of the 1960s pay off?

Reports from the field on programs such as Title I of the Elementary and Secondary Education Act of 1965 are far from promising. There is, in addition, a growing awareness that add-on, compensatory-type approaches to school improvement really result in more money being spent in the same old ways, the very ways that are being subjected to increased criticism by growing numbers of students and parents—the educational consumers themselves.

As Americans recognized the importance of quality education for their own survival—at times in desperation—education vouchers entered the picture. One of today's most controversial reform proposals, vouchers are an attempt to generate needed change by altering existing misallocations of resources between rich and poor children. The voucher increases the purchasing power of the educational consumer, usually the poor, for different forms of education in a type of free market enterprise. Some families that would likely utilize such vouchers are, however, dissatisfied with public schools. The plan would favor private schools, which is why some use the term "external voucher" in referring to such a proposal. The Office of Economic Opportunity, which tested the feasibility of vouchers, reported:

It is readily apparent that the education system is failing the poor—both by failing to provide adequate skills and by failing to retain children in school.

One reason for this disparity could well be that poor parents have little opportunity to affect the type of quality of education received by their children. The poor have no means by which to make the education system more responsive to their needs and desires. More affluent parents usually can obtain a good education for their children because they can choose schools for their children to attend—either by deciding where to live or by sending the children to private schools . . . .

The Office of Economic Opportunity therefore has begun to seek a means to introduce greater accountability and parental control into schools in such a way that the poor would have a wider range of choices, that the schools would remain attractive to the more affluent. This has led to consideration of an experiment in which public education money would be given directly to parents in the form of vouchers or certificates, which the parents could then take to the school of their choice, public or nonpublic, as payment for their children's education.[11]

The voucher proposals suggest that funds devoted to the financing of public schools be transferred to the parents in the form of redeemable coupons. These coupons, worth the cost of a year's schooling per child, are to be used to support the schools of the parent's choice —public or private, parochial, profit-making, and so on. Schools would cash in the vouchers at proposed Education Voucher Authorities, which would supervise the institutions participating in the plan.

The voucher idea sounds simple, but presently none of the several proposals is acceptable to all. The problem lies with both the economics and politics of each.

Milton Friedman, the original contemporary proponent of the voucher idea, eleven years ago introduced a model in which all parents receive a basic voucher that might be supplemented at will from personal income. Better known as the unregulated voucher model, this plan has come under increased criticism, for wealthy parents could easily match the value of the voucher and thus send their children to better, or at least more expensive, schools. If this occurred, Friedman's model would probably broaden the gap between rich and poor. The plan might operate as a "partial" scholarship for a few of the most talented poor to attend expensive schools, but this does not seem a sufficient incentive to recommend the proposal over the present system.

A second voucher plan developed by former Harvard Dean Theodore Sizer and Phillip Whitten proposes that the value of a voucher be invertibly related to family income. That is, families with incomes below $2,000 would receive vouchers worth a set amount; the value of the voucher would decline to zero as the family's income approached the national average. Though this sliding scale voucher would help poor families in purchasing private education, it would be a coarse equalizer, for it would not consider how much personal income a family is willing to spend on education.

... such discrimination in favor of the poor not only raises possible equal protection problems, but may also discriminate against the "near poor" or students of more affluent families who fail to supplement their vouchers as much as was "predicted" for their income level.

Furthermore, experience in other subsidized areas, such as food stamps and housing, provides little hope for legislative adoption of a system that effectively enables poor families to compete in purchasing services. Because the Sizer-Whitten model is not proposed as a substitute for the present system of state administered education, but rather is designed as a supplement in which poor families are subsidized in choosing private schools, the proposal does not discuss state involvement in any nonfinancial areas. Educational standards and equality of educational opportunity, for example, are not considered. [12]

John Coons has proposed a voucher model under which parents would choose schools of various levels of expenditures to which to send their children, the lowest level being roughly that of present public school expenditures. The parent would receive a voucher about equal to the per pupil cost at this lowest level and would have the option of supplementing that voucher. (As in Friedman's plan, the wealthy would be able to choose a more expensive school for their children as they could more easily supplement the voucher.) This system would be combined with a compensatory scheme so that a parent's economic effort in educating his child was measured relative to his income, the result being a wider separation between the "best" and the "worst" schools. Critics of Coons's plan conclude that this model would accelerate the inequalities in outcome of schooling and would penalize children whose parents have little interest in education.

A fourth plan is the achievement model. Under this plan the value of a student's voucher would be determined by the "success" in educating him, rather than by the student's economic qualifications. "A school's income would be determined by how much progress its students need. That progress would be measured by standardized tests. The difficulty of separating aptitude from achievement in such tests, the questionable relationship between high test scores and later success, and the importance of socio-economic status and race as determinants of test results are all reasons why this model is found unacceptable . . . ." [13]

The voucher proposals mentioned here, as well as others, cannot deal in any significant way with the disparity of revenue between school districts either in a state or between states, as long as property taxes are the main sources of school revenue. While there is a general mood of discontent toward the overreliance on the property tax for financing public schools, there is another dimension that may really become the legal basis for reform. This dimension concerns the fact that the way the property tax works within most states results in unequal allocations of educational resources. This unequal allocation arbitrarily discriminates against the poor. That is to say, since property taxes are assessed according to wealth, the richer communities receive more revenues; those "privileged" public school districts can actually afford better educational services than the poor school districts. This unequal allocation of educational resources is considered by some citizens to be unconstitutional on the grounds that the system of property taxes for financing public schools actually denies children equal protection, which is guaranteed under the Fourteenth Amendment.

The problem of differential spending apparently will be resolved by the courts rather than by the use of vouchers. For instance, in a historic decision the Supreme Court of California, on August 30, 1971, tentatively concluded:

We have determined that this funding scheme invidiously discriminates against the poor because it makes the quality of the child's education a function of the wealth of his parents and neighbors. Recognizing as we must that the right to an education in our public schools is a fundamental interest which cannot be conditioned on wealth, we can discern no compelling state purpose necessitating the present method of financing. We have concluded, therefore, that such a system cannot withstand constitutional challenge and must fall before the equal protection clause.

This case, *Serrano* v. *Priest*, has launched a national dialogue on the inequities of the local property tax.[14] New York and New Jersey have proposed similar plans for full state funding to reduce inequities.

The voucher plan is an attempt at equalization, but it faces many difficult problems unless a more equitable framework for school finance is developed. Further:

Carried to its logical conclusion, . . . the parallel-school approach would reduce the scope of public education, if not dispense with it altogether. The establishment of private schools sufficient to handle significant numbers of poor children would require public support and, in effect, establish a private system of publicly-supported schools. Middle-income parents would demand similar privileges. For financial reasons alone, the parallel-school approach is hardly likely to become widespread in the foreseeable future; moreover, the scheme would founder on political, if not constitutional grounds . . . .[15]

At present the voucher plan could widen the gap because it can be used to continue economic segregation within the schools. If this segregation occurs, the vouchers would effectively become a subsidy for the rich and middle class. Vouchers could also lead to further racial segregation within external schools. There is, at present, no framework outside of the public school system that prevents this from happening. The system could, in addition, lead to public support of religious instruction, which might violate the prohibitions of the Constitution. "Several cases now in the judicial works will have a bearing on the legal status of vouchers. One of these is *Flask* v. *Gardner,* which challenges the use of federal funds to pay for educational services conducted in religious-sponsored schools under Title I of ESEA. If the courts should decide that the use of funds in this way is unconstitutional, the legality of the voucher concepts so far as the religious-related schools are concerned would be dubious indeed."[16]

Others question whether parents, particularly low-income parents, are capable or have the desire to choose sources of education for their children. Many wonder, in addition, whether a voucher system would jeopardize the public schools which might be forced to become schools of the last resort.

The Office of Economic Opportunity has financed a voucher experiment in California that comes close to public schools of choice. Faced with resistance to an "external" voucher, and in the absence of enabling state legislation, OEO decided to consider demonstration of a transitional type of voucher. This transitional voucher would involve only public schools (or private schools operating under contract to the public schools) and could serve as a pilot for an expanded effort later on. After feasibility grants had been made in five school districts, OEO decided to implement a transitional plan in the Alum Rock Public Schools (in San Jose, California) for the school year 1972-1973. Surveys conducted in Alum Rock indicated considerable community support for educational experimentation and alternative forms of education. One survey showed, for example, that 56 percent of the parents felt that schools should try new ideas, while 74 percent of the teachers and 78 percent of the administrators thought that experimentation, including experimentation with alternatives, was a good thing. On March 8, 1972, the Alum Rock School Board authorized the superintendent to develop a transitional voucher demonstration. After revision, the proposal specified:

Parents in the attendance areas of the six pilot school districts will receive vouchers worth about $680 for children in kindergarten through sixth grade and about $970 for those in seventh and eighth grades. This amount represents the current average cost of educating a child in the Alum Rock School District.

. . . Each of the six principals (program managers) with their staff will develop two or more alternative, distinct education programs. The programs will operate simultaneously in one or more buildings. The alternatives will be developed with the full cooperation of the community. Efforts also will be made to encourage private organizations and parent and other public groups to develop programs that would be operated under contract with the public school board . . . .

The Alum Rock transition model differs structurally from the original voucher model in four essential ways:

1. The EVA (Educational Voucher Administration) will function as an advisory board to the school board rather than as an autonomous, publicly constituted body.
2. Interested new school groups will have to contract with the school board to become eligible for voucher funds, rather than apply to the EVA for certification.
3. Six schools and approximately 4,000 students will participate in the first year of operation, rather than the original expected 12,000 to 15,000 pupils.
4. Each of the six schools will offer at least two alternative programs rather than one.

Further, the Alum Rock school district has committed itself to expansion during the second year if the demonstration is successful; if not, the project will be phased out.[17]

The true merit of the current interest in educational vouchers is that it has provided a new way of looking at the problem of delivering quality education to dissatisfied consumers. This new viewpoint has stimulated public schools to create educational alternatives themselves. In so doing, the external voucher has prompted the development of the internal voucher plan, which does not demand the creation of still another bureaucratic regulatory agency to facilitate its implementation. The public schools have the capacity and the resources to operate such a system internally; the creation of a system outside the public school system is less necessary and less desirable. The emphasis of vouchers on alternatives has given the public school mechanism a new mission in the use of existing resources. But can available resources—facilities and personnel—be utilized differently, perhaps more efficiently, to provide alternative education within our public schools?

Public Schools of Choice

The alternative public schools plan calls for cooperation of teachers, parents, and students in the development of a variety of legitimate educational options within our public schools. Choice is a key term in this plan: each of the participating groups—teachers, parents, and students (the agents closest to the action)—has a choice of the option that best supports its style.

"Public Schools of Choice," the title we give to the concept, is also based on the assumption that each teacher has a style of teaching and each student a style of learning. Providing opportunities for a more compatible matching of teaching-learning styles can help promote further the long-held educational ideals of individualization and personalization. Teachers will perform a key role, not only in deciding which of the alternatives best supports their teaching style, but also in designing options. Since parents, students, and teachers are brought together by mutual consent and not by chance, the mismatches of the past, which led to frustration for both teacher and student, can be avoided.

The concept of Public Schools of Choice establishes standard education as a legitimate option. We have in the past overloaded the standard pattern of education, expecting this approach to reach all teachers, students, and parents, but no one pattern can reach everyone, and in a diverse society such as ours, a responsive system of public education provides a range of options and choices, including the standard.

To get any new system to operate, participants must agree on ground rules. To make Public Schools of Choice work, the following ground rules are essential:

1. No alternative within a public system of choice practices exclusivity. No school or alternative can exclude a child because of race, religion, financial status, or, within reason, the nature of previous educational background. The schools must be truly open, able to survive on the basis of their educational merits and their ability to meet the needs of the students and the parents they serve.

2. Each school works toward a comprehensive set of educational objectives. These objectives or educational goals must be common to all schools within the system of choice. They should include mastery of the basic skills, nurturing of physical and emotional development, and vocational and avocational preparation. The student must be equipped with a broad range of skills so that he will have as many alternatives and opportunities as possible for social and educational mobility. Within the system the real issue is not what goals to set, but how best to achieve them. The system itself seeks new means of increasing the chances for the student to mature as a maker of choices rather than to be a mere victim of circumstances.

3. *A ground rule intrinsic to the idea of a free and open society and, therefore, to the notion of Public Schools of Choice is that no person or group imposes an educational plan or design.* Within a system of choice, the consumer shops around as in a supermarket or cafeteria, choosing, testing, and finally settling on a school or learning environment that appeals to him. If 90 percent of the consumers settle on one approach and only 10 percent on another, then 90 percent of the system's schools provide the first approach and 10 percent the second. Each community has to determine how many consumers are necessary to warrant setting up a new alternative. The point here, however, is that once the minimum percentage is established, the individual consumer can choose his own option, rather than having to accept one program because there are no alternatives. Teachers are also free to choose the alternatives that best support their style of teaching; no one alternative is imposed on them. New approaches will, of course, necessitate the retraining of teachers, but this can become an integral part of the staff development program of the school district.

4. *Each new alternative can eventually operate on a financial level equivalent to the per capita cost of the school district as a whole.* Although each new option may be permitted some additional costs for initial planning and development, it must within a reasonable period of time conform to the standard cost per student of the total system. This ground rule ensures that a public school system of choice results in a wiser, more productive use of existing monies.

Some may ask whether a Nazi school or an antiwhite school for blacks could exist within the framework of a public system of choice. Obviously it could not because openness is a necessity, and the system values diversity, is democratic, and is unswerving in its recognition of individual worth. Within these bounds, however, there is a full spectrum of alternative possibilities with new forms of education and learning. Schools could, for example, emphasize science or languages or the arts; they could be graded or ungraded, open or traditional, technical or nontechnical; they could seek a multicultural approach or work to strengthen particular ethnic and group identities. Each, however, must meet principles fundamental to a public school system of choice. Respecting the rights and responsibilities of others, for example, cannot work if the option being promulgated is based on a system that advocates the imposition of one's own values on others.

5. Each alternative provides an approach to education alongside the existing pattern, which continues to be legitimate. Every legitimate educational option is equally valid. The standard approach to education, therefore, is an important alternative and should not be eliminated or forced to take the most criticism.

6. Each alternative includes a plan for evaluation. Since each alternative needs to achieve the same ends, assessment is essential for at least two reasons: to gather information as a basis for continuing to improve the option; and to help determine the relative effectiveness of each option.

What constitutes a legitimate educational option under these rules is a critical question.

Public schools have a responsibility to equip each learner with the skills needed for economic, political, and social survival. They must, at the same time, provide him with the tools needed for improving, transforming, and reconstructing elements of the environment generally recognized as inimical to the noblest aspirations of the nation or as detrimental to the growth and development of the individual. Public schools must also provide opportunities for each learner to discover his talents and to link these talents to economic careers. Thus, the objectives of economic "livelihood" form an important set of educational ends. If an educational option discounted this set of objectives, it would be suspect as a legitimate alternative within the framework of public education.

Public Schools of Choice can work only when students, parents, teachers, and administrators all have equal access to educational options at both the conceptual and operational levels. But, unless the parent or consumer is aware of the existence of new alternatives, he is left with only those with which he is familiar and is forced to play by the ground rules established by the existing system. What mechanism must be developed, then, to bring relevant educational information to the public? The administration of a school system might assume the role of leadership by arranging informational meetings with the groups involved. Such meetings could lead parents' associations to hold additional meetings to explore educational options. Students' groups at the elementary, junior high, and high school levels and teachers' organizations could do the same thing. After careful planning, the school system could launch trial programs, either in one school or in a cluster of schools. Under certain conditions, a whole district could mount a special program.

While the system works best when an entire school participates and provides many options for all students and teachers, it may be desirable to start by trying options not too dissimilar to the school's present operational style.

Developing choices at the individual school level can, however, pose a number of problems. For example, as the different segments of the public explore new options, one group might find itself involved in scanning an almost endless list of reading materials. This would not necessarily be bad, but it could leave the participants with a narrow view of the learning process. If, on the other hand, a community undertook a conceptual examination of educational alternatives, participants might indeed achieve a better background for decision making. It is one thing to become knowledgeable about a concept or idea and quite another to become familiar with the intricate details that go into making the idea work. While it is obvious that some knowledge of detail is necessary, students, parents, and citizens in general need not be as well informed about the subtleties of pedagogy as are professionals.

Professional educators have the responsibility for the substance and techniques of education, but the consumers must be responsible for determining the kind of education they want. They must, therefore, have the opportunity to perform this crucial role in the formation of policy. Thus, a new standard of professional and lay participation could lead to more sensible educational conceptions, supported by both groups.

There are various ways of providing educational options based on choice. They can be based on existing teaching styles; classroom patterns (standard, Montessori, behavior modification, British infant); teams of teachers forming schools within schools (Quincy, Illinois, Senior High II with seven subschools—standard, flexible, independent, fine arts, career, special, and vocational); or "new" school options housed in a setting apart from established schools (four "off site" alternative schools located in different areas of the Los Angeles school system).

Once optional education and the ground rules of the system of choice are understood, an entire district may want to develop a framework of alternatives for its schools. The following is a typical list from which parents, students, teachers, and administrators can choose.

The first alternative is a traditional approach. It is graded and emphasizes the learning of basic skills by cognition. The learning environment is the classroom, which functions with one or two teachers instructing and directing students at their various learning tasks. Students are encouraged to adjust to the school and its operational style, rather than vice versa, and those students with recognized learning problems are referred to a variety of remedial and support programs. A central board of education determines the entire educational and fiscal policy for the school.

There has, recently, been a national movement toward returning to the "traditional" or "basic approach" as an alternative to the open education that has become the rule, rather than the exception, in many public school systems. Proponents would substitute the "old" math for the "new" math, would concentrate heavily on reading, writing, and arithmetic, and would even implement dress codes. The school board in Prince George's County, Maryland, recently ordered establishment of three such schools. Skeptics have maintained that the schools these alternatives would replace never really have become open or free and that those promoting the "basics" also favor censorship of textbooks and sex education programs. School districts planning to move in this direction, according to the critics, should first intelligently examine their educational philosophies. But, so long as these basic schools are not forced upon students and so long as there are other choices available, they fall well within our Public Schools of Choice.

The second alternative is the nontraditional and nongraded school. It resembles in many ways the British primary school with a large number of constructional and manipulative materials in each area where students work and learn. The teacher acts as a facilitator—one who assists and guides, rather than directs and instructs. Most of the activity of students is in the form of specialized learning projects carried on individually and in small groups. Many of the learning experiences and activities take place outside the school.

The third alternative emphasizes the development of talent and focuses on creative experiences, human services, and concentration in a particular field, such as art, media, space, science, dramatics, or music. The school defines its role as diagnostic and prescriptive: it identifies the learner's talents and orchestrates whatever experiences seem necessary to develop and enhance them. It encourages many styles of learning and teaching. Students may achieve by demonstration and by manipulation of real objects as well as by verbal, written, or abstract performances.

The fourth alternative is oriented to techniques. It utilizes computers to help diagnose individual needs and abilities and provides computer-assisted instruction based on these diagnoses. The library stocks tape recordings and has carrels in which students, on their own, can talk to and listen to tapes or work with manipulatable objects. In addition, wide use is made of educational media, which enables students and teachers to individualize many of the learning tasks. The school also has facilities for closed-circuit television.

The fifth alternative is a total community school. Operating on a twelve- to fourteen-hour basis at least six days a week throughout the year, it provides educational and other services for children of varying ages from the neighborhood and evening classes and activities for adults. Services in such areas as health, legal aid, and employment are available within the school facility. Paraprofessionals or community teachers contribute to every phase of the regular school program. A community board governs the school. An example is the new Dunbar Community High School in Baltimore.

The sixth alternative has a Montessori environment. Students move at their own pace and are largely self-directed. The learning areas are rich in materials and specialized learning instruments from which the students can select as they wish. Although teachers operate within a specific, defined methodology, they remain in the background, guiding students rather than instructing them. Special emphasis is placed on the development of the five senses.

The seventh alternative, patterned after the Multi-Culture Institute in San Francisco, may have four or five ethnic groups equally represented in the student body. Students spend part of each day in racially heterogeneous learning groups. During another part of the day students and teachers of the same ethnic background meet together and study the culture, language, customs, history, and heritage of their ethnic groups. A policy board made up of equal numbers of parents and teachers runs the school and is only tangentially responsible to the central board of education.

The eighth alternative is subcontracted. For example, a group of teachers, parents, and students could be delegated authority to operate a particular alternative school, or certain private alternative schools can petition to become part of the public school system.

Alternatives help give new direction to pre- and in-service education of teachers. If some options are in greater demand than others, then certain teachers (perhaps those who express the desire) can be helped to staff them. After all, even if there were no options, teachers would still require in-service education.

Public school alternatives can encourage closer ties between the community and the schools and between professionals and laymen. Without professional leadership that promotes cooperation of all parties concerned, alternatives can be imposed and often opposed.

The public school alternatives system would be a renewal system, that is, the options under a broad public framework would be judged by results. As the results associated with quality education were realized more in one model than in another, the attractiveness of the successful model would grow. The options that were more successful would most likely be in more demand, thus triggering a self-renewing process.

The Range of Educational Alternatives

One way to consider alternatives is to place them on a continuum on the basis of how much freedom a student has to choose the elements of learning. How much freedom does he have to choose the teacher, the content, the learning methodology, the time, the place? At one extreme the learner selects what he will learn, with whom, when, where, and how; here he has the greatest freedom. At the other extreme he has no choice of teacher, content, methodology, time, and place; institutional procedures and requirements predetermine the conditions of learning.

Between these extremes is a range of possibilities. The learner can be free to choose certain content areas, but not others, which are required for everyone (reading, writing, arithmetic, physical education, health). He may have some freedom concerning the way he wishes to approach these content areas (by reading a book, by viewing videotapes, by doing research, by listening to a lecture, by discussing with others). He may have some freedom to choose the time and place to learn, for example, by entering into a contract with the teacher to accomplish a project by a certain time.

There are obviously different types of free school alternatives—ranging from an Illich-Reimer model, which deemphasizes schooling, to a Summerhill model, which uses the school as a type of self-governing unit. Free school alternatives are the most difficult to legitimize under a public school framework at this time and will probably remain outside as private alternative schools since they run counter to the emerging ground rules for alternative public schools.

Another way to see the continuum is to consider how resources for education are utilized: by whom, for whom, when, where, how, and why? By focusing on "resource orchestration," we come up with a broadened conception of alternatives. At one end an institution, usually the school, decides what the student is to learn, when, where, how, why, and with whom. At the other the individual learner, at whatever age, orchestrates his own education. He may decide to study Chinese at Berlitz, learn writing from a journalist, listen to the world's great music at a free library, take guided tours of museums of arts and sciences, travel to different countries, assume an apprenticeship in a law office. At this level the learner uses and tailors these educational resources to fit his needs and style. He may prefer to arrange his activities for late afternoon and evening rather than have the time and place imposed. Under individual educational orchestration guidance is available upon request. The learner is a consumer of various educational services, such as seminars and tours, which are purchased as needed.

Most of the alternatives discussed here are impossible without flexible and humane local, state, and national laws and regulations. States may need to reexamine compulsory attendance laws, and their departments of education may need to make more flexible regulations governing graduation from high school. Maryland, for example, recently issued a new set of high school graduation requirements that makes alternative approaches to the diploma possible.

Educational litigation has begun to run in the direction of consumer rights in education. The Peter Doe and Lau cases in California, the Portales case in New Mexico, and the Aspira case in New York, each established an important beginning in guaranteeing each learner the kind of education that he or she needs to achieve quality education. We are at the brink of legally guaranteeing each learner options in public education. These pioneer cases can expand fields of law that are necessary in a period of educational reform.

The inclusion of parents, students, teachers, and administrators in planning choices and decisions will further assure a desirable outcome.

Notes

1. Center for Options in Public Education, Indiana University, *Changing Schools,* a newsletter on alternative public schools (No. 11), 2.

2. Atlanta hearing of NCCE Commission on Educational Governance, August 1974, III, 67.

3. St. Louis hearing of NCCE Commission on Educational Governance, May 1974, 269.

4. Minneapolis hearing of NCCE Commission on Educational Governance, April 1974, 72.

5. Atlanta hearing of NCCE Commission on Educational Governance, August 1974, III, 57, 58.

6. Minneapolis hearing of NCCE Commission on Educational Governance, April 1974, 115.

7. *Ibid.,* 131.

8. *Ibid.,* 70.

9. Allen Graubard, *Free the Children: Radical Reform and the Free School Movement* (New York: Pantheon, 1973), 13.

10. Los Angeles hearing of NCCE Commission on Educational Governance, October 1974, 70-71.

11. Office of Economic Opportunity Report, Washington, D.C., January 1971, 18.

12. Judith Areen, "Educational Vouchers," Hearings before the Select Committee on Equal Opportunity of the U.S. Senate, 92nd Congress, Washington, D.C., December 1, 2, 3, 1971, Part 22, 11133.

13. Irene Solet, "Education Vouchers: An Evaluation," Washington Research Project, Hearings before the Select Committee, 11131.

14. Cal. 3rd. 584. See *Current History* (July 1972), 28 ff., for excerpts.

15. Mario D. Fantini, *Alternatives for Urban School Reform,* reprint (New York: Ford Foundation, Office of Reports, 1974), 9-10.

16. David Selden, "Vouchers—Solution or Sop?" Hearings before the Select Committee, Part 16D, 17741.

17. "A Proposed Demonstration in Education Vouchers," Office of Economic Opportunity, Office of Planning, Research, and Evaluation, Pamphlet 3400-8, April 1972, 16-17, 20-21.

8

THE STRUCTURE OF CITIZEN PARTICIPATION: PUBLIC DECISIONS FOR PUBLIC SCHOOLS

Donald B. Reed   University of California, Riverside

Douglas E. Mitchell   University of California, Riverside

There has never been any doubt that citizen participation is a vital ingredient in American public education. Citizens and schoolmen alike have proclaimed its necessity and virtues in public school affairs. Lay control has been the ideal of school organization since the days of the founding fathers. But despite this tradition, skepticism increased during the last decade.

Citizen participation as a controversial issue in public education has emerged from the turmoil of the 1960s. The failure of desegregation in urban areas and the collapse of the "War on Poverty" both raised widespread doubts about the capacity of the schools to respond to the needs of urban communities and their citizens. These doubts have been joined by strong feelings that the schools are not performing adequately, are inflexible, and are too often unresponsive in their programs. Under these circumstances, citizen participation is no longer taken for granted.

As an issue in school governance, citizen participation has been shaped largely by two substantially independent developments of the post-World War II period: the "community relations" movement in school administration, and the "maximum feasible participation" of recent federal legislation concerning services to the poor. Each of these two broad social developments called for significant changes in the relationship between citizens and the schools. Only when they came together in the operation of Title I of the Elementary and Secondary Education Act of 1965 and its later amendments was it possible to see that, despite similarities in language, they were based on essentially different conceptions of how and why citizens should participate in school policy making.

One movement was based on the professional view of the citizen's role—that the citizen was to be used to buttress the professional's expertise and make the schools fit his image. The other, as seen in the Title I advisory groups that have gained legitimate authority, was based on a presumption of the citizen's legitimate voice in the operation of the schools.

Citizen participation in the schools was a matter of major interest in the early 1950s. One author, writing in 1952, reviewed nearly five hundred publications related to citizen participation. Nearly all of them had been written between 1940 and 1952. In the preface to his work he pointed to the renewed concern of the education profession with citizen participation: "The movement for citizen participation is the most promising educational movement of the day. It must not be allowed to fail."[1]

There were two reasons for this dramatic upsurge of professional interest in citizen involvement. First, schools were facing some very tough problems. There were too few dollars to meet the expanding needs of education, needs that had become urgent in the successful mobilization of the national economy for war. Schools, like other institutions, had been buffeted by the series of national emergencies, including the Great Depression, the Second World War, and the Korean conflict. A number of highly publicized public fights had broken out over school programs, practices, and personnel. Finally, the movement to secure equality of educational opportunity for minorities, which led to the Supreme Court's desegregation decision in 1954, was well under way and exerting substantial pressure for change on the schools.

These problems alone would not account for the widespread interest of professional educators in citizen participation. A second factor was a revolution in the theories of administration being studied and taught in universities training school administrators. The revolution in administrative theory became known as the "human relations" approach to administration. To oversimplify dramatically its central idea, the human relations approach was based on the realization that if people are involved in making the decisions affecting their lives, they will tend to support them. If this is true, the human relations theorists reasoned, citizen participation in school decision making should go far toward increasing support for the public schools. This idea was captured in the title of the 1954 Yearbook of the prestigious National Society of the Study of Education, *Citizen Cooperation for Better Public Schools,* which was devoted entirely to the problems and prospects for citizen participation in education.[2]

This belief that increased citizen participation would lead to greater cooperation and less conflict in the schools accounted for a tremendous growth in the number of citizens' committees created at every level in public education over the past three decades. It is unfortunate that, as we have seen, the confident predictions of the 1950s have not been borne out, and conflict and turbulence increased throughout the 1960s and into the 1970s. Several efforts were made to explain the persistence of conflict in the face of the prodigious efforts of schoolmen to increase citizen participation. Many administrators found citizens uninterested or unwilling to engage in cooperative activities, and by the mid-1960s some observers were beginning to reassess the basis of the participation movement. One book, provocatively entitled *School-Community Relations: A New Approach,* asserted flatly: "The traditional public relations program of the school consisting, as it does, of 'telling and selling' the community on education, is outmoded."[3]

One major problem with the human relations movement seemed to be that it sought citizen participation *in order* to get cooperation and support and thus all too frequently became more a public relations campaign than a process of public participation. But even where participation was serious and not marred by the general tendency of schools to co-opt rather than cooperate with citizens, there were continuing and serious conflicts over school policy. These conflicts might have led to the abandonment of interest in citizen participation had it not been for the growth of federal legislation mandating this participation in the planning and control of federal programs.

Even though this policy has had a tremendous impact on schools, federal interest in citizen participation was not aimed initially at education. Federal policy has been, in fact, more related to the problems of minorities, urban centers, and the poor than to schools directly. Five pieces of legislation chart the history of federal involvement in this area: the Housing Act of 1949, the Juvenile Delinquency and Youth Offenses Control Act of 1961, the Economic Opportunity Act of 1964, the Model Cities legislation of 1966, and the Elementary and Secondary Education Act of 1965.

Federal Legislation Affecting Education

The thrust of Title I of the Housing Act of 1949 was slum clearance and urban renewal. The act was aimed at clearing and rejuvenating blighted urban areas while at the same time raising a city's income potential through increased property valuation. Local implementation of the legislation was motivated not so much by humanitarian ideals, such as providing suitable living conditions for poor people, as it was by the possibility of transforming unattractive city areas into more pleasing ones in a profitable way.[4]

Legislation regarding urban renewal required "citizen participation" in the planning and development projects before federal money could be spent on renewal projects. This participation took the form of "civic leaders" who represented various groups and interests sitting as board members of urban renewal agencies. These agencies or boards were charged with implementing federal policy, setting local policy, and overseeing a professional planning staff. Poor people—the very people affected by urban renewal projects—were generally excluded from these boards. This led to the formation of spontaneous organizations that resisted urban renewal.

The initial burst of enthusiasm for urban renewal from coalitions of "liberals, planners, mayors, businessmen and real estate interests," followed by the gradual demise of these coalitions when "the hidden political costs began to become evident," has been described by James Q. Wilson.[5] He also reported that "Voters who did not like being called slum dwellers and who liked even less being forced out of their old neighborhoods began to complain."[6] Thus, the urban renewal legislation produced a series of important unanticipated consequences with regard to citizen participation.

While those people most affected by the housing aspects of urban renewal were neither consulted nor involved in the planning of the initial projects, this trend was soon to change. "Many of the earliest redevelopment projects were completed with little organized opposition. Somehow, however, people have learned from the experience of others, and today, in cities that have engaged in renewal for several years, the planners often find prospective renewal areas ready and waiting for them organized to the teeth."[7] Those living in neighborhoods slated for urban renewal found that although they did not participate in the planning of the total projects, they had a powerful veto over them. Furthermore, since many urban renewal projects were planned for predominantly black neighborhoods, they were viewed as a program under the guise of slum clearance that was really Negro clearance.

The story of urban renewal is complex and will not be recounted here, but several important points should be made. The blue-ribbon city renewal agencies in many instances were found not to represent the feelings of the residents of the areas affected by renewal projects. These residents discovered that they could veto urban renewal projects in their neighborhoods if they were willing to organize and resist with direct political action. And planners were forced to recognize local neighborhood participation as necessary in order to proceed with projects. Thus, the renewal legislation forced city officials, at least city planners, to rethink their ideas of citizen participation. Participation no longer could be considered solely the domain of a blue-ribbon civic elite, but had to include residents of local neighborhoods.

Another landmark in the recent history of citizen participation came in the Juvenile Delinquency and Youth Offenses Control Act of 1961. The importance of this legislation is its direct stimulation of broad citizen participation. It contained the idea that citizens themselves should help plan welfare and crime-fighting programs.

But the piece of federal legislation that gave real meaning to the term "participation" was the Economic Opportunity Act of 1964. In addition to deepening the federal interest in participation through such programs as Headstart and Follow Through, this legislation provided for the establishment of Community Action Agencies in urban centers. The legislation stated the community action programs were to be "developed, conducted, and administered with the maximum feasible participation of the residents of the area and members of the group served."[8]

It was in this last statement that the legislation mandated a "new" type of citizen participation: the agency boards, unlike the urban renewal boards, were not intended to include only civic leaders, but were to include community members who would be the direct beneficiaries of the programs. This meant that groups that had not formally been included (or as some argue, had been traditionally excluded) in city governance would now be participating members; these were, of course, poor and minority citizens.

The words "maximum feasible participation" prompted much activity following the enactment of this legislation. There were no traditions for including local citizens in policy-making roles in federal agencies, and the legislation did not make it clear how this was to be accomplished; in many instances, the citizen participation generated by the Economic Opportunity Act appeared to local officials, federal officials, and the national administrator of the OEO agency as unpredictable and uncontrollable. Sit-ins, boycotts, and picketing frequently were attributed to the maximum feasible participation section of the legislation. Claims of misappropriation of agency funds were frequently cited and still are, more than a decade later, though most of the OEO programs have been dismantled.

This energetic outburst of total citizen participation was relatively short lived. The 1967 Green Amendment to the Economic Opportunity Act required that one-third of the boards' membership be public officials, one-third community people, and one-third representatives of the poor.

The dismantling of the OEO by the Nixon administration and the transfer of the continuing programs to other federal agencies seem to have brought an end to maximum feasible participation, at least insofar as it was experienced under the Economic Opportunity Act. The effort to involve the poor in designing and administering programs of which they would be the beneficiaries was by and large unsuccessful.

Many of the activities of the Community Action Agencies and the local neighborhood groups were, moreover, viewed by city officials as disruptive and illegitimate. And as the original economic opportunity legislation was written, local officials had no political power in the local Community Action Agencies. As a consequence, the politicians brought pressure at the federal level to change this. Finally, the lifeblood of the citizen participation mandated by the Economic Opportunity Act was the money that came directly from the federal government to the Community Action Agencies. By adjusting the formula for the membership of the Community Action Agencies and their funding, Washington seemed to be able to control to some degree the intensity of citizen participation.

The fourth of the federal acts important to understanding citizen participation is the Model Cities Act of 1966. If the phrase "maximum feasible participation" of the Economic Opportunity Act had passed unnoticed through Congress, just the opposite was true with the Demonstration (Model) Cities Program. Sensitivity to the famous clause and pressure from local politicians led the framers of the Model Cities legislation to restrict and to define more carefully citizen participation. The Model Cities legislation reestablished local control over federal funds and defined citizen participation in such a way as clearly to restore control of the programs generated by the legislation to local officials and administrators.

These four pieces of federal legislation stand as important landmarks in the evolution of citizen participation at the grass roots. In the first—the urban renewal legislation—citizen participation occurred as an unanticipated consequence; in the second—the Juvenile Delinquency and Youth Offenses Control Act—a rationale was given for citizen participation; in the third—the Economic Opportunity Act—citizen participation was mandated, but produced unforeseen consequences; and in the fourth—the Model Cities legislation—guidelines were established to regulate, control, and reduce broad citizen participation.

It was through the fifth Great Society program, the Elementary and Secondary Education Act of 1965, that the federal government finally and fully required a measure of citizen control over federal aid to the schools. Title I of the act was the major federal effort in compensatory education, a program that has greatly altered the landscape of American education, especially in the cities.

Aimed at improving the education of poor (and mostly black) children, Title I has become, in almost a decade of existence, the major federal school aid program. It has become a fixture—but also a political football. Each year, Congress has tinkered with the spending formula of Title I, while local and state school officials complained about the confusion. Title I has managed to survive, however, in spite of, not because of, the yearly battle over its spending formula.

The correlation between poverty and low achievement, of course,

had been obvious to even the most casual observer even prior to
1965. Yet, somehow, people either failed or refused to view this
correlation within the context of overcrowded classes; substandard
curriculum, facilities, and materials; poor teaching; or the deprivation
of children. Because poor children did not achieve in a manner
familiar to or easily recognized by middle-class-oriented teachers, such
children were "excused" from learning. They were regarded as
incapable of academic achievement. Hence, they became part of a
negative cycle. Nothing was expected of them, and so there was no
incentive to prove otherwise. Even more serious was the fact that
poor children, more than any others, must have basic skills acquired
through an education if they are ever to break out of the cycle of
poverty and discrimination.

Title I set out to redress these grievances. Certainly it did not, and
has not, cured all of the problems. A major one it has not cured is
that many schools serving high concentrations of poor children in
run-down and impoverished facilities are usually segregated schools
for blacks.

Perhaps it is not surprising, in retrospect, that Title I was beset by
a series of scandals. Funds from the program, it was discovered, were
used to buy tuxedos for high school proms and band uniforms. It
was alleged that school districts were using the federal money to sup-
plant, rather than to supplement, regular state and local funds. Title
I, in short, was not finding its way to the poor. The federal government did not attempt to correct these problems until the early
1970s, and only then under considerable pressure. District-wide parent advisory councils were ordered as a condition for receiving the
federal aid. Gradually, and reluctantly, the federal government established guidelines for the "comparability" of the spending of Title I;
that is, the federal funds must be spent over and above regular state
and local expenditures for each pupil.

School administrators were slow to establish the required new
advisory councils and even slower to grant them the considerable
authority over Title I that the new guidelines allowed. Title I was a
complicated program; the comparability regulation made it even
more complicated. With some exceptions, the school officials did
little to help citizens to understand the program. Many found it
much easier and more convenient to comply with the letter of the
law without complying with its spirit.

Imagine a new district-wide advisory council meeting with the education "professionals" (with at least six years of experience with Title I) in the early 1970s. The council is handed a 175-page application for the following year's program, full of words, and whole chapters, it cannot understand. It is asked to "sign off" on the application (that is, approve it) after a brief explanation from the superintendent or his delegate.

Information on Title I—the schools designated to receive the funds and what they were to be spent on—was to be readily available to citizens in general, not only to the parents' councils. Usually it was not.

Despite these drawbacks, Title I served to increase significantly the sophistication of inner-city parents across the nation. Over the years these councils have had considerable success. They have forced big-city school administrations to comply with the spirit of Title I guidelines. With much coordinating help from several organizations, including the National Committee for Citizens in Education, a loose network of Title I advisory councils was formed. In its hearings, in fact, the Commission on Educational Governance found considerable knowledge about Title I in the five cities surveyed. The requirements in the federal act for parents' participation have served to thrust several inner-city residents, usually poor and black, to the forefront. Their testimony might not have been smooth and articulate, but it was always succinct and usually dramatic. Significantly missing was similar testimony from suburban witnesses, presumably because in middle-class and affluent districts the pressures exerted by parents upon every aspect of school life, from curriculum to class size to teacher competence, are taken as a matter of course.

Such is not the case in the relationship between school staff and the parents of poor and minority children. This is why the testimony of one witness from St. Louis, who told how the Title I advisory group had recommended returning Title I funds to the government because the parents wanted a say in the hiring of personnel, was so remarkable and refreshing.

Why had the same educators who had embraced human relations as a means to garner support for the schools found it so easy to ignore the spirit, if not the letter, of these federal mandates? The answer may lie in the intent of the federal legislation, whose goal was what might be called political rather than administrative participation. That is, it was far less concerned with the smooth functioning of public services than it was with the representation of poor and minority citizens in decision making. Educators who fostered citizen participation from an administrative point of view in order to produce support for public school policies found in the federal guidelines little assistance in gaining public cooperation.

Citizens who are trying to get the schools to respond to their needs and desires generally do not think about whether they are dealing with political or administrative processes. The hearings showed abundantly, in fact, that citizens feel that administrators are highly political in their activities or that elected officials are sometimes appendages of school administrators. This view is understandable since "politics" in its broadest definition includes all interactions between two or more individuals in any effort to influence or control the decision-making process. However, administrative participation, that is, participation in the decisions made by administrators, yields quite different outcomes from those arising from political participation.

Political Participation in Local School Districts

The focal point for the political participation of citizens in school governance is their selection of school board members. Most such members are elected rather than appointed to office,[9] and they constitute the largest group of elected officials in the United States. The precise method of selecting school boards varies from state to state and is regulated by state laws. Among the approximately 5 percent of appointed boards are those representing some of the largest urban school districts. These appointment procedures are found generally in cities least affected by the urban reform movement that brought nonpartisan elections, civil service, tenure for teachers, and other significant organizational and political reforms into general use in American politics.

Even though a large percentage of board members are elected, actually more than 34 percent have taken their seats on the board by appointment or through uncontested elections.[10] This strange phenomenon occurs because a substantial number of board members who are not going to seek reelection resign from the board shortly before the completion of their term of office, which permits their colleagues on the board to select a successor who will be compatible with the views of the other incumbents. Once appointed to the board, the new member has the opportunity to run for election as an incumbent, an advantage in any popular election.

In the typical school board election, however, the main problem is getting individuals to run for or assume the office; it is not one of unfair competition among potential board members (although the advantage enjoyed by an incumbent may well be partly responsible for discouraging other potential candidates from even running). The normal selection process would perhaps be better described as an "encouraging process." The "encouraging" of school board candidates is accomplished in a number of ways. A few communities use nominating caucuses, which are usually dominated by people who are closely aligned with the schools in the community. Members of these nominating committees frequently include local PTA leaders and past and present school board members. Most communities, however, have no formal mechanism for recruitment of school board candidates that is comparable to either the regular political nominating process or the membership recruitment practices of large social organizations. Most candidates are encouraged through informal friendships and social relationships. A sizable number of new board members are encouraged by either current board members or by professional school personnel.[11]

Participation by citizens in school board election campaigns is not extensive. Campaign workers are frequently PTA members acting together, but independent of their formal organization. Occasionally candidates have the informal assistance of political parties; in these cases the campaigns are run more skillfully and tend to have a higher probability of success.

Probably the most important fact about school board campaigns is that they are almost completely devoid of any real issues. More than half of all candidates report that their ideas about school policy are not significantly different from those of other candidates. And when incumbents are seeking reelection, the level of agreement among all candidates is even higher.[12]

There are a variety of reasons for the bland, noncontroversial nature of most board elections. First, it takes a knowledge of the problems and possibilities of school board decision making before an issue can even be developed, much less become central to the campaign for office. This knowledge is particularly lacking among voters and candidates alike when it comes to public schools. Although candidates typically have more information than voters, they do not have much more. And even though candidates tend to know more about school programs, they generally have very little knowledge of the activities of school boards, and thus cannot turn their knowledge about school programs into campaign issues.

It is not accidental that so few people, even those who regularly attend school board meetings, know so little about school affairs. In many cases information is exchanged and important decisions are made either informally or in sessions closed to the press and the public. The open public meetings of most school boards tend to be concerned with routine matters or those of minor importance.

If neither the candidates nor the public can acquire the information needed to frame an issue intelligently, there will be no way to generate serious public debate on substantive issues during school board campaigns.

It has also been argued that the public dislikes candidates who create division by developing positions on issues and seeking election on those issues. This dislike is the result of the hard-fought battle waged early in the twentieth century by progressives and urban reformers to remove partisan politics and the associated patronage system from the operation of schools. Candidates who state their positions on issues, violating the tradition of "just being for good, sound education," are frowned upon. They are, as a result, unlikely to receive widespread public support and are easily attacked by their opponents, not for being wrong on the issues but for injecting issues into the campaign.

Voting in school board elections has been historically lighter than in general elections. It is hard to be certain why this is true, but a number of contributing factors are easily identified. First, in most school districts elections are deliberately scheduled to be held in the off year and in the off season so as to remove them as completely as possible from any association with regular political elections. Second, the very low level of competition among candidates leads to less excitement and controversy. Third, the nonpartisan nature of school elections makes it difficult for the voter to differentiate among the candidates; he is not able to rely on any perceptions he might have about what sort of policies a Democrat or a Republican might pursue. Fourth, school board members typically do not establish a stable, identifiable constituency; instead, as the hearings confirmed, they tend to insist that they represent equally all segments of the school district. If all the candidates at least profess to represent all the people equally there is little reason to get too excited about which one wins. Furthermore, the absence of a clearly identified constituency undoubtedly reduces the general level of active involvement in campaigning with a consequent reduction in the enthusiasm of voters. Fifth, the mass media devote little attention to these elections. Finally, it is not at all uncommon for school board candidates to run unopposed. When this occurs low voter turnout is perfectly understandable.

Considering only the "typical" school board election, we have found that it is characterized by a high degree of predictability, very few candidates, almost no issues, and very little participation by citizens. The typical school board derived from this process is made up of members of an elite group who generally spend several years on the board and tend to be self-selecting and self-perpetuating.

There are, however, a significant number of atypical school board elections that have been studied fairly carefully in recent years. From time to time school board campaigns become heated and controversial, and incumbent board members are challenged and sometimes defeated by insurgents. One observer described board elections as "arroyos" which, in the normal course of events, channel "a feeble trickle" of citizen input into the school policy system, but which can be hit with sudden and severe storms of local stress followed by flash floods of political turmoil.[13] The frequency with which these dramatic upsets occur in school board elections may be on the increase. One study conducted in 1965 indicated that about once in every six elections held in a school district an incumbent's defeat could be expected.[14] By 1973 a study of the same districts indicated that one or more incumbents were being defeated in approximately every third election.[15]

Whatever its frequency, the defeat of an incumbent school board member by a successful insurgent leader has dramatic consequences on the conduct of the board's business. In the first place, the insurgent leader adds something quite rare to board conduct: a mandate to take action. During the election campaign the insurgent typically concentrates on issues on which he disagrees with the incumbent.

That this strategy works in these cases must be attributed at least as much to widespread dissatisfaction within the district as to the political campaign skills of the insurgent. When the insurgent succeeds in overcoming the natural advantage of the incumbent, both he and the other incumbents know that his views on school policy have been ratified by the voters. Thus when the insurgent takes his place around the board's meeting table, there is an almost irresistible pressure to defer to his judgment about what questions are important and what decisions should be made about them. It is typical that during the two years immediately following the defeat of an incumbent board member there is a series of split votes on various questions, with the insurgent gradually becoming the key member of the majority coalition. With impressive statistical regularity, the school superintendent feuds with the new majority coalition and becomes the victim of an involuntary release from his contract.[16]

The typical school board then can be seen as a tightly closed political system that receives little if any input from more than a handful of residents of the school district.[17] So long as this closed group continues to operate the schools more or less in conformity with the wishes of most of the community, it can proceed undisturbed in the conduct of business. Gradually, because it is not listening to the community and because the community keeps changing, the board loses contact and does not respond to the community's needs and desires. Because of the nature of school elections, and because of the political advantage held by incumbents, the dissatisfaction has to build up to a fairly intense level before any changes can be made. Thus, the defeat of an incumbent tends to be a turbulent process accompanied by exaggerated pressures on the schools and frequently the firing of the school superintendent.[18]

In addition to school board campaigns and elections, citizens participate politically in school policy making through referendums on school budgets, taxes and bond issues. These referendums along with procedures of initiative and recall are a legacy of the urban reform movement. In order to place some controls on public officials in the collection and spending of public funds, voters frequently have to approve school tax increases and budgets.

Referendums, especially budget referendums, serve not only to secure needed capital and operating funds for the school district; they are also a device by which the degree of harmony between school boards and the voters in the community can be assessed. School boards carefully select and schedule the referendums in an attempt to anticipate the reaction of voters. That is, referendums are proposed and campaigns for their passage are conducted with a careful eye to whether the voters can be persuaded to approve them. The successful passage of a referendum issue is not only a legal process that makes the particular issue a matter of school policy; the board and the voters also take the passage of the referendum to be a vote of confidence in the school board. A substantial defeat of a referendum is construed as a rejection of the board's leadership, and marginal votes either for or against the issue are interpreted as signs of a dangerous split in the community.

A few things have been learned about the participation of voters in school district referendums. The most important discovery is that the lower the rate of voter turnout the more likely the referendum will be successful.[19] This is consistent with one theory of democratic political participation that says that high rates of popular participation accentuate the divisions in the community and hostility toward the political leadership. This theory suggests that it is the responsibility of public officials to anticipate the reactions of citizens to any contemplated official action and to take that action in such a way that citizens will find it palatable and will not be inspired to participate actively in the policy-making process.

The amount of money proposed in a tax referendum is also important. A California study found that "seeking the same tax rate is most successful, even more successful than seeking a reduction. It seems as if change of any kind is more opposed than the *status quo*. Moreover, increases have only about half the chance of succeeding as the other options [in general] and the larger the increase sought the lesser the chance of passage."[20] The resistance to higher tax rates is understandable; the resistance to lower rates underscores the tremendous advantage of the status quo in any political process. Change in any direction, it seems, causes anxiety and is difficult to accomplish politically.

The study of school referendums demonstrates that there are good reasons for school boards to keep school policy out of the limelight and to maintain themselves or their friends in power through a policy that is designed to preserve the status quo. It is, from political point of view, unlikely that elected officials will seek to increase sharply the rate of political participation in any system because the dangers to their own control are real and immediate. When participation increases, moreover, so do conflict and discomfort for everyone.

Political participation, of course, need not be limited to election activity related to school board members and school referendums. After the board members have been selected, whether or not that selection involves an incumbent's defeat, it is possible for citizens to seek out the school board members either in private or in public and try to influence their behavior. A number of important inquiries have been made into the ways in which school board members do or do not respond to these efforts to influence their behavior.

In a landmark study first published in 1964 one researcher, using the pseudonym Norman D. Kerr, demonstrated that there are important reasons why we should not expect school boards to be particularly open to the participation of citizens in the policy-making process.[21] In his study Kerr examined the way in which a school board is transformed from a representational structure, which turns the interests of citizens into school policy, into a structure that receives policy decisions from the superintendent and renders them acceptable to the citizens of the school district. Kerr became convinced that even though school board members are not particularly representative of their community, the reasons behind their lack of responsiveness are independent of their personal characteristics and have more to do with the way school boards typically operate in the policy-making process.[22]

The transformation of the board is the natural result of the interactions among board members, the school superintendent, and citizens. It begins when citizens take education very seriously; they have high expectations for education and expect to see significant results from their children's school attendance. The citizens, therefore, have lively interests in school policy and expect the board to represent them. If they discover that they are not being represented, they are likely to exert real political pressure for change. But, at the same time, citizens are largely ignorant of the workings of education or the school system. They do not know how educational results are achieved, and they do not know what impact the board can reasonably be expected to have on the process of schooling. This means that while citizens may know what they want from schools, they do not know how it can be obtained.

Into this setting comes the superintendent of schools, who believes that only professional educators can really understand how the schools work. Thus, he believes he should establish educational policy.

Now we select a school board. They are members of the community and think of themselves as "only laymen" with limited understanding of the schooling process. These board members attend a meeting at which the superintendent is present. Someone proposes a new program. The school board members know they should decide whether to implement it, but they lack confidence in their own judgment of its value. Now what will happen?

First, board members will want the superintendent to evaluate the program for them. He will do so and make a recommendation on its adoption, which usually ends the matter. But suppose a board member, for whatever reasons, does not wish to accept the superintendent's recommendation. What will he do? He will seek to discuss the matter with other board members, with school administrators, or with teachers to see if they agree. He does this outside the regular board meeting at times and places not open to public scrutiny. Because he is frequently unsure of himself, he uses this procedure to avoid embarrassment if he should become convinced that his initial position was wrong. Furthermore, the member, who is uncertain himself, knows that citizens in his community will be even less informed on the program and will not understand any public debate that he might instigate on the matter.

There are two important consequences of the board member's actions. One is his alienation from the community. This happens because he finds it increasingly difficult to explain to citizens how and why he is making the decisions he does, and it is aggravated because citizens continue to make demands he does not believe should be acceded to. Once the feeling of alienation emerges he finds that life is more comfortable for all involved if he simply conceals important policy discussions from everyone but a few "insiders" whom he trusts and with whom he agrees.

Once the board member falls victim to alienation and concealment, it is virtually impossible for him to represent his constituency in any meaningful way. The net result is that, instead of representing his constituents to the board, he argues in the community for the legitimacy of the board's policies. The member now accepts the superintendent's policy recommendations more or less routinely, simply because the superintendent seems to know what he is doing.

A school board that follows this typical pattern normally will reach the point where all voting is unanimous. The unanimity is achieved by taking informal polls of the board members on any issue that will come to a vote. Then everyone votes for the majority position. The board also avoids serious public discussion of the issues. Under these circumstances what started out as citizens' uncertainty about complex problems is almost certainly going to become citizens' ignorance of what the issues really are.

When school board members are asked to indicate whether they view themselves as "delegates" representing their constituencies or as "trustees" responsible for school policy, they tend to view themselves in the latter role. It is interesting that citizens also have a slight preference for board members who will act as trustees rather than delegates.[23] It is not surprising, then, that only about half of all school board members indicate that they believe they either are or should be directly responsive to the desires of their constituents.[24]

On the whole, then, prospects are dim that citizens will be able to influence school board policy through political pressure on board members. But it is important to remember that this is largely because members and their constituents are ignorant of the complex issues in education.

There are at least two ways to solve this problem; both were suggested at the hearing in Los Angeles. One is to assemble competent technical staffs for school boards that are independennt of the school bureaucracy. A witness described how such a council or staff might work:

My concept of the legislative council [to the school board] is not a group of citizens; it is a group of specialists, educational, accounting, economics, and so forth, men and women who are paid by the district to sit continually by the side of the board members in every hearing, at every meeting of the committees of the board to ask the kind of professional questions, do the kind of detailed analysis of a proposal by staff, and so on.[25]

If this strategy worked, it would remove some of the consequences of the school board members' ignorance of technical educational issues.

A second strategy is to take board policy making to the local school level where most of the basic problems of teaching and learning are encountered and where, as one Chicano father confidently proclaimed, "We are conscious that we are not participating in the education of our children, and it is not because we are stupid . . . . We are the experts."[26] By putting the authority for policy making at the local school level, it would be possible to take advantage of the natural confidence parents have that they know what goes on at that level. Even if they are wrong in this confidence, at least the school board would not be caught in the cycle of ignorance breeding ignorance.

Administrative Participation in Local School Districts

The superintendent of schools is the chief executive officer of each local district. As such, he is the central figure in administering policy. It has been frequently pointed out that hiring the superintendent is the most important action taken by any school board. It has only been in the past few years, however, that careful study of the work of the school superintendent has demonstrated just how extensively he influences both the making and the implementation of policy.

Since the superintendent is the single official link between the school board and the schools, how he handles the flow of information and decisions to and from the board does much to shape policy in the school district. The superintendent is, for example, the authoritative interpreter of board policy to the administrative and instructional units in the school system. His interpretation of the intentions of the board and his emphasis on priorities will be taken by most members of the community and the school staff to be the board's intentions.

This role of interpreter becomes more important as districts get larger and more diverse because individual board members are increasingly remote and the news media tend to give prominent attention to the superintendent's public statements. Even in middle-sized and smaller districts the superintendent is a community leader whose opinions and judgments are widely disseminated and seriously considered. Although some studies have found that business and social leaders tend to be more important shapers of some aspects of public opinion than school superintendents, it is nevertheless true that in day-to-day operation of schools, the superintendent's views carry great weight with school board members and community residents alike.

Within the school system the superintendent is not only the authoritative spokesman for the board; he is also the authoritative interpreter and evaluator of school programs for the board. The superintendent generally defines the central issues requiring policy action and specifies what alternatives might be considered. Evidence gathered from other studies confirms the assertion of George Esser, the director of the Southern Regional Council, who said at the Atlanta hearing: "With the help of the school attorney and the help of acquiescence of the school board chairman, it is the superintendent who basically decides where your children go to school, what kind of a budget the system will have, and what kind of education is going to be provided."[27]

One of the major factors contributing to the influence of the superintendent is the way in which he and others typically identify his proper role in the schools. As was pointed out in the last section, school board members tend to see themselves as trustees who should use their own judgment rather than as delegates whose responsibility is to represent their constituents' views. Superintendents overwhelmingly seek trustee boards, and they want the boards to view them as trustees also.[28] That is, the superintendents want the boards to give them great latitude for exercising judgment and taking actions. These actions would not specifically be the result of delegated authority.

Boards view the superintendents, on the whole, as "itinerant professionals" whose expertise is their most important quality and who can be trusted to apply this expertise with political neutrality. Since this is the prevailing view of the superintendent, the board tends to leave in his hands all questions defined as "technical," and since the superintendent himself is most able to distinguish technical from nontechnical issues, he can usually gain control over most policy questions by simply defining them as technical questions requiring expertise. Thus the superintendent is as much a "separator" of the board from the schools as he is a link between them.

Despite the central role of the superintendent in the administration of school policy, there are definite limits on his power to control the school system. Several important studies have shown, for example, that teachers can insulate their classrooms against aggressive intervention by school administrators.[29] Important in insulating the teachers from the superintendent and his staff is the fact that teachers derive much satisfaction from students' response to their teaching efforts as well as from their salaries. As a result, school superintendents tend to use very personal and informal methods of communication with teachers in order to secure their cooperation with district policies. They can rarely rely on the issuance of formal directives in order to secure compliance with policy changes.[30] It is obvious that there are limits on the number of teachers with whom any administration can have and maintain an informal, personal relationship. In larger, urban districts the superintendent is at a decided disadvantage. Two other factors also contribute to the limitation of the relationship between teachers and the superintendent in large districts. One is the emergence of the central office, middle-management staff as a buffer between superintendent and teachers. The other is the difficulty the superintendent has in getting effective feedback on the actual performance of any one teacher or any one school.

There is some participation by citizens in the administration of the school in at least a superficial way. The access of citizens to the superintendent and district staff is of three different kinds: the involvement of citizens in support for the schools, the participation of citizens in district-wide advisory committees, and the pressure brought by individuals and groups of citizens on the administrators for particular causes.

Superintendents take seriously the problem of generating support for public education in general and their own school system in particular. No doubt one major reason for this interest is that school budgets, tax levies, and bond issues are so vulnerable to rejection by voters. Beyond that, however, school-community relations have been frequently punctuated with harsh and turbulent outbreaks ranging from Little Rock to Charleston, West Virginia, and South Boston. These outbursts are of grave concern to school administrators who frequently lose their job if controversy is prolonged or intense. Most observers agree that although citizens may reject the public relations efforts of the superintendent, he does have a tremendous advantage over his critics in any contest for public support. His access to the media, his legitimacy as an expert, and his control over information make it very hard for anyone to argue with him in public and win.

The second type of participation by citizens in the administration is through the activities of various school district advisory committees or task forces. The typical committee is actually an administrative rather than a political device directed toward shaping the thinking and actions of the school superintendent and the school principal and is only indirectly related to the school board. The impact of district advisory committees can be substantial when they are working in harmony with the district superintendent and his staff. When the committee begins to oppose the administrative staff, however, its work quickly comes to a halt.

The third type of participation consists of pressuring the administration for specific decisions or actions. Superintendents report that they experience a great many pressures over a wide range of policy matters from numerous groups and individuals. In one study superintendents said they received more demands for specific actions than board members. Of fifteen policy areas, ranging from demands for changes in courses and programs to pressures on tax and budget matters, only "demanding the introduction of new teaching methods" was more frequently experienced by board members.[31] When these superintendents were queried as to who was responsible for this pressure, they most frequently identified "parents or PTA," "individual school board members," "teachers," "taxpayers' association," "town finance committee or city council," "politicians," "business or commercial organizations," and "individuals influential for economic reasons," in that order. The school administrators are generally responsive to these pressures, at least to some extent.[32]

In the larger urban districts the problems of participation in school administration are complicated by the limited impact of the central administrative staff on the schools. Under these circumstances, the charge that schools are "inflexible" takes on a new meaning. Inflexibility, after all, implies that behavior is being closely controlled. What we find, in fact, is that the structure of educational governance, both political and administrative, greatly limits the ability of everyone to get results. School boards find they have to fire the superintendent and hire an outsider in order to give a clear mandate for change. Then the new administrator has to give orders that call for standardized operational practice throughout the system. Just as the school board election is a powerful but terribly blunt instrument, so also the school superintendent is a powerful but necessarily insensitive executive. If he allows teachers and principals to do whatever they think will achieve results, he must give up his responsibility for carrying out the mandates of the school board. If he frees the teachers and principals from central office constraints, he also removes them, under present governance arrangements, from the political participation that is currently available to citizens only at the school board level.

There have been two broad attacks on these problems. One strategy, seen in the rapid growth of so-called "accountability" laws, seeks to tighten the grip of school boards and superintendents on the performance of teachers and local school administrators. The other strategy is to move policy making to the local school by creating school advisory councils that give citizens an opportunity for direct participation.

As we learned in the early part of the twentieth century, most complex activities like education must be organized so as to give much latitude to the person directly responsible for the work—in this case, the teacher.

Citizen Participation at the Local School Level

One local school board member told the Commission in Los Angeles: "There are essentially two problems in the school system; one of those is the problem at the local building level in the classrooms, where the children and teacher come face to face and where education should be taking place. You have a separate and distinct problem at the district-wide level, and that is where you have to try to find necessary resources . . . to see that all children in the district have equal opportunity for education within the system."[33] For a number of reasons, many citizens are most anxious to participate in educational governance at the level of the school building or site. In the first place, as a Portland school board member pointed out, "Most citizens care about getting involved only when their interests are going to be pretty directly affected by the issues." And, "Generally people only care enough to get involved if it is either their local school or their child that is being affected."[34] This is not surprising. After all, most citizens have no reason to come in contact with the school system beyond its intrusion into their neighborhood and their family. What people think and feel about the central administration or the board of education naturally would depend on how satisfying or distressing this contact is with the local school. There are, of course, many families with special educational problems and needs, and frequently these special needs are initially responsible for involving citizens in broader concerns of school policy. For example, the statewide citizens' groups that have successfully lobbied for various special education programs for physically or educationally handicapped children are often organized and led by parents of such children.

Not only do parents and their children have the most contact with school systems through their local school, but they also get most of their information about schooling from that source. Citizens learn most about public education from their children and through such routine local school activities as printed notices, PTA meetings, "back to school" nights, and other programs including athletic events and graduation ceremonies. Parents report that what information they have about schooling comes directly from their children about twice as frequently as from any other source, including efforts on the part of school personnel to contact them directly.[35]

Not only is the neighborhood school the place where citizens come in contact with the school and the source of their information about the school; the local school is also a place familiar in every citizen's own experience and therefore something he can evaluate by comparison with the schools he attended. This is particularly important in light of the quite limited information most citizens receive regarding the school. Since almost every citizen has been a student and has rich memories of his own schooling experiences, he tends to view the schools on the basis of these memories, not on the basis of official school pronouncements. This is natural, but it creates problems of participation in school policy, since citizens are primarily concerned with this policy through the local school, and since these contacts generally lead to an orientation that is highly idiosyncratic.

The activities in which citizens actually engage at the local school can be divided between those that might be called "traditional" and a number of "new" activities that have begun largely during the last two decades.[36]

First among traditional activities are school-sponsored programs that range all the way from kindergarten Christmas programs to high school graduation ceremonies, including open houses, back to school nights, and athletic events. These programs have two general features: they involve students directly or focus on the activities of the parents' own children, and they emphasize the good qualities of the school and do not involve serious inquiry into most aspects of school programming.

A second kind of traditional participation involves citizens in school-sponsored groups of various kinds. The most widely known of these is the PTA; they also include booster clubs of various types, fund-raising groups, and a wide variety of local variations on the PTA approach. These school-sponsored groups generally share four characteristics: they are at least partly social in nature; they are led by a fairly small ingroup of leaders who do virtually all of the planning for the group; they see themselves, and are seen by school personnel, largely as "communication links" through which information about school programs is disseminated to the community; and they provide auxiliary school services, either directly through contributions of time and talent to the school or indirectly through fund-raising activities. Virtually every school sponsors one or more fairly permanent organization of citizens and at least a few short-term groups that have special purposes.

The third type of contact with the local school centers around relations between parents and teachers. The report card is the most basic form of communication between the teacher and the parent, and most contacts are verbal variations of the report card. In some schools parents only get verbal reports on their children when there is a problem with the child's performance. In a larger number of schools, however, there is at least a minimal level of verbal reporting of teachers to the parents concerning the child. The parent-teacher contacts generally have two common characteristics: the teachers do most of the talking, and the parents are vaguely anxious and a little fearful about their child's performance, but often do not have a clear idea about what might be done to change or improve it. The result is a transaction that confirms a social distance between parent and teacher, leading to parental deference to the teachers, or, less frequently, parental hostility.

The fourth traditional activity is the parents' contacts with the school principal, most of which are the result of a summons to discuss discipline problems or poor academic performance. Principals represent the legal authority of the school. They interpret for the parents what the formal rules of the organization are, what the consequences of the child's behavior will be, and what can or must be done about it. They seek the parents' cooperation. Occasionally citizens initiate contact with the principal. These occasions usually arise because the parent is seeking his authoritative intervention to redress some situation that is causing problems. These contacts will cover anything from complaints about noisy schoolchildren disturbing property owners near the school to an impasse between parent and teacher over evaluation of a child.

In recent years significantly different kinds of activities in and around the school have emerged. The phrase "citizen advisory committee" (CAC) is frequently used as a catchall description, although these groups have a number of different structures, methods of operation, and reasons for coming into existence. Frequently the CACs are mandated in federal legislation, although increasingly state legislative mandates and even local school board action have been responsible for their creation. In some situations, particularly in desegregation cases in the South, the citizen advisory mechanisms have been ordered by the courts. Although there is an increasing tendency to create general CACs, there is also widespread use of special purpose advisory groups for particular school programs or problems, such as early childhood education and curriculum materials.

In order to evaluate new types of citizen participation, it is necessary to examine the nature of the traditional mechanisms and to discover why they are not satisfactory.

In traditional participation, communication is *from* the school principal and other school officials *to* the parents and citizens, and it is either a matter of informing them about school plans and programs or sounding them out on contemplated policy and programs. Communication from parents to the school officials is largely personal and represents complaints or compliments that are evaluative of school programs only in a very narrow sense. In this way citizens rarely, if ever, initiate policy or prevent its implementation.

In the traditional pattern conflict between citizens and school officials is normally intensely personal. When a citizen seeks an arena in which to resolve a problem he is having with the schools, he must directly contact the principal or the teacher involved. As was indicated by a number of witnesses at the NCCE hearings, the traditional process for handling conflict requires a series of personal contacts—first the teacher, then the principal, then the area administration (in decentralized systems), then the superintendent, then an individual school board member. Only after that sequence of four or five personal contacts does it become legitimate to expose the conflict at a public meeting, and the school board is the only appropriate public forum. Such a system normally keeps an individual from exposing conflicts since he will invariably meet at least one (and generally more) person in this sequence who will insist that the trouble derives from the individual's inadequacies rather than from any problem in the system.

It is unfortunate that these informal, traditional ways of resolving conflict work least well in large, urban districts. Here large populations, bureaucratization of school administration, sharp cultural differences, and the remoteness of school board members all contribute to a failure of informal ways in which a citizen might influence school policy.

It is in this context that the new mechanisms have been developed and implemented. So long as informal mechanisms succeeded in resolving conflict, there was little need for basic changes in citizen participation. Urban unrest and violence, the campaign by blacks for "community control" in the mid-1960s, and new federal programs mandating citizen involvement in planning and spending encouraged the development of new types of participation.

How effective have such mechanisms as school community advisory councils been? The public hearings elicited considerable dissatisfaction with the new ways of "involving" citizens in school affairs. These councils, which produce administrative rather than political participation, are founded on an advisory concept rather than one that places them within the decision-making machinery. This "advisory" focus is "outside" of the structure of governance.

When the council is attached to the office of the principal of the local school (by far the most common practice), it can serve as a very important ally for the principal, who is able to secure more immediate and more adequate services from an otherwise slow or insensitive central administration.[37] In order for this to happen, there must be little conflict between the principal and the council, and the latter must be willing to confront the higher levels of the bureaucracy. School officials in the central office can support the request of an advisory group in order to offset strong opposition to their own policies that exists elsewhere in the bureaucracy or in the general public.[38] These two examples are variations on a single theme: advisory groups are viewed as pressure resources that can be brought to bear by one segment of the bureaucracy on another. In the first case the principal uses the council to pressure the higher levels, and, in the other, the central office uses the council for its purposes.

A second consequence of administration-oriented advisory councils is that they continuously face problems of legitimacy and generally fail to gain acceptance from school officials, the community, or both.[39] Councils are, at one extreme, groups with open membership in which any citizen can participate. This gives them legitimacy in the community. School officials, however, think of such self-selected groups as not representing the community and as dominated by a few activists who have their own narrow interests. Councils are, at the other extreme, groups consisting of those who are appointed by the administrator and are viewed by him as legitimate representatives of community interests. Parents who are not on the council regard these groups as co-opted, hand-picked supporters of the principal. A number of alternative strategies for selecting members have been tried, some by elections, some by appointment, some by petition. But no matter how the group is selected, its legitimacy is fragile because its role is confined to being advisory. When the advisory group takes a position on any issue, those who oppose that position, regardless of who they are, can either attack the position or attack the legitimacy of the council in order to discredit the position. As the public debate over policy continues, the legitimacy of the advisory group, even the most prestigious and competent, is bound to be attacked with increasing frequency, and it is destined to collapse under these attacks if it consistently takes unpopular positions.

Another weakness attributable to the fact that these advisory groups are administrative rather than political is that they tend to degenerate into the traditional pattern of participation.[40] Since the new councils exist almost exclusively where administrators bear the final legal and social responsibility for any actions taken, over time the councils will find that they are viewed as useful only by administrators who agree with them, and they will increasingly discover that serious conflicts are taken elsewhere for action. It is just this feature of the PTA-type groups that has made them inappropriate in the urban setting. Though it takes a few years for advisory groups to discover their inability to exert authority if they are without responsibility for the consequences, learning the lesson is inevitable. Advisory councils are decidedly limited in the amount of conflict they can handle. This is because the responsible administrator is unwilling to let an advisory group make decisions when he will have to pay the costs of mistakes in judgment. The administrator may initially find the advisory council a comforting shield against the pressures arising from either the central office or the disenchanted community, but the more he realizes that he will be held accountable for the council's decisions, the more he will accept only their advice and counsel when they agree with him.

A final problem with advisory groups is that they often encourage the very eruptions and open conflict they were created to eliminate.[41] This unpredictable characteristic is one of the reasons why school and political officials have been reluctant to organize councils.

Citizen Participation in the Broader Perspective

Any analysis of citizen participation in school policy would be incomplete without at least some attention to state and federal governments. Although most of the newer efforts have been directed toward the local school and district levels, there have been significant changes at the state level. What is more important, many of the changes that citizens are seeking depend directly or indirectly on statewide policy making.

The federal government, on the other hand, will probably have a far less dramatic impact over the next decade or so than it had in the last two decades. This is because education is left constitutionally to state governments. There is also a fairly wide acceptance of the so-called "New Federalism," which is committed to channeling federal resources through state and local governmental agencies. These observations are not intended in any way to diminish the significance of federal policy during the last decade. Under the impact of the federal legislation outlined at the beginning of this chapter, there has been a profound change in our national views on the participation of citizens in governmental policy making. Under Title V of the 1965 ESEA legislation, there has also been a transformation in the size and professional skill of the typical state department of education. These changes, now firmly established, will continue to shape school programs in the years to come. As federal initiatives they are, however, substantially fulfilled.

Citizens will encounter four key problems when they participate at the state level: cost, the fact that many state officials avoid making management decisions, the diversity and overlapping of state policy structures, and the traditional dominance of state policy by professional educators.

The matter of cost is so obvious that it requires only a passing remark. It is unquestionably true that citizens of modest means, who could easily persuade the local school principal to take their views seriously, and who could generally get the attention of board members in a small or moderately sized district, will find it difficult to get results from state-level policy makers. It is not just the dollar and time costs of getting to the state capital or otherwise communicating with state officials. A citizen must also count the cost of organizing his group, and if he wants his views to be aired widely, he may have to attract the attention of the mass media. State policy makers find it difficult to listen to individual opinions. They are trying to make policy for large groups, and they must determine which citizens actually represent a substantial body of opinion. State policy makers want to know, consequently, how large a group is represented by anyone seeking their response.

The second problem is the lack of a clear management orientation on the part of state executives. The chairman of the Missouri House Education Committee remarked at the Commission's St. Louis hearing: "The first [state] superintendent's . . . view of the office was that of a record-keeping function . . . the current Commissioner of Education is taking much more of a leadership role."[42] This legislative leader added approvingly, however, that the local school boards "run the schools." Many other witnesses in the course of the hearings confirmed this strong support for continuing local control. It is a view shared by state-level executives, who see themselves as consultants and advisers, or perhaps occasionally intervenors in local education, but virtually never as responsible executives or managers. With this perspective on their work, state policy-makers and their staffs do not generally think they need much citizen input, since the citizens control the local district through the local board.

A third major problem is the diversity of state policy agencies and the overlapping character of their powers and responsibilities. Citizens must consider, at a minimum, the state legislature, the state school board, the state department of education, and the governor. Each of these offices has significant impact on policy, and they frequently can effectively veto each other. Theoretically, the state legislature is the starting point for developing policy that will fulfill the state's constitutional mandate in education. In actual practice, however, state legislatures have relinquished extensive policy latitude to state school boards and departments of education. These offices generally must develop the guidelines for implementing legislation. Whether the guidelines actually fulfill the intent of the legislature is frequently an open question. One study of the operation of the California Department of Education found two quite distinct groups within the staff.[43] One was oriented to the legislature and helped write legislation and create guidelines for its implementation. The other was oriented to the school districts and their staffs and sought to provide them with services they would find helpful and valuable. This split served more to sever the connections between the legislature and the schools than to strengthen them. Finding who is in charge of what aspect of state policy is not always easy.

The fourth problem is the traditional dominance of state policy by professional educators. It has been demonstrated repeatedly that by far the strongest influence on state-level policy is the position taken by administrators and teachers. Witnesses at the hearings who claimed that superintendents' or teachers' groups were preventing policy change at the state level confirmed what sociologists and others had been saying for some time.

There is, however, some evidence that state legislators are no longer content to have their agendas developed by professional educators alone. A number of states are searching for new ways to bring other interests to bear on the legislative process. But until the state legislatures substantially strengthen their ability to monitor the laws they pass, they will be forced to depend heavily on the professional educators' judgment of what information is necessary to adjust and refine these laws. This revitalization cannot be a matter of simply turning back the clock to an earlier era. The shift away from representative government to executive and professionally dominated government resulted from the very real complexities of modern society that require competence and large-scale organizations to solve problems.

Summary

Citizen participation is a vital but complex part of American public education. Recent history has seen two significant developments that have renewed interest in the process of participation. From within the education profession there has developed a deep conviction that public cooperation with and support for the schools must be based on increased participation in policy making. And through a series of federal laws political participation by citizens has been mandated and structured.

The simple truth is that not very much in the way of substantive citizen participation has resulted either from the new federal legislation or from the enthusiastic endorsements of it by human relations theories of school administration. Where citizen participation has been tried, it has brought turbulence and controversy and not the cooperation and support that had been confidently predicted in the 1950s.

The problem seems to lie in the failure to differentiate adequately political from administrative processes of participation. Administrative participation works fairly well to provide smooth, supportive school settings where the citizens and school officials are homogeneous in matters of ethnicity, culture, socioeconomic class, and goals for education. The same processes lead to co-optation and public relations gimmickry when the citizens are minorities, poor, or otherwise diverge significantly from existing school officials. Political participation is a potent means of achieving significant influence over school policy. It is unfortunate that present structures of school governance make political participation an increasingly blunt and imprecise instrument for changing policy. Citizens who encounter difficulties largely at the level of the individual local school find that they must mount an effective political challenge to a remote and uninformed school board in order to secure the needed change.

The logic of the available evidence is clear. A school council with genuine legislative policy authority at each school site would go far toward providing an effective structure for citizen participation. If effective technical staff support were also utilized by state legislative committees and local school boards to ensure that their policy mandates were both intelligently constructed and effectively complied with, they would be able to "fine tune" the political participation of citizens at these important but more remote policy levels. Continuing, and even more effective, administrative participation by citizens in understanding and cooperating with school administrators as they seek to provide effective educational services is, no doubt, vital to the ongoing success of education for every student and every citizen. But this administrative participation cannot be expected to substitute for the democratic process of political participation by which, in the words of John Adams, "The whole people must take upon themselves the education of the whole people."[44]

Notes

1. Herbert M. Hamlin, *Citizens' Committees in the Public Schools* (Danville, Ill.: Interstate Printers and Publishers, 1952), i.

2. *Citizen Co-operation for Better Public Schools*, Fifty third Yearbook of the National Society for the Study of Education, Part I, ed. Nelson B. Henry (Chicago: University of Chicago Press, 1954).

3. Merle R. Sumption and Yvonne Engstrom, *School-Community Relations: A New Approach* (New York: McGraw-Hill, 1966), 2.

4. Scott A. Greer, *Urban Renewal and American Cities: The Dilemma of Democratic Intervention* (Indianapolis: Bobbs-Merrill, 1965), 91-97.

5. James Q. Wilson, "Planning and Politics: Citizen Participation in Urban Renewal," *Journal of the American Institute of Planners* 29 (November 1963), 243.

6. *Ibid.*

7. *Ibid.*

8. Title II-A, Section 202(a) of the Economic Opportunity Act.

9. Harmon Zeigler *et al.*, *Governing American Education* (North Scituate, Mass.: Duxbury Press, 1974), Part I.

10. *Ibid.*, 38.

11. *Ibid.*, 35.

12. *Ibid.*, 43.

13. Frederick M. Wirt and Michael W. Kirst, *The Political Web of American Schools* (Boston: Little, Brown, 1972), 66.

14. Richard S. Kirkendall, "Discriminating Social, Economic, and Political Characteristics of Changing versus Stable Policy-Making Systems in School Districts," unpublished doctoral dissertation, Claremont Graduate School, 1966.

15. Richard R. Thorsted, "Predicting School Board Member Defeat:

Demographic and Political Variables that Influence School Board Elections," unpublished doctoral dissertation, University of California, Riverside, 1974.

16. John C. Walden, "School Board Changes and Involuntary Superintendent Turnover," unpublished doctoral dissertation, Claremont Graduate School, 1966.

17. Laurence Iannaccone and Frank Lutz, *Politics, Power, and Policy: The Governing of Local School Districts* (Columbus, Ohio: Charles E. Merrill, 1970), 52-68.

18. *Ibid.*, 173-174, 215-217.

19. Wirt and Kirst, *The Political Web of American Schools,* 100.

20. *Ibid.*, 105.

21. Norman D. Kerr, "The School Board as an Agency of Legitimation," in *Sociology of Education,* ed. Ronald M. Pavalko (Itasca, Ill.: F. E. Peacock, 1969), 361-388.

22. *Ibid.*

23. Zeigler *et al., Governing American Education,* 121.

24. *Ibid.*, 78.

25. Los Angeles hearing of NCCE Commission on Educational Governance, October 1974.

26. *Ibid.*

27. Atlanta hearing of NCCE Commission on Educational Governance, August 1974.

28. Zeigler *et al., Governing American Education,* 121.

29. Dan C. Lortie, "The Balance of Control and Autonomy in Elementary School Teaching," in *The Semi-Professionals and Their Organization,* ed. Amitai Etzioni (New York: Free Press, 1969), 34.

30. Richard O. Carlson, *School Superintendents: Careers and Performance* (Columbus, Ohio: Charles E. Merrill, 1972), 98-104.

31. Neal C. Gross, *Who Runs Our Schools?* (New York: John Wiley, 1958), 45-60.

32. *Ibid.*

33. Los Angeles hearing of NCCE Commission on Educational Governance, October 1974.

34. Portland hearing of NCCE Commission on Educational Governance, June 1974.

35. Paul F. Kleine, Raphael O. Nystrand, and Edwin M. Bridges, "Citizen Views of Big City Schools," *Theory into Practice* 8 (October 1969), 225.

36. Luvern L. Cunningham and Raphael O. Nystrand, *Citizen Participation in School Affairs: A Report to the National Urban Coalition* (Washington, D.C.: National Urban Coalition, 1969), 1-19.

37. *Ibid.*, 31.

38. *Ibid.*

39. *Ibid.*, 21-28; also Leila Sussman, "Community Participation in Schools: The Boston Case," *Urban Education* 7 (January 1973), 348-349.

40. Dale Mann, "Political Representation and Urban School Advisory Councils," *Teachers College Record* 75 (February 1974), 279-307.

41. Cunningham and Nystrand, *Citizen Participation in School Affairs,* 26-28, 34-35; also Joseph L. Falkson and Marc A. Grainer, "Neighborhood School Politics and Constituency Organization," *School Review* 81 (November 1972), 46-48.

42. St. Louis hearing of NCCE Commission on Educational Governance, May 1974.

43. Thomas R. Collins, "An Organizational Study of the California State Department of Education," unpublished doctoral dissertation, Claremont Graduate School, 1973.

44. Quoted in Hamlin, *Citizens' Committees in the Public Schools,* 2.

9

A PLAN FOR GOVERNANCE:
RECOMMENDATIONS AND DISSENT

What should be the role of citizens in education? The answer is so complex that a complete one may never be possible. The recommendations in the following pages are, however, a first step toward returning control of American schools to the people they serve.

Previous chapters have concentrated on at least three major forces in education: the teachers, whose organizational strength and bargaining power are gaining rapidly; state legislators, who are beginning to do more acting than reacting in the political arena of education; and "citizens"—surely a broad and partially indefinable group but one whose frustration with the schools has grown especially deep. That frustration is, of course, shared by legislators and teachers, not to mention many school administrators and school board members.

One root of the problem is the failure of some of the reforms, such as citizens' advisory councils. We have heard much about the operations of the councils and have concluded that they are most effective where the local school or schools are under the guidance of strong and dedicated principals who are willing to heed advice. But, in most instances in an enterprise that is more pervasively public than perhaps any in America, the professionals, for all the previously stated complex reasons, are showing strong resistance to sharing a portion of control. There are, to be sure, exceptions.

There are outstanding examples of citizens sharing in budget decisions and program development. For the most part, however, reforms related to the participation of citizens propose an advisory rather than a policy-making role. This is an inversion of the historical and legislative concept of the citizen as the policy maker. And it is equally an inversion of our more modern notion that the skilled technician or administrator presents the alternatives and consequences of proposed policies while the citizens and their representatives set policy.

The concentration of power in the administrative branch of government is not only at the school level; it is at the local and state school board levels as well as at the legislative level. The Commission learned how administrative control has been brought about by efforts to "depoliticize" and "professionalize" the schools. These gradual changes in policy have largely altered the representative functions of local and state school boards. They have become trustees of administrative policies through formal delegation of authority and informal reliance on the professional judgments of the educational technicians. At the same time state legislative enactments to guarantee uniformity of schooling and to assist in making schools efficient and productive have weakened the economic strength of local school boards in collective bargaining.

Chapter 6 stated that "collective bargaining has produced a dramatic change in the governance of American schools." The Commission suggests that legislatures are allowing the balance of power to tip in favor of professional organizations. There is a need for planned governance to avoid the further exacerbation of problems concerning collective bargaining. Collective bargaining is an important model of democratic decision making and has contributed to the improvement of American public education. In most states, however, the models used for teachers' negotiations are fashioned after industrial labor relations models, which are not suitable for the public sector. Closed bargaining meetings, weakened economic leverage for local school boards, and contractual agreements on issues of public policy further remove the citizen from the decision-making process. It should be emphasized that the citizen has nothing to fear from collective bargaining if it is carried out in the open.

The Commission feels that the judicial branch of government not only has been contributing to responsible policy but that it has had to bear too much responsibility for school policies that should have been shaped, and then monitored carefully, by legislative bodies. In many school districts the courts have had to lead the way in deciding issues such as fluctuating enrollments, school consolidation and re-organization, desegregation, teachers' assignments, and curriculum organization.

Information is the legitimate currency of power. Gathering information, distributing it, and making it democratically available are crucial activities in modern democracies. It is unfortunate that almost no public policy exists for gathering information on the effectiveness of educational programs and alternatives and providing it to parents and other citizens. This needs to be corrected. The burden of responsibility for disclosures of information needs to be clearly and effectively placed on those who have the information.

One important lesson to be drawn from the study has been that add-on, patch-up approaches to restructuring school governance are not working well now and cannot be expected to work well in the future. What is called for is a solid grasp of the essential problems confronting the present structure.

A plan for restructuring school governance must focus on the relationship between the administrative and legislative functions of government and must include a reconsideration of current policy and administrative arrangements. A policy model for educational services must assure that the legitimate rights and interests of individuals and communities are adequately represented.

The Commission offers what it believes to be a sound Governance Plan that embodies the above considerations.

Recommendations

1. *The NCCE Commission on Educational Governance recommends that steps be taken to improve the "legislative process" in educational policy making. The Commission further recommends a redistribution of responsibilities for policy decisions at each legislative level: state, local district, and school.*

There are three distinct levels at which school policy is formulated: the school level, where parents, students, teachers, and principals are the key actors; the school district level, where the crucial actors are boards of education, teachers' organizations, superintendents, and citizens' groups; and the state level, where state boards of education, state legislators, state-level educational executives, statewide education groups, school board associations, and various state-level interest groups are the actors.

Legislation and policies have been designed over the years to increase the efficiency of management and to "professionalize" school operations as populations have grown and have become more diversified and as the needs of the community have changed. The effect has been to remove from the citizen much of his traditional role as decision maker in school affairs. This development has transformed a historical legislative model for school governance into a modern professional-industrial model.

Deliberation is inherent in the legislative process and is a component of its structure. A legislative body functions as a policy maker and then monitors carefully the implementation of its policies. In the former role it deliberates the goals to be reached through statutory authority and sets policy with the help of competent technical advice. In the latter role it reviews legislation to assess the appropriateness and wisdom of its policy and to see that the administrative branch is carrying it out diligently and following the original intent.

Findings indicate these democratic principles are not part of the operations of many school systems. It is essential that at each level the legislative process for policy making and monitoring be guaranteed. In order to develop democratic school policy that is flexible and technically competent, it is necessary to have a deliberating legislative body at each level.

2. *The NCCE Commission on Educational Governance recommends a council at each school with appropriate responsibility and authority. The school council should be elected and should share authority and responsibility for curriculum, school program budgeting, school progress reports, and personnel evaluations.*[1]

Under present governing structures the local school board or district is the primary unit for school decision making. This has several drawbacks, particularly in school districts with more than a thousand students. Parents, students, teachers, and principals are in the best position to make judgments about local programs. Parents hold a strong allegiance to their local schools. The important contact between the professional and the parent does not take place at the district level but at the school site. While the school district is too large and often too far distant to make decisions for local schools, the classroom is too small. Students are frequently in contact with more than one teacher, especially in the era of team teaching and specialization. The individual school is, therefore, the most reasonable and manageable unit for decision making.

The electoral process never guarantees perfect representation, and it has disadvantages. It is, nevertheless, far preferable to appointment by principals, the central office staff, or the school board. Appointed members would be open to substantial criticism, not the least of which that they are dominated by the appointer. This criticism weakens the legitimacy of the appointed group and reduces its ability to represent citizens' interests effectively. Elections provide more effective representation in the legislative process, and, though they can be time consuming and cumbersome, they are consistent with democratic principles.

School budgeting is yet another tool to provide the flexibility necessary to match the tastes of clients with programs. It is best accomplished through a system of allocating lump sums to school sites based upon formal, district-wide rules. An equal amount of money for each pupil, exclusive of federal, state, and local categorical funds for specialized programs or populations, should be allocated to each school for its discretion in selecting programs. The school council, principal, and faculty would then be free within state and local budget guidelines to determine how they want to spend funds. Purchasing and payments should remain a function of the central school district; school-by-school accounting procedures can, however, also assist school councils, principals, and teachers in their policy decisions. School-by-school fiscal reporting is a critical step in achieving a better understanding in education of the linkage between resources and school performance.

An important function of the school council is to participate in the selection of the principal. Over and over again the principal has been cited as the single most important component of a school's success. Sometimes it is possible to identify a capable principal in a bad school; in the view of the community, however, it is extraordinarily rare to identify a "good" school which has an incompetent principal.

A formal, deliberative school council working to balance professional and client interests will, by its nature, also balance individual and community interests.

3. *The NCCE Commission on Educational Governance recommends:*
   a. *That responsibility for negotiations with teachers remain with the local school board, and, further, that local school boards be adequately provided with independent staffs or consultants to assist in analyzing the impact of bargaining demands and in developing strategies and policies; and*
   b. *That school boards should seek independent advice or staff to develop policies that represent a balance between professional and lay concerns.*[2]

There is a need to revitalize the legislative powers of school boards, which are constrained by restrictive state regulations and prohibitions. In collective bargaining, the board needs an independent staff to develop bargaining demands and strategies without relying on the school administration.

School administrators often lack resources needed to bargain in good faith or to implement program priorities. As the rights of collective bargaining have been extended to administrators, moreover, they find themselves frequently in a conflict of interest when they sit across the bargaining table from teachers. Principals and others in a middle-management role are finding increasingly that they are neither management nor labor but, rather, in an awkward position somewhere between. An independent advisory staff for the school board should alleviate at least part of this problem.

The Commission is aware that there is a danger in such a plan of adding still another level of bureaucracy to the central administration. That is why the proposal stipulates that the consulting staff be independent of the administration and that it be charged with balancing, as much as possible, professional and lay concerns. Adequate safeguards must be provided against staff abuse for personal or political purposes by individual school board members.

4. *The NCCE Commission on Educational Governance recommends that the local school board establish procedures to involve the public responsibly in the process of negotiations. These should include:*
   a. *Inclusion of citizens in the development of school bargaining positions;*
   b. *Public hearings;*
   c. *Broad dissemination and distribution of the board's position on the major bargaining issues;*

d. Open and publicized negotiations;
e. Press notification of meetings.[3]

Negotiators must learn that public awareness, involvement, and opinion are as crucial to successful bargaining in the public sector as the marketplace has been in the private sphere. They must learn to bargain in public when using public funds and establishing public policy, just as city councils and legislative committees are learning to function in public under recently enacted open-meeting laws. Democratic decision making is not easy, but the added trust and support that result from open negotiations and meetings are well worth the added effort.

Yet, as an earlier chapter makes clear, opening negotiations to public scrutiny is far from reality in America. This is because collective bargaining in education is based on the private industrial model. Neither school boards nor teachers' unions are anxious to conduct open bargaining, even though there are significant differences between private-sector and public-sector negotiations, not the least of which is that vast amounts of public money are involved. And the public has a stake in a number of matters that are considered negotiable, such as policies regarding discipline, size of classes, and length of the school year.

5. *The NCCE Commission on Educational Governance recommends that state legislatures substantially increase the power of and the staff support for education committees so that there can be effective legislative monitoring.*

The legislature oversees and reviews the establishment and maintenance of a thorough and efficient system of free public schools to provide for equality of educational opportunity through funding, programs, and services. State boards of education have legal responsibility for guaranteeing adequate and equal educational services; providing for minimal state standards and requirements; evaluating and disseminating information on school performance; ensuring equity in allocating resources; and guaranteeing the constitutional rights of parents, students, and teachers.

The hearings have indicated that citizens are increasingly calling upon legislators to resolve conflicts that the state and local boards are unwilling or unable to resolve. Educational and fiscal priorities have further increased the need for improvement in the monitoring and review functions of the legislature. In the absence of adequate legislative review, too much responsibility for setting substantive policy has fallen upon administrators even though the legislature is especially suited to representing the collective will of the citizenry in establishing educational policy. The growing complexity of both the educational process and the society it serves makes it essential that legislators have available to them high-quality and independent information.

Currently some states perform these functions much better than others. A legislative committee must have a competent and dedicated professional staff whose services are available directly to the legislative branch of government. Monitoring education legislation must be accomplished independently of the executive branch to determine the wisdom of the original mandate and the need for modified or corrective legislation.

6. *The NCCE Commission on Educational Governance recommends that state legislatures seek to coordinate all education-related services.*

Most states have a hodgepodge of educational services that are usually under several departments of government, are frequently uncoordinated, and are too often competing for resources. Both the intense interest of citizens in alternative educational experiences and the recent court decisions mandating education for previously neglected groups make statewide coordination vital.

The state legislative standing committee on education is the appropriate body for the coordination of education-related services in libraries, museums, and state hospital and social welfare programs, as well as all other educational services for children and youth.

7. *The NCCE Commission on Educational Governance recommends that the state guarantee the right of teachers to organize and negotiate on matters relating to teachers' wages, welfare, and benefits.*[4]

Teachers throughout the country are already negotiating in many school districts where negotiations are not permitted by state law. Governments that continue to resist efforts at collective bargaining can expect defiance from teachers and resulting administrative problems at the district level. The state's major responsibility in collective bargaining in public education is to establish a set of rules that is fair to all sides and guarantees adequate public access. Once a fair and rational model is approved, the state should carefully monitor the collective bargaining law to assure that local districts comply with it and to provide equal protection and advantage for school boards, teachers, and citizens.

8. *The NCCE Commission on Educational Governance recommends that basic ground rules for bargaining be established to provide each side with balanced incentives to reach agreement.*[5]

Most states have enacted laws that limit the economic advantage of school boards in the negotiating process; the public needs guarantees that its interest and values will have an equal voice in the process. Previous chapters have shown the citizens cannot influence public-sector collective bargaining in the same manner as they influence private-sector collective bargaining. The public must have an opportunity to influence public decisions through direct participation, thus strengthening the citizen's voice.

Basic ground rules must be carefully designed to provide each side with incentives to reach agreement. The state must balance the teachers' right to negotiate against the public's rights in collective bargaining. Laws that constrain school boards and that have removed their economic power in negotiating should be reviewed.

The following are examples of laws that could be examined for more balance: laws that specify the numbers of days in the school year; tenure laws; state regulations for granting credentials and certification; pupil-teacher ratios; incentive pay and differentiated staffing requirements.

Many of these laws as they are presently written remove a measure of economic leverage from the local school board. For example, the laws requiring the numbers of school days minimize the risk of loss of salary to striking teachers and prevent local decisions on teaching options. Under most present laws teachers know that salary lost during a strike will be made up at the end of the school year. Local school boards should be able to determine how the community wants to spend the money not used during a strike, perhaps to develop new programs or for teachers' aides. Likewise, laws concerning credentials and certification are an additional constraint on the local school boards' decisions about classroom aides, teaching techniques, assistants, and resource persons. These are only a few examples of the disadvantages the citizen has at the school board bargaining table.

Questions have been raised regarding what—beyond salaries, benefits, and working conditions—is fair game for teacher-school board bargaining. Some states have left these decisions to local school districts. The Commission believes this is a good start, and since many of these issues—the length of the school year, for example—are of abiding public interest, the citizens should have a say in this decision.

9. *The NCCE Commission on Educational Governance recommends that each state align its budgetary procedures to guarantee that neither side is unfairly constrained in reaching a collective bargaining agreement.*[6]

Different states have different laws for local and state school budgeting. Most states set some demands for budget submission dates and the forms required. Evidence exists that teachers' organizations consider these budgetary laws in planning their bargaining strategies, which may give them an unfair advantage. The effects of budgetary laws on collective bargaining should be taken into consideration, and efforts should be made to isolate the budgetary process from the negotiating process.

10. *The NCCE Commission on Educational Governance recommends that states set rules and guidelines that guarantee fairness to all sides, public access, and public influence. The Commission further recommends that open-meeting laws be established at all levels to encourage public discussion and dissemination of information.*[7]

An important reform at the state level is to provide an open atmosphere that enables the public to participate in and gain information about school negotiations. State and local provisions that exempt bargaining sessions from open-meeting laws should be removed. Regulations prohibiting discussion of contract proposals before, during, or after negotiations should be changed to encourage dissemination of information about the negotiations. A fundamental principle of democracy is the right of citizens to share in the process of governing their institutions; an open-meeting law is one means for citizens to share in the governance process.

Secrecy and closed procedures are the antithesis of democratic proceedings. Public interest and faith in the institution are difficult to maintain without openness and access to information. What is needed is a reasonable, rational mechanism that provides fairness, humaneness, and justice for all sides.

11. *The NCCE Commission on Educational Governance recommends that the state ensure adequate and proportional repre-*

*sentation in the political process through the election of all
local school and school council members.*[8]

The declining number of school districts has had a dramatic impact on citizens' ability to influence schools. Schools touch citizens
more directly than any other arm of government. The number of
school districts has dropped markedly over the last twenty years
from approximately 55,000 to approximately 16,000, while the
country's population has risen to 210,000,000. Many present-day
school districts are large, sprawling, and frustratingly bureaucratic.
The statistics give heightened meaning to the numbers of citizens
unable to have a part in school decisions. Of the 16,000 school
boards, 95 percent are elected, and approximately 5 percent are
appointed, but approximately 15 percent of the country's student
population attend schools in districts where school boards are appointed.

Of the 90,000 school board members, 34 percent of those members on elected boards actually have been appointed to fill unexpired
terms or have run for office uncontested. In a recent Gallup survey,
63 percent of the public surveyed were unable to cite anything their
school board had done in the past year, and 40 percent either admitted they do not know or were wrong about whether their school
board was elected or appointed. On the other hand, 60 percent of
school board members surveyed separately did not believe their role
is to represent citizens.

The National School Boards Association believes that "local
school boards exemplify American principles of representative
democracy." However, "40 per cent of the people in the United
States don't know how they got the school boards they have."[9]

Recent widespread attention to the problems related to the lack of
citizen representation on school boards has produced suggestions
ranging from partisan and ward-based elections to notions that election or appointment will not make a difference.

Present methods used to nominate, appoint, and elect school
board members are clearly not functioning to produce desirable
representation. There is abundant testimony in the hearings of the
many different cultural and ethnic views on parents' participation
and representative democracy. The smaller a school community is,
the more likely are its residents to feel their school board will listen
to an appeal. The perceived ability of the citizen to influence his

schools is closely related to smaller school populations with proportional representation. Electing school boards with adequate and proportional representation is an essential part of representative democratic procedures.[10]

12. *The NCCE Commission on Educational Governance recommends the appointment of a gubernatorial task force in each state to revitalize the educational system as an accessible and responsive democratic institution providing equal educational opportunity for all. The task forces should include representation from broad citizen interest, including ethnic and minority representation, students, legislators, teachers, business, professional, and university representation, and school administrators. The task forces on governance reform should be provided with independent staff.*

The Commission recognizes the prior recommendations for reform are a conceptual framework for the governance structures of public schools. A conceptual framework is a statement of what needs to be accomplished; it is not a statement of how to get it done. The diversity of a state's population, regional interests, and existing state laws must be taken into consideration. It is the Commission's belief that each state should review and reform public education. One of the strengths of the American system is our pluralistic society. This pluralism also means that few universal policies are workable. A spectrum of varied state educational systems, each reflecting its own unique contribution in creativity and quality, could serve to revitalize the American educational experience.

Dissent

Mrs. Merrimon Cuninggim

My concern in general deals with the adversary posture and the degree of change recommended, and the little recognition given to conscientious administrators and school board members all over this country who are making great efforts to provide access and responsiveness to the citizenry. For example, the sentence used in introducing the recommendations—"The recommendations in the following pages are . . . a first step toward returning control of American schools to the people they serve"—implies there is no such control now. Most communities, however, do have elected school boards where orderly change is always possible through the democratic process. I would prefer to emphasize the need to increase the citizens' participation and the boards' responsiveness, and the need to find strategies to accomplish this end as a collaborative effort on the part of citizens, students, administrators, and boards, with structures designed to build trust.

This leads me to express the following specific concerns:

1. In re the role of the citizens' advisory councils: Recommendation Number 2 suggests they be given "appropriate responsibility and authority." I agree, so long as it is understood that school boards cannot legally delegate their decision-making powers. If boards are to be held accountable, they must have ultimate responsibility, including the right to say no—though, of course, they should give great weight to considered opinions of local school councils. I raise this question because of the lack of specificity as to what "appropriate responsibility and authority" means, and because Dr. Pierce, in Chapter 6, states, "These school councils would have *full* legislative authority over curriculum, school program budgeting, school progress reports, and personnel evaluation [italics mine]." With this statement I cannot agree.

2. In re staffs for boards of education that are independent of school administrations: More information and more staff availability are certainly needed by boards, and by advisory councils as well. But before adopting such an expensive, and adversary, stance, I would hope existing staff could be shared. This might well lead to greater understanding and collaboration. If, on the other hand, a superintendent were to suggest such a separate staff, particularly with reference to negotiations, that should be considered. Other circumstances could also dictate such a procedure. It is, however, the automatic nature of the separate staff suggested for boards and advisory councils that concerns me.

3. In re the involvement of the public in staff negotiations: Amen to the public's presence at formal sessions where negotiations occur! But I would hope that recommendation Number 10—"open-meeting laws be established at all levels"—would not prevent confidential explorations before arriving at formal positions. For it would seem to me that the public's interest is better served when opportunity can be given to each side to explore the other's points of view and to change opinions without losing face.

4. In re the implication that matters other than salaries, benefits, and working conditions are "fair game" for teachers' negotiations: Other matters are, of course, of legitimate concern to teachers. Their input on all academic matters is essential, but not as subjects for negotiation. If the balance needs to be redressed at this point—and I do believe it does—it should come through procedures other than bargaining. Where policies for consultation with teachers do not exist, boards have the duty to initiate them. But negotiations on such matters would contradict the very effort the study makes to strengthen the hands of school boards so that they may be more responsive to the varying needs of the community at varying school locations.

5. In re the election of school board members by proportional representation: In certain cases this works very well. On the other hand, it occurs to me that objectivity and concern for all the children (And is this not the ideal posture for all school board members?) will be enhanced if at least some members are elected at large.

In conclusion, let me say that the hearings were extremely helpful to me. It is my hope and belief that the efforts made by NCCE in this governance project will provoke lively public discussion and perhaps some solutions to our many problems in constructively strengthening the citizen's role in public education in this country.

Dissent

Frederick T. Haley

Recommendation Number 2. The key words in this recommendation are "appropriate responsibility and authority" and "share[d] authority." Experience thus far in our recent period of turbulent educational history suggests that a good deal of trial and error might well precede wholesale adoption of this somewhat basic reform, that is, elected members of advisory councils. I think also that such a reform will be found best suited to elementary education, less suitable at secondary levels, and quite unworkable in many special circumstances.

Recommendation Number 12. Since every state's problems are unique to that state, it might be unwise to circumscribe a governor's selection of the membership of a "blue-ribbon" commission. Such a task force might well include the representation here suggested,

though I tend to be somewhat skeptical of these standard genuflec-
tions to "ethnic and minority representation, students, legislators,
teachers, business, professional, and university representation, and
school administrators." Since real reform is implied, equally as important in the variety of representation will be the stature of the
members, knowledgeability, commitment to a formidable task, and
requisite time and dollars to fulfill the very difficult objective.

Dissent

Mary Conway Kohler

I find myself in a peculiar position in relation to this report. I am
deeply committed to helping citizens participate more fully in decisions that affect education. For this reason I have remained a member of the Commission on Educational Governance. While I was not
able to attend any of the hearings, I have read the transcripts available and have studied all staff reports.

The condemnatory tone that permeates the hearings and now the
final report is unacceptable to me.

My own experience suggests that hearings of this kind draw com-
plainants instead of persons with constructive ideas for change. It is
questionable whether hearings are ever the best method to ferret out
public opinion on controversial issues unless they are backed by
intense study of the type that the Fleischmann Commission conducted. It is unfortunate that the Commission on Educational Governance had neither sufficient funds nor time to make such a study.

While some of the recommendations in this report may have a
basis in fact, their effect is so sweeping and authoritarian as to add to
the confusion that now exists around school governance.

I will always be sympathetic to the motives behind this report, but I
cannot endorse a document that so readily condemns existing structures and practices without developing those positive solutions which
have already been adopted by many concerned with public education.

Dissent

Charlotte Ryan

Political solutions for school governance problems are more appropriate at district and state levels than at the local level, in the school

itself. Here the quality of education is directly related to the quality of interaction between teacher and student, and, only second to this, in the quality of the relationships between principal and faculty, and between principal, faculty, and parents. An elected citizens' council for each school, such as is suggested in Recommendation Number 2 with the objective of citizens' control of school-level decisions, is unlikely either to foster collaborative relationships or to achieve the desired citizens' influence in school operation.

The practical alternative is to bring together all interested individuals, lay and professional, in developmental discussions, where they can learn to understand each other and influence each other's thinking. Out of this comes real "power," if power is significant, to influence curriculum and school practices.

Provision for ad hoc groups, with open membership and open agenda, would recognize the practical certainty that parents and other citizens will wish to pursue different interests at particular times and, further, that students and teachers will similarly differ in their choices for concentrated activity. Such groups could be initiated by any interested parents, teachers, students, or other citizens who raised a concern of sufficient interest to attract others to a discussion. Matters of individual interest could still be handled on an individual basis. Guidelines would include provision for whatever preparation may be needed in the skills of assessment of needs, fact-finding, study, and group decision making. Such training could come through existing PTAs, central school staff, or other resources.

Evaluation can be provided by annual reports, jointly submitted by officers of active groups and school administration, reviewing the objectives, procedures, and progress of current activities. Complaints of nonparticipation or other obstruction by school administration could be appealed, by majority vote of the group concerned, to the school board and thence if necessary to the department of education.

These procedures carry their own safeguards. The reality-testing of any proposals in an open-membership, lay-professional group provides the principal with ample screening of recommendations for wisdom and feasibility. The same open membership prevents suppression of innovation, on the one hand, or unreasonable appeals on the other, but rather invites both lay and professional participation in a climate productive for education.

Notes

1. For more detailed information on school councils, see Chapter 5.
2. For more detailed information on bargaining, see Chapter 6.
3. *Ibid.*
4. *Ibid.*
5. *Ibid.*
6. *Ibid.*
7. *Ibid.*
8. See Chapter 5.
9. Dr. Harold V. Webb, Executive Director, National School Boards Association, news release, March 24, 1975.
10. The data in the eleventh recommendation can be found in Harmon Zeigler *et al.*, *Governing American Education* (North Scituate, Mass.: Duxbury Press, 1974); and Gallup Organization, Inc., *Public Knowledge and Attitudes Concerning Local School Boards*, conducted for National School Boards Association, 1975.

APPENDIXES

APPENDIX A. NATIONAL COMMITTEE FOR CITIZENS IN EDUCATION CHARGE FOR THE COMMISSION ON EDUCATIONAL GOVERNANCE

Much has been written about the problems confronting American education today. In spite of a decade of creative energy, the expenditure of vast sums of money, and widespread research, however, these problems have not diminished. The result has been confusion, frustration, and despair and a critical loss of confidence in the schools by the American people.

Now, more than ever, there exists no mechanism for public concerns to be expressed in any systematic, meaningful, and productive way on the issue of educational changes or for redressing the balance of power in American education.

In 1973 the National Committee for Citizens in Education received Ford Foundation support to develop as an action-oriented, public-interest organization. Its purposes would be to build a broad-based constituency for education and to press for educational reforms and to help citizens to act on future alternatives.

It is in the furtherance of these purposes that the National Committee for Citizens in Education has established a Commission on Educational Governance.

The Committee believes the governance of education, involving a state structure working toward equal educational opportunity, cannot and should not be arbitrarily or capriciously altered without input and understanding from the community it serves.

The task before the Commission will be to conduct six public hearings sometime between April and September 1974 in the following locations: Minneapolis, Minnesota; St. Louis, Missouri; Los Angeles, California; Portland, Oregon; Atlanta, Georgia; New York, New York.

The Commissioners will collect information on citizens' experiences in conjunction with the federal, state, and local educational agencies in the governance of public education.

They will assure full opportunity to hear from teachers, educators, administrators, students, citizens, and experts on the following issues:

Who controls public education?

Who should control public education?

What are or should be the roles of citizens in public education?

How is the system changing?

Is change desirable; what are the factors causing and governing these changes?

Following the six public hearings, the Commission on Educational Governance will develop a report and recommendations addressing the concerns raised in the public hearings. The report and recommendations will be made available to appropriate executive educational committees, federal and state legislative education committees, professional organizations, citizens and civic groups, and all interested citizens.

APPENDIX B. PROJECT DESIGN AND EXECUTION

The Commission on Educational Governance set out to gather information to document citizen decision making in the existing legal and administrative structures, including procedural practices and the role of the citizen in decision making within the educational institution.

Criteria were established to choose the location for the public hearings. They were the presence of citizen activity and interest in educational change, active local citizen organizations and community support, availability of press and media coverage, and regional diversity and accessibility.

The goals for the design of the public hearings were to assure the fullest opportunity to question and hear from teachers, students, educators, administrators, legislators, and citizens in order to afford the fullest opportunity for a diverse and broad representation of individuals who had influence or desired influence in the public schools.

The Commission on Educational Governance has taken testimony from more than 190 witnesses which includes eight state or local school board members, seventeen official community advisory council members, thirty-five legislative or executive commission or committee members, six ad hoc legislative or executive committee members, six Title I committee members, ten official teachers' organizations or students' organizations representatives, four representatives of Parent-Teacher Associations, six representatives of the League of Women Voters, four quasi-official advisory committee members, two American Friends Service representatives, one quasi-official teachers' organization representative, three quasi-official citizens' organizations members, thirty-six representatives of unofficial organizations, and forty-nine unorganized witnesses or those who testified as private citizens.

The overall site design was developed to identify resource people, key leaders in the educational and legislative areas and in community-interest organizations and citizen leaders. These resource people were interviewed to develop historical background, perspectives about the area, and knowledge about and identification of community leaders and organizations and issues that were of major concern to the schools. More than 540 people were contacted by various types of communications and by personal interviews by the staff.

Initial contacts were made with the local and state superintendents to introduce the NCCE, explain our hearing goals, and seek the local superintendent's assistance and cooperation.

Interviews were held with the superintendent's staff and community leaders in each city to identify resource people, key leaders in the educational and legislative areas, community activists, and leaders of various organizations. Two or three groups were contacted to provide background information, secretarial or clerical assistance, personal contacts with media and resource people, and information for local mailings.

To maintain objectivity in the collection of testimony the NCCE decided to accept the assistance of local community organizations, but would avoid cosponsorship with a local group or organization.

High schools and community colleges were asked to provide students for administrative assistance during the hearings and video-taping services.

All field interviewers received background information on the organizations, the schools, and the community and the questions to be explored in interviews.

Interview information obtained from resource persons and background materials resulted in identifying two or three issues currently of concern to the school communities. This served a dual purpose. First, it provided an opportunity for witnesses to relate personal knowledge and experience to larger issues of control and process. Second, it afforded the fullest opportunity to gather information and to hear from a diverse and broad representation of individuals who had influence or desired influence in the public schools. The design included witnesses to represent the following pressure groups at each hearing: teachers' organizations, school administrations, school boards, legislators, elected city or state officials, students, parents, community- and ethnic-interest groups, quasi-official organizations, unclassifiable. Approximately 2,350 organizations or individuals were contacted or interviewed.

Mayors and other city officials were asked:

Would you describe the structure within city government for dealing with the school system and school-related problems?

What role does the city play in the public schools?

Would you give examples of the role of city government in regard to two or three major issues in the past few years?

Could you provide any recommendations for changing the relationship between the city and the schools?

State officials were asked the same questions as city officials except at the state level.

Teachers and administrators were asked:

What mechanism or pattern of interaction do you recommend as the most effective way for the parent and student to influence the teachers, the local schools, and the policies of the school district?

Do you feel that existing teachers' organizations properly represent your interests?

What issues are of major concern to you at present?

Would you describe a recent change that has occurred in your school system and how it came about?

Local superintendents and administrators were asked:

What mechanisms do you use to involve citizen participation in your schools? What have been your successes and failures? Give examples of ways that these mechanisms have helped to inform your decision-making process.

What is your relationship to city government, and how could it be more helpful to you? (This question refers to structure and not to particular incumbents.)

What is your relationship to the teachers and other professional staff?

Are there any problems of policy implementation?

What changes would you recommend to enable the superintendent to exercise his leadership more effectively and to make certain that his leadership reflects the interests of the community?

Are there any legal restraints that currently prevent the superintendent's office from performing effectively?

What do you see as the future of community or alternative schools?

What are the problems you are dealing with presently in your schools? What do you see for the future?

State and local school board representatives were asked:

Does your local board have adequate range of decision-making authority to reflect local interests and needs?

Does the level of state funding affect in any way the areas focused on by the board or its powers?

Are the mechanisms for relating to teachers' unions adequate?

What recommendation does the board have in terms of: enlarging its power; reducing its power; enabling it to represent more effectively the people who elected its members?

What steps or structures do you recommend for making the local schools more responsive to neighborhood interests and requests?

What do you see as the future of "community" or "alternative" schools?

Community or citizen groups were asked:

What have been (are) the major issues with which you have been concerned over the past few years, and what response has the school system made in regard to them? (Describe the steps taken, the road-blocks encountered, and the eventual decision-making process.)

Do you feel there is adequate power in your school board? local superintendent? teachers? other local officials?

Do you know anything about the negotiating process used by the school board and the teachers' organizations? Do you feel represented in this process?

Would you describe the most appropriate role for a group such as your own in regard to shaping the public schools and suggest how that role could be more effective?

What, in your view, has been the impact of litigation in regard to desegregation, school finance, or other issues on your school system?

What do you see as the future of community or alternative schools and why?

How does your parent advisory council operate? How are the members selected and for what length of time? What are its authorities and responsibilities? How do you communicate with your school community? with your school board? with the principal and teachers? Have the advisory committees been successful? If so, how? If not, why not? (These questions were asked when advisory committees were extant.)

Three classifications were made for purposes of selecting witnesses to testify at the hearings: personal characteristics, organizations, pressure groups.

Our purposes were to identify witnesses to represent the pressure groups or individuals that affect or are desirous of affecting the structure. Personal characteristics of sex and race or ethnicity were identified as well as occupations when available. Another classification for selection of witnesses was the formally organized structures within the school system and the community, which were composed of official groups, quasi-official groups, unofficial groups or organizations, and the unorganized. The purpose of dividing organizations and groups into these four categories is to define the legal, political, and administrative relationships within the existing structure of boards, groups, organizations, and committees.

An official organization is defined as one where the roots, authority, status, or existence is either prescribed, authorized, or mandated. The authority and responsibilities given to an "organization" or its counterpart will not affect the "official" designation of the group. An advisory committee or its counterpart can be one or another classification. If an advisory committee has its origins in a legislative mandate, it is an "official" group. Examples of this are the Title I Advisory Committees that are mandated under federal guidelines. A parent advisory committee that has been convened by a school board directive or bylaw is also an example of an "official" group.

The quasi-official group classification is more complex. There is a strong sense of similarity between a quasi-official group and an official group. The quasi-official group, however, is not prescribed, authorized, or mandated for a specific intent, but rather gains the appearance of being official by its operation or construction. Since each school may have a PTA organized by state and local charter, rather than a mandate, the nature and acceptance of its operation and construction make it a quasi-official organization. This is not unlike citizens' organizations that have come into being with local and business support, local charter, and public acceptance of the organizations within the school structure. Thus, the school board, mandated advisory committees, and ad hoc committees or commissions are official organizations, while PTA, LWV, and administrator-created advisory committees are classified as quasi-official organizations.

The unofficial groups or organizations do not possess any of the above attributes; they are self-appointed and do not receive organizational or financial support from outside their membership or from general fund raising. Self-appointed citizens' groups, grass-roots organizations, and self-styled community and neighborhood groups are examples of unofficial organizations.

Those falling under the heading "unorganized" testified as individuals (private citizens) representing no specific organization, group, board, or committee.

The pressure systems classification enabled us to view and analyze the realignment and reorganization of the individuals and groups in a different way from their more formally structured official, quasi-official, and unofficial nature.

An example can be found in Title I Advisory Committees, which, in the existing structures, are classified as "official groups." By definition they are "official organizations" because their roots, authority, status, or existence is prescribed, authorized, or mandated.

Under the pressure systems classification, although Title I Advisory Committees do not lose any of their official nature, their purpose and power are delegated outside of the system into the classification of community-interest groups. Another example of reorganization of pressure groups is seen in school administrators' and teachers' organizations, both of which are classified as official or quasi-official depending upon state regulations. The purposes and goals of middle management and teachers' organizations are diverging, however, which results in a conflict of interest. For the purpose of testimony, therefore, the two groups are separated.

State education laws, local governing structures, administrations, regulations, socioeconomic data, site information, and relevant issues were used in preparation for briefings prior to each public hearing. These briefings, held the evening before each public hearing, lasted approximately two to two and a half hours and were used to develop the commissioners' knowledge about the schools, the community, and the witnesses. The data presented included the staff's overview on the school community, profiles of witnesses, demographic and geographical charts and graphs, and prefiled testimony. In addition, local resource people were available at each briefing to answer the commissioners' questions.

Witnesses selected to testify received formal letters of request along with guidelines on procedures for the hearings.

Of major importance to the project were the ways to identify issues and witnesses that were representative of the community. If we failed to identify a large portion of the community, the significance of the public hearing could be seriously minimized. The inclusion of many parts of a community in the public hearings was also a way of enlisting the support of the community in the work of the Commission. Two vital questions for the Commission were, thus, Who is the community? and What are its views?

The staff and the Commission questioned whether we could use the term "community" in the same context as we had in the 1950s and 1960s. How would we assure representation of all communities in the hearing process? What constitutes a community, and were there regional or local differences? Do ethnic and minority communities view influence, power, representation, and participation differently from predominantly white, middle-class communities?

Some of our experiences in fieldwork and in preliminary interviewing showed the complexity of the task. In one city we found traditionally conservative, tax-minded senior citizens' groups coming together with younger, liberal, neighborhood-oriented groups. Their efforts to coalesce were based on an economic issue. Though their basis for agreement transcended color lines, it did not transcend economic lines. Their efforts were ultimately more successful at bringing about change in the economic sphere than in the educational sphere.

Outside of the major eastern cities where there are large numbers of minorities to account for ranges of differences in community values, the black communities with which we came in contact had values and expectations for their schools that were more akin to the middle-class white population than the other ethnic groups. The Indians, Spanish-speaking, and Oriental communities appear to be at the level of the black community of the early 1960s. Some ethnic groups worked through different modes to achieve their goals. For example, some of the Chinese community who were concerned with bilingual practices (or lack of them) in public schools worked through the courts. Chicano groups, along with some black community groups, for the most part sought legislative redress. The Indian activists we encountered were going outside the local school level to work at the federal level.

It was clear that although the makeup of communities had already changed, they were continuing to change at varying rates, and their goals and values would influence their problems and solutions. Recognizing these changing concepts of "community," the staff undertook to develop the information and testimony received at many different levels. Every effort was made to receive testimony that would assure a very broad base of information, divergent views, ethnic and minority differences, and school community differences.

Letters to Announce Hearings

1. To School Superintendents

I have recently assumed leadership in the National Committee for Citizens in Education which is a nonprofit, nonpartisan citizen organization formed in 1973. Membership is nationwide. It is an outgrowth of the National Committee for Support of the Public Schools. I am enclosing some additional information on the National Committee for your perusal to give you a better understanding of our organization.

Several months back, the board of directors of the National Committee established a Commission on Educational Governance. The Commission consists of twenty persons including some members of the board of directors of the National Committee. The makeup of the Commission consists of lay citizens with a demonstrated broad interest, nationally, regionally, or locally on the issue of governance. They include representatives of minorities, women, students, Spanish-speaking peoples, and a broad geographic diversity.

The Commission on Educational Governance will conduct six national public hearings at different locations sometime between April and September 1974. The Commission has as its purpose the examination of these issues:

1. Who controls American education?
2. Who should control the public schools?
3. What are or should be the roles of citizens, parents, and students in that governance?

(Site city) has been selected as a possible site for one of the Commission's national hearings. The criteria used in our site selection are as follows: Local citizen organization and community support; citizen activity and interest in educational change and improvement; personal contacts; availability of good press and media coverage; and regional diversity and accessibility.

The Commission is considering a hearing in (site city) sometime during the month of _____ . Your input and advice are of utmost importance to the work of the Commission. We are seeking information about the PTA and citizens' and community organizations in your locale. In addition, your knowledge and understanding of the issues confronting your schools and their communities are of major concern to us. We will also be gathering information about the size, structure, and organization of the schools in your area and state. Whatever resources you may have available for our use to develop this information will be of great assistance.

The hearings are national in scope, and, therefore, in addition to your staff's expert knowledge and information about their local school issues, we will be seeking testimony from the State Superintendent's office and staff along with some assistance from the city government. Efforts are being made to have the hearings covered by the local educational television station.

The issues confronting educational governance and the significant changes taking place are of extreme importance to the growth and development of our country and the vitality of public education. Your cooperation and contributions to the work of the Commission will add greatly to the depth of its understanding of the problem.

We will contact you sometime within the week, and perhaps at that time you might find it feasible to assign one person to work directly with our office to facilitate the communications between our offices. Thank you for your time, which we are sure is in short supply, and your efforts on our behalf.

Looking forward to speaking with you within the week.

2. To Citizens and Organizations

The National Committee for Citizens in Education, like many others, is concerned with the absence of citizen decision making in our public schools. The National Committee for Citizens in Education is doing something about its concern.

The NCCE has established a Commission on Educational Governance. The Commission is holding a series of public hearings around the country developing information and testimony on the citizens' experiences in participating with the federal, state, and local educational agencies. Along with citizen testimony, we take testimony from educators, teachers, legislators, and students. Following the public hearings, in the spring of 1975, a report and recommendations will be available. We are enclosing literature on the Commission and the NCCE.

The Commission on Educational Governance will hold a hearing in (site city and date). The hearing will be held in _____ where the Commission will engage in dialogue with concerned witnesses. We hope you will take the opportunity to observe the hearings.

In addition, your knowledge and information on the educational issues in (site state and city) will be of great help to us. We would appreciate hearing from you at the earliest possible time with comments and materials.

We look forward to meeting you.

3. To State Legislators

I am enclosing material about the Commission on Educational Governance and the public hearing we will be holding in (site city, date, and place).

It has been our experience that the hearings offer an unusual opportunity to bring together those with the responsibility for public education and those who wish to have a role in the decision making. The views of legislators, educators, teachers, students, and citizens should provide the _____ legislature with invaluable information.

Along with our Commissioners we have a panel of observers attending all of our hearings. They are The National Legislative Conference, Citizens Conference on State Legislatures, Education Commission of the States, and National Urban Coalition.

The Commission on Educational Governance and the observers sincerely hope you will take the opportunity to spend the full day observing the hearings. If this is possible the Commissioners and observers would like you to join them for lunch.

We look forward to meeting with you.

Letters to Prospective Witnesses in Atlanta

1. To Students

The Commission on Educational Governance has been working in your state for several months. We have been gathering information and knowledge about your public schools for the purposes of our hearings to be held on August 22, 23, 1974.

We are holding these public hearings in Atlanta and four other cities for the purposes of gathering information and testimony on citizens' experiences in conjunction with the federal, state, and local educational agencies.

As a student will you please focus your testimony on the role of the student on citizen advisory committees, and the students' role in the decision-making process at all levels. You may wish to discuss these things with personal experiences and from issues you have been dealing with.

We look forward to your testimony on August 22 in the morning at the City Council Chambers, City Hall. We will notify you of the approximate time of your testimony by mailogram on August 19.

We are enclosing information on the National Committee for Citizens in Education, a list of procedural guidelines, and an Atlanta Hearing Announcement. Following the five public hearings the Commission on Educational Governance will publish a full report on the proceedings at the five sites.

2. To Elected City Officials

The Commission on Educational Governance has been working in your state for several months. We have been gathering information and knowledge about your public schools for the purposes of our hearings to be held on August 22, 23, 1974.

We are holding these public hearings in Atlanta and four other cities for the purposes of gathering information and testimony on citizens' experiences in conjunction with the federal, state, and local educational agencies.

As a City Council member if you would share with us in your

testimony your knowledge and experiences in developing citizen participation and citizen councils under the existing structure it would be extremely helpful to our work. How citizen councils evolved and examples of their successes and failures are the kind of questions which need addressing.

We look forward to your testimony on August 22 during the morning at the City Council Chambers, City Hall. We will notify you of the approximate time of your testimony by mailogram on August 19.

We are enclosing information on the National Committee for Citizens in Education, a list of procedural guidelines, and an Atlanta Hearing Announcement. Following the five public hearings the Commission on Educational Governance will publish a full report on the proceedings at the five sites.

3. To Citizen Activists

The Commission on Educational Governance has been working in your state for several months. We have been gathering information and knowledge about your public schools for the purposes of our hearings to be held on August 22, 23, 1974.

We are holding these public hearings in Atlanta and four other cities for the purposes of gathering information and testimony on citizens' experiences in conjunction with the federal, state, and local educational agencies.

Your testimony focused on the roles, successes, and failures of citizen advisory councils and community participation within the public school system would be extremely helpful to the work of the Commission.

We look forward to your testimony on August 23 sometime during the morning at the City Council Chambers, City Hall. We will notify you of the approximate time of your testimony by mailogram on August 19.

We are enclosing information on the National Committee for Citizens in Education, a list of procedural guidelines, and an Atlanta Hearing Announcement. Following the five public hearings the Commission on Educational Governance will publish a full report on the proceedings at the five sites.

4. To Representatives of Teachers' Organizations

The Commission on Educational Governance has been working in your state for several months. We have been gathering information and knowledge about your public schools for the purposes of our hearings to be held on August 22, 23, 1974.

We are holding these public hearings in Atlanta and four other cities for the purposes of gathering information and testimony on citizens' experiences in conjunction with the federal, state, and local educational agencies.

Your testimony focused on the teachers' needs and personnel policies of the Atlanta school system will enable the Commissioners to understand more clearly the role of the citizen and teacher in public education.

We look forward to your testimony on August 22 sometime during the afternoon at the City Council Chambers, City Hall. We will notify you of the approximate time of your testimony by mailogram on August 19.

We are enclosing information on the National Committee for Citizens in Education, a list of procedural guidelines, and an Atlanta Hearing Announcement. Following the five public hearings the Commission on Educational Governance will publish a full report on the proceedings at the five sites.

5. To School Board Members

The Commission on Educational Governance has been working in your state for several months. We have been gathering information and knowledge about your public schools for the purposes of our hearings to be held on August 22, 23, 1974.

We are holding these public hearings in Atlanta and four other cities for the purposes of gathering information and testimony on citizens' experiences in conjunction with the federal, state, and local educational agencies.

As a school board member if you would share with us in your testimony your knowledge and experiences in developing citizen participation and citizen councils under the existing structure it would be extremely helpful to our work. How citizen councils evolved and examples of their successes and failures are the kinds of questions which need addressing.

We look forward to your testimony on August 22 sometime during the morning at the City Council Chambers, City Hall. We will notify you of the approximate time of your testimony by mailogram on August 19.

We are enclosing information on the National Committee for Citizens in Education, a list of procedural guidelines, and an Atlanta

Hearing Announcement. Following the five public hearings the Commission on Educational Governance will publish a full report on the proceedings at the five sites.

6. To School Administrators

The Commission on Educational Governance has been working in your state for several months. We have been gathering information and knowledge about your public schools for the purposes of our hearings to be held on August 22, 23, 1974.

We are holding these public hearings in Atlanta and four other cities for the purposes of gathering information and testimony on citizens' experiences in conjunction with the federal, state, and local educational agencies.

Your testimony is of utmost importance to the work of the Commission. Your information, knowledge, and experiences in developing the role of the citizen and citizen advisory councils in public education will be most helpful to the hearing. You have the distinction of having an outstanding community affairs department within your administration. Testimony on its operations, goals, and procedures would enable the Commissioners to understand the administration's focus on community participation.

We look forward to your testimony on August 22 in the City Council Chambers, City Hall, sometime during the afternoon session. Please advise us as to what time is best for your schedule during the afternoon.

7. To Participants in Community Organizations

The Commission on Educational Governance has been working in your state for several months. We have been gathering information and knowledge about your public schools for the purposes of our hearings to be held on August 22, 23, 1974.

We are holding these public hearings in Atlanta and four other cities for the purposes of gathering information and testimony on citizens' experiences in conjunction with the federal, state, and local educational agencies.

As a community leader your experiences in presenting community-developed alternative plans to existing or proposed administrative plans would be very helpful in your testimony. We would like to share in your knowledge and information on the successes and failures of community participation within the Atlanta school system.

We look forward to your testimony on August 22 sometime during the morning at the City Council Chambers, City Hall. We will notify you of the approximate time of your testimony by mailogram on August 19.

We are enclosing information on the National Committee for Citizens in Education, a list of procedural guidelines, and an Atlanta Hearing Announcement. Following the five public hearings the Commission on Educational Governance will publish a full report on the proceedings at the five sites.

8. To an Individual Involved in an Alternative School*

The Commission on Educational Governance has been working in your state for several months. We have been gathering information and knowledge about your public schools for the purposes of our hearings to be held on August 22, 23, 1974.

We are holding these public hearings in Atlanta and four other cities for the purposes of gathering information and testimony on citizens' experiences in conjunction with the federal, state, and local educational agencies.

As a community leader your experiences in presenting community-developed alternatives plans to existing or proposed administrative plans would be very helpful in your testimony. We would like to share in your knowledge and information on the successes and failures of community participation within the Atlanta school system.

We look forward to your testimony on August 22 sometime during the morning at the City Council Chambers, City Hall. We will notify you of the approximate time of your testimony by mailogram on August 19.

We are enclosing information on the National Committee for Citizens in Education, a list of procedural guidelines, and an Atlanta Hearing Announcement. Following the five public hearings the Commission on Educational Governance will publish a full report on the proceedings at the five sites.

Questions for Prospective Witnesses

The following lists of questions were used in letters to prospective witnesses in the various cities or regions where the hearings were scheduled. The questions were proposed as suggested topics of interest to the Commission on Educational Governance as a means to give focus to the testimony of the witnesses.

*Similar letters were sent to a lawyer involved in a desegregation case, former leaders of national organizations, citizens who have been affected by changing school policies, and so forth.

For Mayors and Other City Officials

1. Could you describe the structure within city government for dealing with the school system and school-related problems?

2. Would you give examples of the role city government has played in regard to two or three major issues in the past few years?

3. Could you provide any recommendations you might have for changing the relationship between the city and the schools?

4. Do you feel that the school system should be a part of city government?

For State Officials

These individuals received the same questions as city officials except "state government" was substituted for "city government."

For School Principals and Teachers

1. Would you describe the role of: state regulations; local board policies or administrative determinations in guiding the work of the teacher or inhibiting the teacher from conducting his classes in the manner that he deems most effective?

2. What mechanism or pattern of interaction do you recommend as the most effective way for the parent and student to influence the teachers, the local schools, and the policies of the school district?

3. Do you feel that existing teachers' organizations properly represent your interests? Describe any instances in which you feel their efforts have been frustrated and the reasons therefor.

4. Does your school system deal adequately with problem children (behavioral, learning, or health problems)? If not, what changes would you recommend?

5. Could you describe a recent change that has occurred in your school system and how it came about?

For City Superintendents

1. Would you describe the relationship of your office to the state? (Does the state preempt too many areas of decision making? If so, which ones? Is your relationship to the state affected by the level of state funding? If so, how and what changes have occurred recently?)

2. What is the relationship of your office to sources of federal funding?

3. What are the major problems in regard to the federal government, and how could the situation be improved?

4. Could you describe your relationship to the local school board? (Is the legal balance of power between you and the board appropriate? If not, how should it be changed?)

5. Similarly, what is your relationship to city government, and how could it be more helpful to you? (This question refers to structure, not to particular incumbents.)

6. What is your relationship to the teachers and other professional staff?

7. Are there any problems of policy implementation in regard to the professionals?

8. What mechanisms exist for you to relate to the community, particularly parents and students? (Give examples of ways that these mechanisms have helped to inform your decision-making processes.)

9. What changes would you recommend to enable the superintendent to exercise his leadership more effectively and to make certain that his leadership reflects the interests of the community?

10. Are there any legal restraints that currently prevent the superintendent's office from performing effectively?

11. What do you see as the future of community or alternative schools?

12. What has the impact of desegregation, school finance, or other litigation been on your school system?

13. Does your school system deal adequately with problem children (behavioral, learning, or health problems)? If not, what changes would you recommend?

For Local School Board Representatives

1. Does the local board have an adequate range of decision-making authority to reflect local interests and needs, or is too much authority vested in the state, the superintendent, or other institutions?

2. Does the level of state funding affect in any way the areas focused on by the board or its powers?

3. Does the board have adequate powers or mechanisms for relating to teachers' unions? If so, please describe.

4. How does the board relate to federal funding agencies?

5. What is the major input of the board in regard to the operation of the schools?

6. What recommendation does the board have in terms of: enlarging its powers; reducing its powers; enabling it to represent more effectively the people who elected its members?

7. What steps or structures do you recommend for making the

local schools more responsive to neighborhood interests and requests?

8. What do you see as the future of community or alternative schools?

9. Does your school system deal adequately with problem children (behavioral, learning, or health problems)? If not, what changes would you recommend?

For State School Board Representatives

These individuals received the same questions as local school board representatives except "state board" was substituted for "local school board."

For Community or Citizen Groups

1. What have been (are) the major issues with which you have been concerned over the past few years, and what response has the school system made in regard to them? (Describe the steps taken, the roadblocks encountered, and the eventual decision-making process.)

2. Do you feel there is adequate power in your school board? local superintendent? teachers? other local officials?

3. Do you feel you are able to approach and influence these officials in regard to either specific problems or broad policy evolution?

4. What mechanisms or structures would you recommend to change your relationship to these officials?

5. Do you feel that the school board adequately represents your interests in its negotiations with the teachers' union? If not, how would you change the present situation?

6. Would you describe the most appropriate role for a group such as your own in regard to shaping the public schools and suggest how that role could be more effective?

7. What, in your view, has been the impact of litigation in regard to desegregation, school finance, or other issues on your school system?

8. What do you see as the future of community or alternative schools and why?

9. Does your school system deal adequately with problem children (behavioral, learning, or health problems)? If not, what changes would you recommend?

Testimony

Procedures *

In order to provide the fullest opportunity for as many people as possible to testify and for the Commission to gather relevant information, we have established the following guidelines for witnesses to follow:

1. Whenever possible, your testimony should be submitted in writing to our Columbia, Maryland, office a week in advance of the hearing. If you have been unable to submit it prior to the proceedings, bring the written testimony with you to the hearing.

2. You are specifically requested to summarize your testimony. *DO NOT READ VERBATIM.* The Commissioners will want time to ask questions. (Reading your testimony is not necessary. A court stenographer will incorporate your written testimony directly into the record.)

3. You will be given approximately three to five minutes for summation of written testimony; ten to fifteen minutes for questions and answers.

4. Prior to the hearing you will be informed of the approximate time for your testimony. It is advisable, however, that you plan to be present for the full morning, afternoon, or evening.

5. Owing to the press of our hearing schedule, in the event that you are not called to testify your written testimony will be included in the court stenographer's minutes for the hearing. We will do everything in our power to prevent this kind of schedule change. If this does happen, however, please accept our apologies for the inconvenience.

Analysis

The actual analysis of the public hearing transcripts was at once a simple, spontaneous process and a complex, technical one. Some of the interpretation resulted from a careful reading of what was actually said since it was understood that the people who spoke said meaningful things. These words were then subjected to a deeper study to see if style, tone, and reaction to questions were in tune with the spoken words.

It is natural to doubt that any interpreter has really grasped the essence of another person's speech, and so there is another, more

*These procedures were enclosed with the letters asking people to be witnesses at the public hearing.

systematic way to be reasonably sure that we *understand* the significance of the public hearings. The technical processes by which field data can be effectively analyzed have been the object of extended scholarly inquiry and analysis during the past half century and have led to a substantial body of technical literature, but, unfortunately, space does not permit a detailed treatment of this complex subject.

It may be helpful in understanding the application of this technique to the public hearing testimony if we outline the assumptions and the principles of interpretation that were central to the analysis of the videotapes and transcripts. These technical notes may be useful both to the general reader and to the policy makers and scholars who wish to expand this inquiry. For the critical reader the notes may lead to alternative interpretations that were not apparent to the Commission members and staff. For the policy maker and scholar they will be a guide to the reliability and the limits of the public hearing process in shaping questions concerning public school governance.

We were able to make five assumptions that seemed reasonable and necessary in order to analyze effectively the public hearing testimony:

1. The witnesses who appeared before the Commission spoke seriously about matters that they considered important.

2. Education is a national experience for all of its regional variations. Since "going to school" has the same basic meaning throughout the nation, the differences among school systems can be compared for improvements, shortcomings, or accommodations to variations in local settings.

3. Because governance and control are sufficiently broad concepts, the testimony of some witnesses may not touch directly on that of some others. Educational governance, like any experience, is approached from a particular perspective; thus, the witnesses spoke about those matters that were important to them.

4. The witnesses who testified were representative of many others who might have spoken from a broad cross section of occupations and ethnic interests.

5. In public testimony people are trying to "say something," that is, express an opinion; and "do something," that is, make something happen. They expect that their words will influence policy changes.

Principles of Interpretation

On the basis of the above assumptions, we derived the following principles:

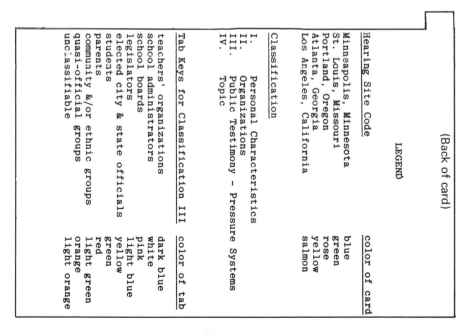

Figure B-1
Functional role groupings of witnesses

1. People with similar views will use words and phrases in a similar way. A comparison of the uses of key words and phrases not only clarifies meanings but often identifies the point of view of the speaker.

2. There are certain patterns that emerge in the videotapes and transcripts that help to disclose the way each witness approaches general issues. The perspectives and life-styles of the witnesses account for their different beliefs about an issue.

3. It is possible to distinguish between the witnesses' views about how educational governance is and how it might or should be, although this is not always explicit in the testimony.

4. Conflicts can be identified and organized according to meaningful groupings of witnesses. As we said in Chapters 2-4, there are both functional role groupings (Figure B-1) and ethnic groupings (Table B-1) for the witnesses. If we had had more complete information about the witnesses, we might have found other important groupings as well. It seems likely, for example, that political orientations, religious affiliations, and age groups may help to shape ideas about school governance and policy making. Our data on these factors are too limited, however, to use them effectively. What is important for this analysis is that there are meaningful associations among the groups we identified and we can describe the agreements and conflicts among the witnesses.

5. All of the testimony is meaningful and should be interpreted with care.

Table B-1
Role-ethnicity groupings of witnesses

Witnesses	Majority	Minority	Unknown
Students	12	11	1
Parents-citizens	55	37	2
Teachers	15	7	3
Administrators	6	4	0
School board members	4	3	0
State executives	8	2	0
State legislators	10	1	0
Others	5	4	0

Resource and Contact People*

Minneapolis, Minnesota†

Wendell R. Anderson, Governor of Minnesota
Daryl Carter, President, Minneapolis Education Association
Howard P. Casmey, Commissioner of Education, State of Minnesota
Gerald Christenson, Director of State Planning
John B. Davis, Superintendent of Schools
W. Harry Davis, Chairman of School Board
Alvin Hofsted, Mayor of Minneapolis
Dean Honetschlager, Director, Minnesota Human Resources
Carl Johnson, Chairman, Minnesota House Education Committee
Larry Leventhal, attorney
Norman Moen, President, Minneapolis Federation of Teachers
Anthony Morley, Director, Southeast Alternative Program
Maxine Nathanson, Minneapolis Citizens Committee on Public Education
August Rivera, Minneapolis school system, Information Service
Bruce Quackenbush, Assistant to the Mayor
Samuel Richardson, State Department of Human Rights
August Rivera, Minneapolis school system, Information Service
Betty Svetnson, Director, St. Paul Volunteer Services
Ralph Ware, clinical psychologist

St. Louis, Missouri‡

W. C. Banta, State Board of Education
James Barnes, KETC-TV
Zack Bettis, State Board of Education
Michael Bingman, Executive Secretary, St. Louis Teachers' Association
Anita Bond, State Advisory Committee, U.S. Civil Rights Commission
Christopher S. Bond, Governor of Missouri
Danforth Foundation
Demosthenes DuBose, President, St. Louis Teachers' Union
Joseph W. Fordyce, St. Louis Jr. College

*Purpose for contact: Develop information, gather data, encourage local support, identify resource and community organizations, media contacts, potential witnesses, and so forth.

†Forty-nine people were contacted by communications and personal interviews by members of the staff.

‡Sixty-one people were contacted by communications and personal interviews by members of the staff.

Frankie Freeman, United States Civil Rights Commission
P. Wayne Goode, State Representative
Arthur L. Mallory, Commissioner of Education
Clyde Miller, Superintendent of Schools
Alice Muckler, White House Conference on Education
Robert Osborne, Education Aide to the Mayor
William Pearson, Assistant Superintendent of Schools
John H. Poelker, Mayor of St. Louis
Irene M. Wright, Dean of Instruction, Harris Teachers College

Portland, Oregon †

Donald Barney, Mayor's office
Robert Blanchard, Superintendent of Schools
Ernest Bonner, Director of City Planning
Charles Clemman, Legislative Lobbyist, Department of Education
Howard Cherry, State Senator
John Danielson, Oregon Education Association
Jesse Fasold, State Superintendent of Schools
Cleveland Gilchrease, Portland Community Action Agency
William Gunn, President, Portland Association of Teachers
Gladys McCoy, School Board
Donald McElroy, Assistant Superintendent of Schools
John Nellor, Portland Public School Office of Public Information
Thomas Owens, Northwest Region Education Laboratory
Mary Rieke, State Representative
Wanda Silverman, Schools for the City

Atlanta, Georgia ‡

Junie Brown, *Atlanta Journal*
K. C. Chavitz, Leadership Development Program
Alonzo Crim, Superintendent of Schools
William Denton, Director, Center for School and Community Services, Atlanta University
Hugh Fordyce, Citizen Advisory Committee
Winifred Greene, Director, S.E. Public Education, American Friends Service Committee
Rufus Huffman, Southern Education Field Director, NAACP
Goldie Johnson, Center for School and Community Services, Atlanta University

†Forty-nine people were contacted by communications and personal interviews by members of the staff.

‡One hundred and sixty-eight people were contacted by communications and personal interviews by members of the staff.

Tom Keating, *Your Community Schools,* Newsletter
Esther LeFevre, Director, Community Learning Center, Cabbage Town
Jack Leppert, Senate Education Committee, Florida
Larry Linker, Georgia State University
Roger Mills, Education Task Force, Southern Regional Council
Terry Peterson, South Carolina
Dorothy Routh, Leadership Development Program

Los Angeles, California†

Roy Azarnoff, Mayor's office
Rosalind Cooperman, Education Chairman, Women For
Clive Hoffman, public relations
William Johnston, Superintendent of Schools, LAUSD
Walter Jones, Black Education Committee, LAUSD
Ethel Lichtman, Commission on Educational Governance
Robert Loveland, Chairman, Goals Committee, LAUSD
Ruth March, National Committee for Citizens in Education
Jack McCurdy, *Los Angeles Times*
Lois Nevius, Community Relations Council of Southern California
William Rivera, Assistant Superintendent of Schools
Connie Schiff, LWV
Robert Scott, San Francisco Service Center
Robert Singleton, Director, Education Finances and Resources Project of California
James Taylor, Deputy Superintendent of Schools, LAUSD

†Two hundred and fourteen people were contacted by communications and personal interviews by members of the staff.

APPENDIX C. HEARING SCHEDULES, GUIDELINES, AND WITNESSES

Schedules

Minneapolis, Minnesota

"Who Controls American Education?"

Heritage Hall, Public Library
April 22, 1974
9:30-4:00 and 7:00-9:00

Impaneled Commissioners
Sarah Carey, chairperson
R. Stephen Browning, hearing
  counsel
Karen Blank
Daniel A. Collins
Calvin J. Hurd
Susanne Martinez
Phyllis Wiener

Observers
Citizens Conference on State Legis-
  latures
Education Commission of the
  States
National Legislative Conference

St. Louis, Missouri

"Who Controls American Education?"

Theatre Building of Forest Park Community College
May 21, 1974
9:30-4:00 and 7:00-9:00

Impaneled Commissioners
Sarah Carey, chairperson
R. Stephen Browning, hearing
  counsel
Karen Blank
Charles Bowen
Daniel A. Collins
Frederick T. Haley

Observers
Citizens Conference on State Legis-
  latures
National Legislative Conference
National Urban Coalition

Portland, Oregon

"Who Controls American Education?"

Auditorium, Bonneville Power Building
June 26, 1974
9:30-4:00 and 7:00-9:00

Impaneled Commissioners	*Observers*
R. Stephen Browning, hearing counsel	Education Commission of the States
Karen Blank	
Daniel A. Collins	
Mrs. Merrimon Cuninggim	
Frederick T. Haley	
Ethel Lichtman	

Atlanta, Georgia

"Who Controls American Education?"

City Hall, Council Chambers

August 22, 1974	August 23, 1974
9:00 a.m.-10:00 p.m.	9:00 a.m.-4:00 p.m.

Impaneled Commissioners	*Observers*
Karen Blank	Education Commission of the States
Mrs. Merrimon Cuninggim	
Susanne Martinez	
Charlotte Ryan	
Paul Ylvisaker	

Los Angeles, California

"Who Controls American Education?"

Board of Public Works Room, City Hall
October 17, 1974   October 18, 1974
9:00 a.m.-10:00 p.m.   9:00 a.m.-4:00 p.m.

Impaneled Commissioners
Calvin J. Hurd, chairperson
  (October 17)
Phyllis Wiener, chairperson
  (October 18)
Karen Blank
Susan Blaustein
Frederick T. Haley
Ethel Lichtman
Susanne Martinez

Observers
Citizens Conference on State Legislatures
Education Commission of the States
National Urban Coalition

Guidelines*

This is one of five nationwide public hearings conducted by the National Committee for Citizens in Education on the subject of educational governance.

1. These hearings, open to the public, are divided into two segments—a day session running from 9:30 a.m. to 4 p.m., and an evening session running from 7 p.m. to 9 p.m.

2. The day session will be to hear invited witnesses who have been selected by the Commission on the basis of interviews. Witnesses will make a brief presentation followed by questions from the panel.

3. The evening session will be conducted under an open format, whereby any citizen, student, or representative of any group will be allowed to testify on a first-come basis.

4. Evening session witnesses are asked to sign up on the sheets provided at the witness tables at the hearing room door. These witnesses will be called in the order they signed up, subject only to a time limit and order rulings from the chair.

5. The exact time limit for evening witnesses will be announced at the beginning of the session and will depend on the number of witnesses who wish to testify.

*The guidelines were placed on a table outside the door of the hearing room along with attendance sheets.

6. Each witness will be subject to questions only from the chair and the members of the hearing panel. No questions from the floor will be permitted.

7. A timekeeper will indicate when the witness has thirty seconds of his or her allotted time left and again when the witness must conclude testimony.

8. All witnesses are encouraged to submit written statements or exhibits in addition to, or instead of, oral testimony. Written statements will carry the same weight as oral presentations and will be made part of the hearing record. Written material should be handed to the stenographer, and it should be clearly marked with the name and address of the witness.

9. A hearing counsel will assist the chairperson in the conduct of this hearing, which is operated under standard rules of order.

10. Members of the hearing panel have been selected from the attached list. All Commissioners listed will attend at least two of the six hearings, and all of them will actively participate in the preparation of the final report of findings and recommendations.

Any inquiries on these hearings should be directed to:

Ms. Shelly Weinstein
National Committee for Citizens in Education
Suite 410, Wilde Lake Village Green
Columbia, Maryland 21044

Witnesses

Minneapolis, Minnesota

Mindy Peabody, student
Frank Wilderson, Jr., student
Jeffrey Indek, student
Jerome M. Hughes, State Senator
James O'Brien, Director, Heart of the Earth Survival School
Brad Sonogles, student, Heart of the Earth Survival School
Mark Self, student
John B. Davis, Jr., Superintendent of Schools, Minneapolis
James Kent, Director, Southeast Alternatives
Margaret Schryer, staff, Teacher Center
Timi Stevens, Parent Council, Southeast Alternatives
Jane Starr, parent, Teacher Center Board
Gleason Glover, Executive Director, Minneapolis Urban League
Ann Darby, Director of Community Organizations, Urban League
Dean Honetschlager, Office of State Planning

Dwayne Dunkley, Director of Indian Education, Department of Education

Helen Miller, representing State Representative Lynda Berglin

Howard Casmey, State Commissioner of Education

Barbara Schwartz, Citizens for Integrated Education

Jan Hively, Minneapolis Accountability Project

Nathan Miller, Minneapolis Accountability Project

James Hetland, Minneapolis Accountability Project

Joseph Howard, Minneapolis Accountability Project

Bryant Peterson, citizen activist

W. Harry Davis, President, Minneapolis Board of Education

Marvin Geissness, Citizens' League

Roger R. Palmer, Citizens' League

Norman Moen, President, Minneapolis Federation of Teachers

Dale Holstrom, Minneapolis Federation of Teachers

Ervin Gaines, Director, Minneapolis Public Library

Mary Tjosvold, Women's Education Action Group

Anthony Zaragoza, President, League of United Latin American Citizens

Joyce Klep, teacher, alternative school

Claudia Furlong, parent

St. Louis, Missouri

Chandra McFarland, student

Jean Tecku, student

Wayne Goode, State Representative

Ms. J. Robert Trevor, Education Alliance of Citizens' Groups

Elma Myers, citizen

Percy Green, A.C.T.I.O.N.

James Conway, State Representative

Anita Bond, State's Advisory U.S. Civil Rights Commission

Charles Oldham, attorney with State's Advisory U.S. Civil Rights Commission

Deverne Calloway, State Representative

Zack Bettis, State Board of Education

Demosthenes DuBose, President, St. Louis Teachers' Union

Carol Losos, Vice-President, White House Conference on Education

Vera Burke, Education Chairman, State LWV

Jan Schoenfeld, Metropolitan Council, LWV

Dorothy Springer, Parents' Congress

Tom Keating, *Your Community Schools,* Newsletter, Atlanta

Al Chappelle, Director, Sophia, Inc.

Mary Ellen Stanwick, Institute for Responsive Education, Connecticut

Josie Thomas, Parents' Congress

Al Katzenberger, teacher

Portland, Oregon

Donald Barney, Education Assistant, Mayor's office

Cecil Hammond, Assistant Superintendent of Education, Washington State

Thomas Rigby, Executive Director, Oregon School Board Association

Robert Dahlman, Executive Secretary, Portland Association of Teachers

William Oberteuffer, teacher

Milton Baum, representing State Superintendent of Education Jesse Fasso

Mary Rieke, State Representative

Sylvia Gates, student

Mark Cogan, student

Kenneth Clarkson, student

Robert Ridgely, Vice-Chairman, Portland School Board

Gladys McCoy, member, Portland School Board

Robert Blanchard, Superintendent, Portland Public Schools

Mattie Spears, Chairperson, Parents' Advisory Council Board, Elliot School

William Siverly, Title I Advisory Committee

Sharon Siverly, Title I Advisory Committee

Charlotte Brown, Title I Advisory Committee

Richard Roy, Area-wide Advisory Committee

Liz Shepherd, Chairperson, King School Advisory Board

Robert Shoemaker, Executive Officer, Schools for the City

Wanda Silverman, Executive Officer, Schools for the City

Julie Sterling, Executive Officer, Schools for the City

McKinley Burt, Oregon Black Educators' Association

C. Leroy Hite, parent and music teacher, Portland schools

Jeri Cook, parent

Keith Cook, parent

Howard Cherry, State Representative

Mrs. O. J. Gates, parent

Margaret Oberteuffer, citizen

Walter F. Morris, U.S. Postal Service, Equal Employment Specialist

Hildress Benson, citizen

Peter Blumquist, parent
Louise Weidlich, Mothers for Children

Atlanta, Georgia

Frances Paulley, citizen
Lonnie King, NAACP
Mary Sandford, Chairman, Advisory Council
Hugh Fordyce, Chairman, Sutton School Community Council
Betty Cantor, Anti-Defamation League of B'nai B'rith
William Denton, Center for School and Community Services, Atlanta
    University
Goldie Johnson, Center for School and Community Services, Atlanta
    University
Alonzo Crim, Superintendent of Schools
Esther LeFevre, Director, Community Learning Center, Cabbage
    Town
June Cofer, member, Atlanta School Board
Maggie Moody, citizen activist
Lydia Bivins, student
Rochelle Glover, student
Alfreda Brown, student
Dolores Grizby, student
Dorothy Samples, Atlanta Title I Advisory Committee
Eleanor Richardson, DeKalb Citizens for Quality in Public Education
Ryburn Stevens, American Federation of Teachers
Victor Ware, Atlanta Street Academy
Jesse Moore, Atlanta Association of Educators
Miriam Grayboff, Intergrand Planning Institute
Nathaniel Ingram, Atlanta Association of Educators
Christina LeFevre, student
Richy Jones, student
Mike Tims, student
Austin Ford, Emaus House
Maynard Jackson, Mayor of Atlanta
Neil Shorthouse, Exodus
Rufus Huffman, Southern Education Field Director, NAACP
Robert Graham, State Senator, Florida
Panke Bradley, Atlanta City Council
Winifred Greene, Director, S.E. Public Education, American Friends
    Service Committee
George Esser, Director, Southern Regional Council
Jules Sugarman, citizen
Ruby Lyells, citizen activist, Jackson, Mississippi

Los Angeles, California

Emma McFarland, Special Assistant to the Mayor of Los Angeles

W. Z. Hirsch, attorney for State Legislative Committees

E. Maylon Drake, Assistant Superintendent for Los Angeles County Schools

Clive Hoffman, citizen

Donald Newman, President, Los Angeles School Board

William Spellman, student

Mimi Wagner, student

Rory Kaufman, student and Chairman, Black Education Committee, Youth Council

Eugenia Huston, student

Kim Caldwell, student

Charlotte Tysen, student

Tony Allen, student

Julia Luna Mount, Chairman of School Advisory Councils

George Mount, Mexican-American Education Committee

Raoul Delber Wilson, Chairman, Magnolia School Advisory Committee

Julia Flores, member, Albion School Advisory Committee

Ms. Wilson, member, Magnolia School Advisory Committee

Connie Schiff, Education Consultant, Los Angeles LWV

Jackie Berman, Director of Education, California LWV

Robert House, Executive Secretary, Black Education Committee

LaVerne La Motte, Pasadena Board of Education

Robert Unruhe, President, United Teachers' Association

John Vasconcellos, State Representative

Rosalind Cooperman, Education Chairman, Women For

Rita Walters, citizen

Max Mont, Los Angeles County Federation of Labor

Walter Jones, Black Education Committee, LAUSD

Lois Nevius, Community Relations Council of Southern California

Eleanor Blumenberg, Antidefamation League of B'nai B'rith

Robert Singleton, Director, Education Finances and Resources Project of California

Ernest Aubry, Counsel, Education Finances and Resources Project of California

E. Bonilla, Chairman, Mexican-American Commission, LAUSD

Ernest Smith, Parents' Action Committee of South Central Los Angeles

Gary Goldsmith, Chairman, Micheltorena School Advisory Committee

Tom Robischon, Antioch College-West
I. J. Kenny, parent
Mattie Netterville, parent
Sue Adkins, Title I parent
Larry Kessler, citizen
Vahoc Mardirosian, Hispanic Urban Center
Margaret Wright, United Parents' Council
David Gonzalez, parent, Area B, Florence Avenue School District
Mercedes Cardiel, Advisory Council, Florence Avenue School
Celia Garcia, parent
Rosa Lopez, Parents Involvement in the Community Action
Robert Loveland, Chairman, Goals Committee, LAUSD
Jessie Heinzman, representing State Superintendent Wilson Riles
James Taylor, Deputy Superintendent, LAUSD
James Ballard, San Francisco Federation of Teachers
Betty Kozasa, Asian-American Voluntary Action Center
Pegge Lacey, President, San Francisco PTA
Nicky Salan, Chairman, Zone 7 Council, San Francisco PTA
Mary Byrd, President, San Francisco Urban School Administrators
Robert Grant, President, Professional Educators of Los Angeles
Leo Lopez, Director, Migrant Education for California
Barbara Boudreaux, teacher
Al Boudreaux, teacher
Betty Blake, Thirty-first District, Los Angeles PTA

Written Testimony*

St. Louis, Missouri

Clyde Miller, Superintendent of Schools
Robert Elsea, Cooperating School District
Marlene English, Parkway Community School
Andrew Doyle, St. Louis University

Portland, Oregon

Jean Bucciarelli, Community Advisory Council
William Gunn, Portland Association of Teachers
Jesse Fasold, State Superintendent of Education

Los Angeles, California

Betty Simons, teacher
Jo Celio, parent

*These people submitted written testimony, but did not appear in person.

Elliot Medrich, California Master Plan Citizens' Committee
James Ware, consultant to Assemblyman Leon Ralph
Edward Robinson, Neighborhood Adult Participation Project

APPENDIX D. MINIHEARING AND LEADERSHIP DEVELOPMENT PROGRAM CONFERENCE, BLACKSBURG, VIRGINIA, AUGUST 9, 1974

Witnesses

Joy Sovde, LWV, Rock Hill, South Carolina

Paul A. Judkins, Leadership Development Program, Northeast, Fannington, Maine

Dexter Montgomery, Leadership Development Program, Amory, Mississippi

J. C. Taylor, Florence, South Carolina

Aaron Jones, Moss Point, Mississippi

Rufus C. Huffman, Southern Education Field Director, NAACP

M. Hayes Mizell, American Friends Service Committee, Columbia, South Carolina

W. Al Schuler, Administrative Assistant to Superintendent of Schools, Cobb County, Georgia

Robert J. Armour, Principal, Goodwater Elementary School, Goodwater, Alabama

Questions Distributed to Potential Participants

1. Does your school community provide some form of citizen advisory committees? At what level are they? District-wide or community? Are they effective? What are their responsibilities?

2. Could you describe briefly the profile of your community (ethnic, minority, economic, occupations, and so forth)?

3. What are the community's concerns about its schools?

4. How does it deal with these concerns? How does it communicate with the school administration or the school board?

5. How does the school administration, central staff, teacher, or principal communicate with the citizens?

6. Could you explain briefly how your community pays for its schools?

7. Is the present financing and school districting a deterrent to equality of programming? What other influences determine the programs afforded?

8. Do parents or students have a share in the decisions determining the courses available to them?

9. What issues are the teachers presently concerned with?

10. There may be one incident or issue that you believe can best describe the role of the citizen in the decision-making process of your schools. Could you use it as an example to illustrate your views on community participation?

APPENDIX E. STATE COLLECTIVE BARGAINING LAWS AFFECTING EDUCATION

December 1974

State and Statutory Reference; Identification	Coverage; Employe Classification; Level	Bargaining Unit; Type of Representation; Union Security	Administration	Scope of Bargaining; Management Rights	Bargaining Impasse Procedures	Grievance Procedures	Unfair Practices, Penalties; Strikes	Final Form; Deadline Dates For Completed Agreements	Comments
ALABAMA									A statutory prohibition of public employe membership in labor unions was declared unconstitutional in 1972. State has firefighters bargaining: Tit. 37, § 450(3)
ALASKA § A 14.20.550 through A 14.20.610 CB | P K-12	All certified employes K-12 level	All certified employes; superintendents excluded. Certified administrative personnel, including principals, asst. principals may bargain separately. Exclusive representation; no union security	Local school boards or directors of state-operated schools	Matters pertaining to employment and fulfillment of professional duties	Mediation Board; recommendations to be made public	Must be bargained	No specific provisions	Final agreement must be made at public meeting. No deadline specified	
ALASKA Public Employment Relations Act: § 23.40.010 through 23.40.240 CB | P-C PS	All public employes, including professional and classified postsecondary personnel	Units determined by Labor Relations Agency. Exclusive representation; union shop, dues checkoff, service fees permitted	Labor Relations Agency; Department of Labor	Wages, hours, terms and conditions of employment. Merit system retention	Mediation; arbitration	Must be bargained. Must provide binding arbitration	"Standard" provisions (no interference, restraint, coercion, discrimination, etc.). Injunctive relief. Strikes permitted after mediation; to be followed by binding arbitration	Written agreement not to exceed 3 years. No deadline specified	Bargained items requiring funding are subject to legislative approval.
ARIZONA									State has no public employe collective bargaining legislation.
ARKANSAS									State has no public employe collective bargaining legislation.

State and Statutory Reference; Identification	Coverage: Employe Classification; Level	Bargaining Unit; Type of Representation; Union Security	Administration	Scope of Bargaining; Management Rights	Bargaining Impasse Procedures	Grievance Procedures	Unfair Practices; Penalties; Strikes	Final Form; Deadline Dates For Completed Agreements	Comments
CALIFORNIA West's Annotated California Education Code: Winton Act: § 13080 through 13090. MC / K-12 / P-C	All public school employes except those elected by popular vote or appointed by governor. K-12 level, professional and classified	Any number of public school employe organizations permitted. Proportional representation with single certificated employe council. No "management" on council; separate management group permitted	Public school employer to adopt rules and regulations. County board of education is employer for multi-organization council	All matters relating to employer-employment conditions, employer-employe relations, procedures relating to definition of educational objectives, course content, curricula, textbooks, etc. If permitted by law, Certificated employes may bargain above; classified employes may not bargain undefined items, or "other terms and conditions of employment"	No specific provisions	Resolution procedure for persistent disagreements to be established by meeting and conferring. Provision for factfinding committee; nonbinding recommendations	Standard provisions for unfair practices. No specific provisions for strikes	No legally enforceable contracts, written resolutions, regulations or policies permitted. Written memorandum of understanding may be presented to governing body	A meet and confer law. Other bargaining laws not covering education are: Public Employes; § 3500-3510 of Government Code; State Employes, § 3525-3526 of Government Code; and Firefighters, § 1960-1963 of Labor Code. A 1971 governor's executive order called for meeting and conferring with non-academic university and college employes on general salary increases, inequities, and general benefits.
COLORADO									State has no public employe collective bargaining legislation.
CONNECTICUT General Statutes Annotated: § 10-153a through 10-153g. MC / K-12 / P	All certified professional employes of town and regional boards of education except administrators and persons responsible for budget preparation, personnel relations and temporary substitutes. K-12 level	Separate units for administrators and non-administrators may be combined only by mutual agreement. Exclusive representation. No union security	Local and state boards of education	Salaries and other conditions of employment about which either party wishes to meet and confer	Mediation by secretary of state board of education. Arbitration with nonbinding recommendations	No specific provisions	Standard provisions for unfair practices. Strikes prohibited; no penalties specified	Written agreement to be completed in time for budget-making process	Agreement is binding on legislative body of town or regional district unless rejected by such body; renegotiation prescribed. A meet and confer law. State has Municipal Employes Relations Act: PA 159, L 1969.
DELAWARE Code: Tit. 14, Ch. 40, § 4001-4013. MC / K-12 / P	All certificated non-administrative employes, excluding supervisory and staff personnel. K-12 level	All covered employes. Exclusive representation. Dues checkoff permitted	Local boards and state board of education	Salaries, employe benefits, working conditions must be bargained. May meet and confer on other matters as defined in act	Mediation, factfinding, nonbinding recommendations	No specific provisions	Unfair practices defined as any tactic which circumvents teacher contracts. Strikes prohibited, with loss of unit recognition for violation	Form of minimum 2-year agreement not specified. No deadline specified	A meet and confer law.

State and Statutory Reference; Identification	Coverage: Employee Classification; Level	Bargaining Unit; Type of Representation; Union Security	Administration	Scope of Bargaining; Management Rights	Bargaining Impasse Procedures	Grievance Procedures	Unfair Practices; Penalties; Strikes	Final Form; Deadline Dates For Completed Agreements	Comments
DELAWARE Code: Right of Public Employees to Organize: Tit. 19, Ch. 13, § 1301 through 1313 MC PS	Any certificated professional employee of public school system of state; includes postsecondary	Unit determination not specified. Exclusive representation. Dues checkoff permitted	Department of Labor and Industrial Relations	Employee relations, wages, salaries, hours, vacations, sick leave, grievance procedures, other terms and conditions of employment	State mediation service or arbitration. Wages and salaries excluded	May be bargained	Standard provisions for unfair practices. Strikes prohibited; no penalties specified	Written agreement. No deadline specified	A meet and confer law.
FLORIDA Statutes: Public Employe Relations Act: § 447.001 through 447.023 CB K-12 P-C PS CC	Public employees; K-12 and postsecondary levels included; professional and classified	Criteria listed for appropriateness of unit. Final review of unit determination by Public Employe Relations Commission. Exclusive representation. Dues checkoff permitted	Public Employe Relations Commission: 5 members appointed by governor	Wages, hours, terms and conditions of employment. Extensive management rights; merit system protected	Mediation, "special master" for public hearings, factfinding. Settlement by appropriate legislative body	Must be bargained; must provide for binding disposition	Standard provisions for unfair practices; injunctive relief. Strikes prohibited, listed as unfair practice; injunctive relief; fines, damages, probation, loss of unit recognition for violation	Written contract. No deadline specified	Impasse to be declared if no agreement after 60 bargaining days or 70 days prior to budget submission date. Legislative last resort settlement of impasse. Legislature has right to approve, amend or rescind all rules of PERC.
GEORGIA									State has Firefighters Bargaining Law: Code of Georgia Annotated, § 54.1301 through 54.1315
HAWAII Statutes: Public Employees Act: § 89-1 through 89-17 CB K-12 P-C PS	Any person employed by a public employer except elected and appointed officials and top level management. K-12 and postsecondary levels; professional and classified	13 categories for appropriate units listed, including teachers and other personnel on same salary schedule; education officers and others on same salary schedule; faculty of University of Hawaii & Community College System; other postsecondary personnel. Exclusive representation. Dues checkoff, service fee permitted	Public Employment Relations Board: 3 members, 1 management, 1 labor, 1 public, appointed by governor	Wages, hours, other terms and conditions of employment. Specific exclusions. Extensive management rights; merit system protected	Mediation, factfinding; may culminate in binding arbitration by mutual agreement	May be bargained. Must culminate in final binding agreement	Standard provisions for unfair practices. Strikes permitted after factfinding if no arbitration occurs	Written contract. Reasonable effort must be made to conclude prior to legislative appropriation of cost items	Students and student help of state institutions excluded from act. Terms of agreement within legal scope of bargaining prevail over existing rules and regulations of employer. Act takes precedence over all conflicting statutes; preempts all contrary local regulation.

State and Statutory Reference; Identification	Coverage: Employee Classification; Level	Bargaining Unit; Type of Representation; Union Security	Administration	Scope of Bargaining; Management Rights	Bargaining Impasse Procedures	Grievance Procedures	Unfair Practices; Penalties; Strikes	Final Form; Deadline Dates For Completed Agreements	Comments
IDAHO Code; § 33–1271 through 33–1276 **MC** K-12 | P	Certificated employes of school districts. K-12 level	Superintendents, supervisors and principals may be excluded from professional employe group by agreement. Exclusive representation. No union security	Local board of trustees of school district	Specified in agreement. School board "necessary action" protected	Mediation, factfinding, nonbinding recommendations	No specific provisions	No specific provisions	Final form not specified. No deadline specified	A meet and confer law. Powers, duties and responsibilities of legislature, state board of education, local boards are protected State has firefighters bargaining act: Ch. 138, L1970.
ILLINOIS									State has no public employe collective bargaining legislation. Under a 1966 judicial ruling, teachers and local employes may bargain collectively. State universities have conducted bargaining under personnel code. State executive branch employes, under 1973 executive order, may negotiate wages, hours and certain conditions of employment not regulated by law.
INDIANA Burns Annotated Statutes: § 28–4551 through 28–4564 **CB** K-12 | P	Certificated employes. Supervisors, confidential employes, security employes and noncertificated employes excluded. K-12 level	Certificated employe organization. Exclusive representation. Dues checkoff permitted	Education Employment Relations Board: 3 members appointed by governor	Salaries, wages and related fringe benefits, hours. Deficit financing prohibited. Extensive management rights listed	Mediation and factfinding by Education Employment Relations Board	May be bargained. May be subject to binding arbitration; change in contract prohibited. Complaints to and hearing by EERB	Standard provisions for unfair practices. Strikes prohibited, with no makeup time; salary loss, loss of dues checkoff for violation	Written contract. If agreement is not reached 14 days before budget submission date, tentative individual contracts authorized; bargaining to continue	A 1969 attorney general's opinion states that public employers, including boards of higher education, may not engage in collective bargaining until authorized by legislature. Contracts may not include provisions in conflict with rights or benefits established by federal or state law.

State and Statutory Reference; Identification	Coverage; Employe Classification; Level	Bargaining Unit; Type of Representation; Union Security	Administration	Scope of Bargaining; Management Rights	Bargaining Impasse Procedures	Grievance Procedures	Unfair Practices, Penalties; Strikes	Final Form; Deadline Dates For Completed Agreements	Comments
IOWA SF 531 of 1974 CB K-12 | PS	Public employes, excluding administrators, superintendents, principals, asst. principals, elective officials, certain students. K-12 and postsecondary levels; professional and classified	Professional and nonprofessional employes; separate or single unit by agreement. Exclusive representation. Dues checkoff permitted	Public Employment Relations Board: 3 members appointed by governor	Wages, hours, terms and conditions of employment, including health, safety, evaluation, in-service training, mutually agreed-upon matters. Retirement excluded. Extensive management rights listed	Mediation, factfinding, binding arbitration	May be bargained; may provide binding arbitration	Standard provisions for unfair practices. Strikes prohibited; injunctive relief. Fines, dismissal, loss of organization recognition for violation	Final form not specified, must be made public. Impasse procedures must begin 120 days before budget submission date	Contract is not to be inconsistent with statutory limitations on public employer funds. If provisions of act jeopardize federal funds to state, they are inoperative.
KANSAS Revised Statutes: §72-5413 through 72-5425 MC K-12 | CC	All professional employes. K-12 and community college levels	Separate teacher and administrator units. State board to settle unit determination disputes. Exclusive representation. No union security	State board of education	Terms and conditions of professional service	No specific provisions	May be bargained; may provide binding arbitration	No specific provisions for unfair practices. Strikes prohibited: no penalties specified	Final form not specified, but not to exceed 2 years. No deadline specified	A meet and confer law. Supreme court ruled in 1973 that Act requires negotiation, not merely meeting and conferring; written agreement in master or individual contracts; binding on both parties.
KANSAS Public Employe Law: Revised Statutes: §75-4321 through 75-4337 MC K-12 | C PS | P-C	Public employes. Classified K-12; professional and classified postsecondary included	Public employes, including supervisors by agreement. Exclusive representation. No union security	Public Employe Relations Board: 5 members; 1 public employe, 1 management, 3 at-large, appointed by governor	Conditions of employment, including salaries, wages, hours, etc.	Mediation, factfinding	May be bargained	Standard provisions for unfair practices. Strikes prohibited; injunctive relief	Written memo of agreement to be completed 14 days before budget submission date	A meet and confer law.
KENTUCKY									State has Firefighters Collective Bargaining Act: Kentucky Revised Statutes, Ch. 345 (cities over 300,000 or by petition); county policemen's collective bargaining (over 300,000); KRS Ch. 78. A 1965 attorney general's opinion (65-84) indicated a right of teachers to bargain collectively. Recent teacher attempts to organize have been refused by the courts and attorney general.

State and Statutory Reference; Identification	Coverage: Employee Classification; Level	Bargaining Unit; Type of Representation; Union Security	Administration	Scope of Bargaining; Management Rights	Bargaining Impasse Procedures	Grievance Procedures	Unfair Practices, Penalties; Strikes	Final Form; Deadline Dates For Completed Agreements	Comments
LOUISIANA									State has no public employe collective bargaining legislation.
MAINE Municipal Employe Law: Revised Statutes: Tit. 26, § 961 through 972 **CB** **K-12** | **P-C**	Any municipal or political subdivision employe except superintendent, asst. superintendent, asst. principals, supervisory teachers. Principals, supervisory teachers may be included in teacher unit. Exclusive representation. No union security	Employer or Executive Director of Public Employes Labor Relations Board to determine unit. Principals, asst. principals, supervisory teachers may be included in teacher unit. Exclusive representation. No union security	Public Employes Labor Relations Board: 3 members, 3 alternates appointed by governor: 1 employer, 1 employe, 1 public	Must bargain wages, hours, working conditions and grievance arbitration. Must meet and confer on educational policies. Merit system protected	Mediation and/or factfinding. Maine Board of Conciliation & Arbitration available. Binding arbitration on all matters by mutual consent; if no consent, binding arbitration on matters other than salaries, pensions, insurance	Parties may enter into binding arbitration agreements on meaning or application of specific terms of contract	Standard provisions for unfair practices. Strikes prohibited, listed as unfair practice; injunctive relief	Written contract not to exceed 3 years. No deadline specified	
MAINE State Employe Law: Revised Statutes: Tit. 26, § 979 through 979n **CB** **PS** | **C**	Any state employe except: elected or appointed. Interpretation includes postsecondary classified personnel, excludes faculty	All covered employes. Exclusive representation. No union security	Public Employes Labor Relations Board: 3 members, 3 alternates appointed by governor: 1 employer, 1 employe, 1 public	Wages, hours, working conditions, contract grievance arbitration, employe-employer relationships; other items not controlled by law. Merit system protected. Eligibility of state for federal grants in aid and assistance programs protected	Mediation and/or factfinding. Maine Board of Conciliation & Arbitration available. Binding arbitration on all matters by mutual consent, if no consent, binding arbitrat on on matters other than sa aries, pensions, insurance.	May be bargained. Binding arbitration may be included to supersede other procedures in statutes. State Employe Appeals Board to resolve if grievance procedures not bargained	Standard provisions for unfair practices. Strikes prohibited, listed as unfair practice; injunctive relief, court review	Written contract not to exceed 3 years. Cost items must be submitted to governor 10 days after ratification	Legislature has right to reject cost items; renegotiation required. It is responsibility of legislature to act on tentative agreements which require legislative action. To coordinate employer position in negotiation of agreements, legislative council is to maintain liaison with employer relative to cost items. Prior to 1974, 6 vocational institutions under state department of education voluntarily negotiated faculty contracts. University of Maine was excluded as not directly under governor.

State and Statutory Reference; Identification	Coverage; Employee Classification; Level	Bargaining Unit; Type of Representation; Union Security	Administration	Scope of Bargaining; Management Rights	Bargaining Impasse Procedures	Grievance Procedures	Unfair Practices, Penalties; Strikes	Final Form; Deadline Dates For Completed Agreements	Comments
MARYLAND Annotated Code: Art. 77, § 160-160a **MC** K-12 / P / C*	All certificated professional employees of public schools except superintendents and persons designated by their negotiators. In all but 6 counties, non-certificated employees are included. K-12 level	Unit determined by employer; no more than 2 units per district. Exclusive representation. Dues checkoff permitted	Local boards and state board of education	Salaries, wages, hours and working conditions	Mediation by mutual agreement; non-binding recommendations	Binding arbitration of grievances may be bargained	Standard provisions for unfair practices. Strikes prohibited; loss of dues checkoff and exclusivity rights for 2 years for violation	Written agreement. No deadline specified	A meet and confer law.
MASSACHUSETTS General Laws Annotated: State-County-Municipal Employe Law: Ch. 150-E, § 1-15, 1974 **CB** K-12 / P-C / PS	All state, county and municipal employes, including teachers, and excepting elected officials, board and commission members, police and executive officers. K-12 and postsecondary levels; professional and classified	State Labor Relations Commission to determine appropriateness of units. Exclusive representation. Service fees, dues checkoff permitted in specified areas	Labor Relations Commission: 3 members appointed by governor	Wages, hours, standards of productivity and performance and other conditions of employment	Board of Conciliation and Arbitration mediation, factfinding, binding recommendations if mutually agreed by parties and authorized by legislature	May be bargained; binding arbitration permitted. Board of Conciliation and Arbitration available	Standard provisions for unfair practices. Strikes prohibited; injunctive relief. Salary loss, no makeup, discipline and discharge for violation	Written contract not to exceed 3 years. No deadline specified	Legislature authorizes binding arbitration of contract disputes. Request for funding to be submitted to legislature within 30 days after agreement. If rejected, renegotiation prescribed.
MICHIGAN Statutes Annotated: Public Employe Relations Act: § 423.201 through 423.216 **CB** K-12 / P-C / PS / P	All public employes except those in state classified service. K-12 professional and classified; post-secondary professional	Determination of unit by MERC. Executives and supervisors excluded from employe unit; execs may form own unit. Exclusive representation. No union security	Michigan Employment Relations Board: 3 members appointed by governor, confirmed by senate	Wages, hours and other terms and conditions of employment	Mediation and factfinding; nonbinding recommendations via MERC	May be bargained. Mediation via MERC	Standard provisions for unfair practices. Strikes prohibited; discipline, dismissal for violation	Written contract. No deadline specified	
MINNESOTA Statutes Annotated: Employment Relations Act: § 179.61 through 179.67 **CB** K-12 / P-C / PS	All public employes except elected officials, election officers, National Guard and some temporary or part-time employes. K-12 and post-secondary levels; professional and classified	Public employe organizations. Principals, asst. principals, supervisors and confidential employes excluded, but may form own unit. Determination of units by PERB. Exclusive representation. Dues checkoff permitted	Public Employment Relations Board: 5 members appointed by governor, 1 at large, 2 employer, 2 employe	Matters pertaining to terms and conditions of employment and grievance procedures. Employer is not required to negotiate inherent managerial policy	Final and binding arbitration	Must be bargained; must provide compulsory binding arbitration	Standard provisions for unfair practices. Strikes prohibited; loss of unit recognition, dismissal for violation	Written contract. No deadline specified	Agreements on wages and economic fringe benefits are subject to legislative approval; renegotiation prescribed.

State and Statutory Reference; Identification	Coverage; Employe Classification; Level	Bargaining Unit; Type of Representation; Union Security	Administration	Scope of Bargaining; Management Rights	Bargaining Impasse Procedures	Grievance Procedures	Unfair Practices, Penalties; Strikes	Final Form; Deadline Dates For Completed Agreements	Comments
MISSISSIPPI									State has no public employe collective bargaining legislation.
MISSOURI Vernon's Annotated Statutes: Public Employe Law: § 105.500 through 105.540 MC | P-C K-12 | PS	Public employes, excluding K-12 and post-secondary teachers and certain others. K-12 and post-secondary classified included	Appropriate unit; community of interest. State Board of Mediation to resolve unit disputes. Exclusive representation. No union security	Public employer	Proposals relative to salaries and other conditions of employment	No specific provisions	No specific provisions	Standard provisions for unfair practices. Strikes prohibited; no penalties specified	Written agreement. No deadline specified	Agreement to be presented to appropriate legislative body in proper form for adoption, modification or rejection. A meet and confer law. A 1968 attorney general's opinion (#276) stated: "teachers may join in groups and unions for making proposals to school boards, but boards cannot enter into binding agreements with such groups."
MONTANA Revised Code: Professional Negotiations Act for Teachers: § 75-6115 through 75-6128 CB K-12 | P	All certificated employes of public school system except chief administrative officers. K-12 level	Principals may be part of teacher unit or may form own group. Exclusive representation. No union security	Local school board	Salary, hours and other terms of employment	Fifty days after beginning of negotiations either party may request factfinding by Committee or Impasse	No specific provisions	Standard provisions for unfair practices. Strikes considered unfair practice; salary loss, suspension, dismissal for violation	Written contract for a maximum of 2 years. No deadline specified	State also has public employe law which excludes teachers, professional instructors, school clerks, school administrators and paraprofessionals employed by school boards: MRC § 59-1601-16.
MONTANA Educational Employes Law: HB 1032 of 1974, Secs. 1-12 CB PS | CC K-12 | P	All resident personnel half-time or more; teachers, counselors, librarians, researchers, chairmen, deans. Students excluded. Post-secondary level; professional	Any group of covered employes on any one campus. Exclusive representation; consultative rights of faculty senate or similar groups protected. No union security	Commission on Higher Education and Board of Personnel Appeals	Wages, hours, fringe benefits and other conditions of employment. Academic freedom protected	Mediation, factfinding, voluntary binding arbitration. Recommendations requiring legislative enactment to be advisory only	Must be bargained	Standard provisions for unfair practices. No specific provisions for strikes	Written contract should be completed in time for governor's budget planning session	Contract agreements do not limit authority of legislature on appropriations.
NEBRASKA Revised Statutes: Teachers Professional Negotiations Act: § 79-1287 through 79-1295 MC K-12 | P	Certificated employes in Class III, IV, V school districts. K-12 level	Unit not specified. Exclusive representation. No union security	Local school board	Employment relations and mutually agreed-to matters	Factfinding board and non-binding recommendations	No specific provisions	No specific provisions	Written agreement. No deadline specified	A meet and confer law.

State and Statutory Reference; Identification	Coverage: Employe Classification; Level	Bargaining Unit; Type of Representation; Union Security	Administration	Scope of Bargaining; Management Rights	Bargaining Impasse Procedures	Grievance Procedures	Unfair Practices, Penalties; Strikes	Final Form; Deadline Dates For Completed Agreements	Comments
NEBRASKA Revised Statutes: Public Employes Act: § 48-801 through 48-837 CB / PS / P-C	Public employes, postsecondary professional and classified included	Unit not specified. Exclusive representation. No union security	State Court of Industrial Relations: 5 judges appointed by governor	Conditions of employment, including wages and hours	Binding arbitration by Court of Industrial Relations	May be bargained	Standard provisions for unfair practices. No specific provisions for strikes	Written contract required to cover biennial period coinciding with state budgeting period. No deadline specified	Written contract is subject to legislative approval.
NEVADA Revised Statutes: Local Government Employe Management Relations Act: § 288-010 through 288-280 CB / K-12 / P-C	Local government employes. K-12 level: professional and classified	Principals, asst. principals or other administrators below may not be in teacher unit unless district employs less than five principals. Separate units otherwise. Exclusive representation. No union security	Local Government Employe Management Relations Board: 3 members appointed by governor	Wages, hours, conditions of employment. Written notice of negotiation to employer by December 1 if funds involved	Mediation and factfinding mandatory by various dates. Governor has authority to make factfinder recommendations binding within 10 days of legislature's adjournment	Appeals and disputes may be made to Local Government Relations Board	Standard provisions for unfair practices. Strikes prohibited; no strike pledge required for recognition. Fines, salary loss, dismissal for violation; injunctive relief	Written contract at request of either party; complete by May 5 or within 10 days of legislature's adjournment	Governor has authority to make contract impasse factfinding recommendations binding within 10 days of legislature's adjournment. Contrary to earlier reports, the community college system is part of the University of Nevada system and all of its employes are not covered under this act.
NEW HAMPSHIRE Revised Statutes Annotated: Public Employe Law: § 98-C:1 through 98-C:7 CB / PS / C	Classified state employes, nonacademic excluding department heads and executive officers of University of N.H. Keene State, & Plymouth Colleges. Postsecondary level	Not less than 10 employes on campus or division of university system. Exclusive representation. Dues checkoff permitted	Public Employe Commission: 3 members, 1 chairman of state personnel commission: 1 secretary of state; 1 commissioner of labor; or designees	Conditions of employment. Extensive management rights listed	Mediation and factfinding	May be bargained. Binding arbitration for non-fund items; otherwise, advisory	No specific provisions for unfair practices. Strikes prohibited; agreements must contain no strike clause. Discipline, loss of contract for violation	Written agreement not to exceed 5 years. No deadline specified	By statute: Revised Statutes Annotated: 31.3, school board has authority but is not required to deal with teacher organization representatives. State also has municipal police officers collective bargaining: Ch. 64, L. 1972.
NEW JERSEY Statutes Annotated: Employer-Employe Relations Act: § 34:13A-1 through 34:13A-13 CB / K-12 / PS / P-C	All employes: state, county, municipal. Superintendents and nonsupervisory chief administrators excluded. K-12 and postsecondary levels; professional and classified	No unit may contain supervisors and nonsupervisors. Exclusive representation. No union security	Public Employment Relations Commission: 7 members: 2 employer, 2 employe, 3 public appointed by governor	Grievances and terms and conditions of employment	Mediation, factfinding and arbitration	Must be bargained. May provide for binding arbitration	Standard provisions for unfair practices; injunctive relief. No specific provisions for strikes	Written contracts. Deadline date regulated by PERC	

State and Statutory Reference; Identification	Coverage; Employee Classification; Level	Bargaining Unit; Type of Representation; Union Security	Administration	Scope of Bargaining; Management Rights	Bargaining Impasse Procedures	Grievance Procedures	Unfair Practices Penalties; Strikes	Final Form; Deadline Dates For Completed Agreements	Comments
NEW MEXICO									State has no public employee collective bargaining legislation; but an April 14, 1971 attorney general's opinion indicates a limited collective bargaining right for public employes and teachers. State personnel board rules include limited bargaining procedure for classified state employes
NEW YORK McKinney's Consolidated Laws Annotated: Taylor Act: Secs. 200-214, Civil Service Law **CB** K-12 / PS / P-C	Any person holding a position by appointment or employment in a unit of government. K-12 and postsecondary levels; professional and classified. Managerial, confidential, militia excluded	Community of interest. Final decision by Public Employment Relations Board. Exclusive representation. Dues checkoff permitted	Public Employment Relations Commission: 3 members appointed by governor	Terms and conditions of employment; grievance procedures	Parties to develop own procedures; may include voluntary arbitration. Mediation and factfinding available. Impasse declared 120 days prior to FY; 10 days after factfinding, legislature may intervene	Must be bargained	Standard provisions for unfair practices. Strikes prohibited; no strike pledge required for recognition; salary loss for violation	Written contract. No deadline specified	Any agreement requiring legislative action to permit implementation or additional funds must be approved by legislature.
NORTH CAROLINA General Statutes									State has no public employee collective bargaining legislation.

NCGS: § 95-85 through 95-88, barring public employee membership in national labor organizations was declared unconstitutional by U.S. District Court in 1970; section forbidding state contracts with unions was upheld. |
| **NORTH DAKOTA** Century Code: § 15-38-1.01 through 15-38-1.15 **CB** K-12 / P | All classroom teachers and administrators employed by a public school system. K-12 level | Teachers and administrators may not be in same unit. Employer determines appropriate unit. Exclusive representation. No union security | Education Fact-finding Commission: 3 members; 1 appointed by state education superintendent; 1 by governor; 1 by attorney general | Terms and conditions of employment; employer-employe relations, salaries, hours. Extensive management rights listed | Mediation, fact-finding with nonbinding recommendations via Education Fact Finding Commission. Parties may agree to own procedures | May be bargained. Board required to meet and negotiate any question arising out of interpretation of agreement | Standard provisions for unfair practices. Strikes prohibited; salary loss for violation | Written contract. No deadline specified | State also has public employe law dealing with mediation of disputes which would cover postsecondary classified employes: NDCC: § 31-11-01 through 31-11-05 |
| **OHIO** | | | | | | | | | State has no public employee collective bargaining legislation |

State and Statutory Reference; Identification	Coverage; Employe Classification; Level	Bargaining Unit; Type of Representation: Union Security	Administration	Scope of Bargaining; Management Rights	Bargaining Impasse Procedures	Grievance Procedures	Unfair Practices, Penalties; Strikes	Final Form; Deadline Dates For Completed Agreements	Comments
OKLAHOMA Statutes Annotated: § 509.1 through 509.10. CB | P-C. K-12	All employes in district. Those not wishing representation may so state in writing to local board. K-12 level: professional and classified	Separate units for certified teachers and nonprofessional employes. Exclusive representation. No union security	Local boards of education	Items affecting the performance of professional services	Parties must develop procedures. 3-member factfinding may be used on impasse	No specific provisions	Discrimination against employes exercising rights is unfair practice. Strikes prohibited; salary loss, loss of unit recognition for violation	No specific provisions	State has fireman, policeman and municipal employe collective bargaining: CSA: § 548.1 through 548.14
OREGON Revised Statutes: Public Employer Law: § 243.711 through 243.795. CB | P-C. K-12 | PS	Public employes excluding elected, appointed, confidential or supervisory. K-12 and postsecondary levels; professional and classified	No specific provisions for unit. Exclusive representation. Dues checkoff, service fees, union or agency shop permitted	Public Employe Relations Board: 5 members appointed by governor	Including but not limited to salaries, benefits, hours, terms and conditions of employment	Mediation, factfinding, binding arbitration	May be bargained	Standard provisions for unfair practices plus refusal to write and sub-contract and violation of contract. Strikes permitted if not in violation of public well-being. Enjoined strikes must be submitted to binding arbitration	Written contract if requested by either party. No deadline specified	
PENNSYLVANIA Purdon's Statutes Annotated: Public Employe Relations Act: § 43, §§ 1101.101 through 1101.2301. CB | PS. K-12	Public employes, excluding elected, governor appointed, management, confidential. K-12 and postsecondary levels; professional and classified	Appropriate units. Disputes to be settled by Labor Relations Board. Exclusive representation. Dues checkoff. Membership maintenance permitted	Labor Relations Board: 3 members appointed by governor	Wages, hours and terms and conditions of employment. Extensive management rights listed	Mutual voluntary binding arbitration permitted. Mediation, factfinding mandatory to budget submission date timetable	May be bargained. Arbitration mandatory	Standard provisions for unfair practices. Strikes prohibited if "clear and present danger" to public well-being. Otherwise permitted after exhaustion of bargaining procedures	Written contract. No deadline specified	Contract may not violate statutes. State has separate collective bargaining laws for (1) police and firemen: SB 1343 L. 1968; and (2) municipal transit employes: Act 228 L. 1967.
RHODE ISLAND General Laws: School Teachers Arbitration Act: § 28-9.3-1 through 28-9.3-16. CB | P. K-12	Certified teachers employed in any public school system, excluding superintendents, asst. superintendents, principals, asst. principals. K-12 level	All covered employes. Exclusive representation. No union security in law, but state supreme court approved agency shop contracts (with limitations) in 1972	State Labor Relations Board: 3 members appointed by governor; 1 management, 1 labor, 1 public	Hours, salaries, working conditions, terms and conditions of professional employment	Mediation if requested within 30 days of start of bargaining. Ad hoc panel to provide binding arbitration on all non-fund matters	No specific provisions	No specific provisions	Written contract not to exceed 3 years. No deadline specified	In January 1973, the state supreme court ruled teacher strikes illegal and subject to injunction.
RHODE ISLAND General Laws: State Employes: § 36-11-1 through 36-11-12. CB | P-C. PS	All public, state employes, including postsecondary level; professional and classified	All covered employes. Exclusive representation. Service fees permitted	State Labor Relations Board: 3 members appointed by governor; 1 management, 1 labor, 1 public	Wages, hours, working conditions	Mediation, factfinding, binding arbitration on non-fund matters	May be bargained	No specific provisions for unfair practices. Strikes prohibited; no penalties specified	Written contract. No deadline specified	State has fireman collective bargaining law: § 28-9.1-2 through 28-9.1-14 and policeman collective bargaining law: § 28-9.2-2 through 28-9.2-14

State and Statutory Reference; Identification	Coverage: Employee Classification; Level	Bargaining Unit; Type of Representation; Union Security	Administration	Scope of Bargaining; Management Rights	Bargaining Impasse Procedures	Grievance Procedures	Unfair Practices, Penalties; Strikes	Final Form; Deadline Dates For Completed Agreements	Comments
RHODE ISLAND General Laws: Municipal Employes Arbitration Act: § 28-9.4-1 through 28-9.4-19; CB; K-12 | C	Any employee of municipal employer (including school boards), except elected, management, etc., and teachers. Covers nonteaching K-12 personnel	All covered employes. Exclusive representation. No union security	State Labor Relations Board: 3 members appointed by governor; 1 management, 1 labor, 1 public	Hours, salary working conditions all other terms and conditions of employment	Mediation, conciliation, binding arbitration on non-fund matters. State director of labor available	No specific provisions	No specific provisions for unfair practices. Strikes prohibited; no penalties specified	Written contract not to exceed 3 years. No deadline specified	
SOUTH CAROLINA									State has Grievance Procedures Acts for state, county and municipal employes: SB 121 and SB 124, L1971; but no public employe collective bargaining legislation.
SOUTH DAKOTA Compiled Laws: Public Employe Negotiation Law: § 3-18-1 through 3-18-20; CB; K-12 | P-C; PS	Any person holding a position by appointment or employed with state public service. K-12 and postsecondary level; professional and classified	Appropriate unit; dispute to be resolved by Commissioner of Labor and Management Relations. Exclusive representation. No union security	Commissioner of Labor and Management Relations	Wages, hours and other terms and conditions of employment	Mediation with Commissioner of Labor and Management Relations available; other procedures optional	Employer to establish grievance procedures; binding decision by Commissioner of no local solution	Standard provisions for unfair practices. Strikes prohibited; injunctive relief; court review	Written contract. No deadline specified	Agreements must be submitted to appropriate legislative body, governing body or officer for approval and necessary implementation.
TENNESSEE									State has no public employe collective bargaining legislation.
TEXAS Vernon's Codes Annotated	Boards of trustees and administrative personnel of school districts may consult with teachers on matters of educational policy and conditions of employment: VTCA § 13.901. In May 1967 (#M-77) attorney general ruled that public employes have the right to present grievances concerning wages, hours or working conditions through a union not claiming the right to collective bargaining or strikes. VTCA § 22.278 forbids public employe collective bargaining contracts or strikes. State has Fire and Police Employe Relations Act permitting collective bargaining in local jurisdictions only after petition and public referendum: HB 185 of 1973.								
UTAH									State has no public employe collective bargaining legislation. The Right to Work law allows organization but not negotiation.

State and Statutory Reference; Identification	Coverage; Employe Classification; Level	Bargaining Unit; Type of Representation; Union Security	Administration	Scope of Bargaining; Management Rights	Bargaining Impasse Procedures	Grievance Procedures	Unfair Practices, Penalties; Strikes	Final Form; Deadline Dates For Completed Agreements	Comments
VERMONT Statutes Annotated: Labor Relations Act for Teachers: Tit. 16, § 1981 through 2010 **MC** K-12 | P	All certified teachers and administrators in publicly funded schools	Separate units for teachers and administrators. Exclusive representation. No union security	No specific provision	Salaries, related economic conditions of employment, grievance procedures, other mutually agreed items not in conflict with statutes. Extensive management rights	Mediation, factfinding, nonbinding recommendations. American Arbitration Association may assist. Employer decision final	Must be bargained	No specific provisions for unfair practices. Actions posing "clear and present danger to sound program of school education" prohibited; injunctive relief	Written agreement. No deadline specified	A meet and confer law.
VERMONT Ch. 7, L 1969 State Employe Labor Relations Act **CB** K-12 | P-C PS Coverage is selective: all state university personnel excluded	State employes including: certified primary and secondary teachers at state hospital, state training school for retarded, state juvenile correctional institution; faculty and nonfaculty at state colleges; state police. Excluding: certain tax exempt personnel, administrative, management, etc. Excluding: all personnel at state university	Appropriate unit determined by Employe Labor Relations Board. Exclusive representation. No union security	State Employe Labor Relations Board: 3 members appointed by governor	Wages, salaries, hours, other terms and conditions of employment not in conflict with statutes. Merit system principles protected	Factfinding by panel to ELRB; ELRB recommendations binding only by mutual agreement; may not conflict with statutes	Rules and final determination by ELRB	Standard provisions for unfair practices; implied discipline prohibited; listed as unfair practice; implied discipline	Written contract not to exceed 3 years	
VERMONT Statutes Annotated: Municipal Employe Relations Act: § 21-1701 through 21-1710 **CB** K-12 | C	Municipal employes, including school district classified personnel; excluding: elected, supervisors, confidential, certified, etc. K-12 level	Separate units for professional and nonprofessional. Exclusive representation. Dues checkoff, service fees permitted	State Employe Labor Relations Board: 3 members appointed by governor	Wages, hours, conditions of employment	Mediation, factfinding, advisory recommendations; voluntary binding arbitration	May be bargained. Binding arbitration of contract interpretation grievances may be included. Voluntary binding arbitration of tenure grievances must be only procedure for such; supersedes state law	Standard provisions for unfair practices. Strikes permitted only: 30 days after factfinding, after binding arbitration award, and if no danger to public well-being. Injunctive relief	Written contract. No deadline specified	Contracts must not violate state law. Contracts which violate state ordinance, by-law, rule or regulation must be approved by appropriate legislative body. Voluntary binding arbitration awards in tenure grievances may supersede state law.
VIRGINIA									State has no public employe collective bargaining legislation. In July 1962 and February 1970, attorney general's opinions ruled that local employes and teachers have the right to bargain.

State and Statutory Reference; Identification	Coverage; Employee Classification; Level	Bargaining Unit; Type of Representation; Union Security	Administration	Scope of Bargaining; Management Rights	Bargaining Impasse Procedures	Grievance Procedures	Unfair Practices, Penalties; Strikes	Final Form; Deadline Dates For Completed Agreements	Comments
WASHINGTON Revised Code Annotated: § 28A.72.010 through 28A.72.100 **MC** | **P** **K-12**	All regularly certificated employees except chief administrative officers. K-12 level	All covered employees. School principals and asst. principals may form separate unit. Exclusive representation. No union security	Local school board and state superintendent of public instruction	Consult on curriculum, text-books, inservice training, student, teaching, personnel hiring and assignment practices, leaves of absence, salaries, noninstructional duties, etc. Principals and assistants limited to compensation, hours, contract duration	Ad hoc committee appointed by state superintendent to make nonbinding recommendations	No specific provisions	No discrimination because of exercise of rights. No specific provisions for strikes	No specific provisions	A meet and confer law
WASHINGTON Revised Code Annotated: Community College Negotiations Act: § 28B.52.010 through 28B.52.200 **CB** **CC** | **P**	Academic employees of community college district	All covered employees. Chief administrators may be included in academic unit by election	Director of state system of community colleges	Curriculum, textbooks, inservice training, student teaching, personnel hiring and assignment practices, leaves of absence, salaries, noninstructional duties	State director may conduct mediation, fact-finding, appoint ad hoc committee to make nonbinding recommendations	No specific provisions	No discrimination because of exercise of rights. No specific provisions for strikes	Written contract not to exceed 3 years. No deadline specified	Contract is not binding on future actions of legislature.
WASHINGTON Revised Code Annotated: Public Employee Collective Bargaining Act: § 41.56.010 through 41.56.950 **CB** **K-12** | **C**	Public employees with specific exceptions. Act includes K-12 classified personnel	Appropriate units. Exclusive representation. Dues checkoff, service fees permitted. Union security provisions prevail over charter, ordinance, rule or regulation	Department of Labor and Industry	Grievance procedures, wages, hours, working conditions. Excludes matters delegated to other authority by ordinance, resolution or charter	State mediation service, arbitration	Must be bargained. May provide binding arbitration on disputed interpretation of agreement	Standard provisions for unfair practices; injunctive relief. Strikes prohibited, no penalties specified	Written contract not to exceed 3 years. No deadline specified	State also has Port District Employee Act: SB 34, L 1967
WASHINGTON Revised Code Annotated: § 28B.16.100 **CB** **PS** | **C**	State classified employees including postsecondary	Appropriate units. Exclusive representation. Dues checkoff permitted	State Personnel Board	Grievance procedures and all personnel matters over which institutions or related boards may lawfully exercise discretion	No specific provisions	May be bargained	No specific provisions for unfair practices. Strikes prohibited; no penalties specified	Written agreement. No deadline specified	Fund matters subject to approval of chief financial officer.
WEST VIRGINIA									State has no public employee collective bargaining legislation.

State and Statutory Reference; Identification	Coverage; Employe Classification; Level	Bargaining Unit; Type of Representation; Union Security	Administration	Scope of Bargaining; Management Rights	Bargaining Impasse Procedures	Grievance Procedures	Unfair Practices, Penalties; Strikes	Final Form; Deadline Dates For Completed Agreements	Comments
WISCONSIN Statutes Annotated: Municipal Employe Relations Act: § 111.70 through 111.71 CB | K-12 | P-C	Any employe of a political subdivision with specific exceptions. Includes teachers and classified. K-12 level	All employes of one employer except executives, supervisors. Exclusive representation. Dues checkoff, service fees permitted	State Employment Relations Commission: 3 members appointed by governor	Wages, hours, and conditions of employment. Extensive management rights listed	Mediation, fact-finding, arbitration. Employment Relations Commission available	May be bargained	Standard provisions for unfair practices; no specific, penalties. Strikes prohibited; injunctive relief, fines deducted from salaries	Written and signed document. No deadline specified	State has policeman and fireman collective bargaining: WSA § 111.77.
WISCONSIN Statutes Annotated: State Employment Labor Relations Act: § 111.80 through 111.97 CB | P-C | CC PS | C	All state employes except 4-year postsecondary teachers. Includes 2-year postsecondary teachers, all postsecondary classified employes. Supervisors, management, etc. excluded	Statewide basis: 1 unit for education employees. Exclusive representation. Dues checkoff, service fees permitted	State Employment Relations Commission: 3 members appointed by governor	Wages, employe classification, fringes, hours and conditions of employment. Extensive management rights listed. Merit system protected	Mediation, fact-finding, arbitration. Employment Relations Commission available	May be bargained	Standard provisions for unfair practices; no specific penalties. Strikes prohibited; fines, suspension, lawsuit for violation	Written and signed document. No deadline specified	Tentative agreements must be submitted to Employment Relations Commission and Legislature for approval, implementation on cost or statutory matters. If rejected, renegotiation required.
WYOMING									State has no public employe collective bargaining legislation.
DISTRICT OF COLUMBIA Public employes have bargaining rights by executive order of the Commissioner of D. C.									
VIRGIN ISLANDS Public employes have right to organize, join, meet and confer by executive order of governor.									

Source: Doris M. Ross, "State Collective Bargaining Laws Affecting Education," in *A Legislator's Guide to Collective Bargaining in Education* (Denver: Education Commission of the States, 1975).

APPENDIX F. SENATOR HUMPHREY'S LETTER

HUBERT H. HUMPHREY
MINNESOTA

United States Senate
WASHINGTON, D.C. 20510

April 10, 1974

Mrs. Shelly Weinstein
National Committee for Citizens in Education
Village of Wild Lake Green
Columbia, Maryland

Dear Mrs. Weinstein:

I want to take this opportunity to welcome
the National Committee for Citizens in Education
to Minneapolis, Minnesota, on April 22nd, when it
will sponsor a hearing on the subject, "Governance
in Education."

I commend highly the effort of the National
Committee to develop public hearings across the
nation on this highly important subject. The
problems and demands confronting education in America
today require the attention and concern of our
citizens. There is a clear need now for thoughtful
public debate on constructive modes of citizen
participation in the evolution of improved educational
programs and systems.

With best wishes.

Sincerely,

Hubert H. Humphrey